# A PROFILE OF ANCIENT ROME

# A PROFILE OF ANCIENT ROME

Flavio Conti

THE J. PAUL GETTY MUSEUM
LOS ANGELES

### *About the Author*

An architect, Professor Flavio Conti is a graduate of the School of Architecture of the Milan Polytechnic Institute and the head of an associated studio based in Milan and specializing in architecture, restoration, industrial design, and publishing consulting services. Along with his professional activities, he teaches at the university level and is seriously involved in publishing activities, with more than a hundred books to his credit. His main intellectual concerns are the continuity of history and the history of architecture, with a focus on the field of medieval architecture. While in high school he became fascinated with the work of Edward Gibbon and enthusiastically delved into late antiquity and the Dark Ages, areas that he later approached on a professional level, writing, among other things, numerous popular works that have been translated into various languages. For years, his book on the forms of Greek art has been a bestseller in several countries. Since his university years, Professor Conti has devoted himself to the study, recognition, and protection of fortified architecture. He is the president of the Istituto Italiano dei Castelli and director of the magazine *Cronache Castellane*.

First published in the United States of America in 2003 by
Getty Publications
1200 Getty Center Drive, Suite 500
Los Angeles, California 90049-1682
www.getty.edu



Christopher Hudson, Publisher
Mark Greenberg, Editor in Chief

Pamela Heath, Production Coordinator

Eriksen Translations, Inc.:
Marguerite Shore, Translation; David Auerbach, Editing

Hespenheide Design, Graphic Design and Typesetting
Printed in Italy by Officine Grafiche De Agostini, Novara

**Library of Congress Cataloging-in-Publication Data**
Conti, Flavio, 1943-
[Atlante dell'antica Roma. English]
A profile of ancient Rome / Flavio Conti.
p. cm.
ISBN 0-89236-697-4
1. Rome—History. 2. Rome—Civilization.
I. J. Paul Getty Museum. II. Title.
DG209 .C66613 2003
937—DC21

2002013420

# Table of Contents

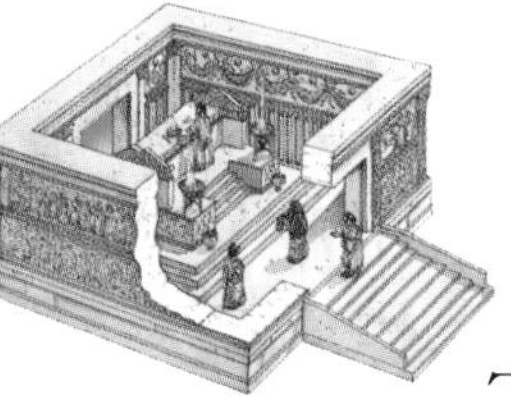

## Religion



## Language and Literature



## Political and Legal System

## Armies and Weapons



## Economic and Social System

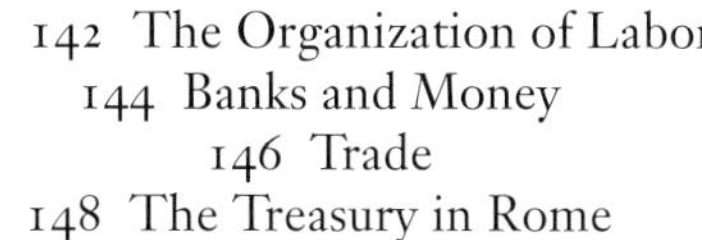



## Architecture and Art



## Large-Scale Projects



## Everyday Life



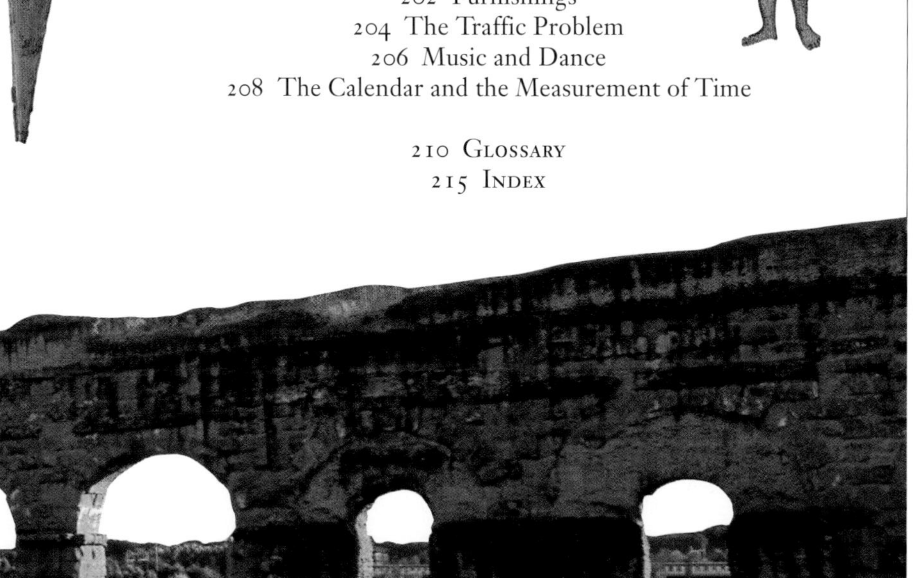

# Introduction

During its more than one-thousand-year history, Rome not only created an empire but made contributions to political, military, social, and cultural life that are still unparalleled. The splendor of its civilization was such, and its connections to the present day so numerous and profound, that we all assume that we are familiar with it in a general sense. But this is mistaken. The many aspects of Roman life that are surprisingly similar to today's world give a misleading impression of absolute, complete continuity. Other features seem remote and foreign to our sensibility, however, and create a daunting sense of the vast distance of the centuries that separate us from our ancestors. This book attempts, within the space available, to heal this often unobserved but ever present fracture. It intends to familiarize the reader with the history and great events of Rome. It will also delve into more significant, unknown, surprising, and compelling aspects of the everyday life of Rome's citizens—how they ate and slept, studied and loved, fought and traded, read and calculated time, dressed and amused themselves. In other words, more than a history book, this is a sort of reportage on the Roman world and its manifestations.

The most obvious manifestations of Roman society—political and civil life, the military, religious life, art and culture, and the economy—and its most important and significant creations—cities and roads, baths and amphitheaters, villas and forums, fortifications and aqueducts—as well as public figures—from Julius Caesar to Diocletian, Cicero to Seneca, Messalina to Galla Placidia—unfold in the pages of this book. Attention is also given to the customs, quirks, idiosyncrasies, beliefs, and lifestyles of the common people: matrons and children, soldiers and tax collectors, musicians and craftsmen, slaves and peasants, moneychangers and poets.

Alongside the general text designed to give an overall picture of specific aspects of society, each chapter contains a wealth of iconographic data, accompanied by brief but illuminating insights into

singular, curious, and amusing implications related to the theme in question. This provides a means to feel more closely connected to the circumstances and lives of our Roman forefathers. It is, in short, a surprising and fascinating voyage, rich with discoveries and unexpected facets, into the world of ancient Rome and its inhabitants.

**Flavio Conti**

# *PARCERE SUBIECTIS, DEBELLARE SUPERBOS*

"Others (I have no doubt) will better know how to model statues of bronze that seem to breathe, or to sculpt living images in marble; they will know how to use the most pointed oratory to defend legal cases; they will know how to map out the movements of the sky with a compass and predict the rising of the heavenly bodies: but you, Roman, remember to govern the people with firm laws (these will be our arts), to impose your peace on the world, to spare the vanquished, to curb the proud."

**PAQUIUS PROCULUS AND HIS WIFE**
This young married couple, immortalized in a fresco in Pompeii, seems to be observing us matter-of-factly from the depths of history.

Thus in Book VI of the *Aeneid*, the elderly Anchises, visited by his son Aeneas in Hades, sketches a portrait of the people who will be born from his progeny. *Parcere subiectis, debellare superbos* (to spare the vanquished, to curb the proud): this is a maxim of extraordinary, compelling pride, which expressively summarizes the meaning of the Roman empire, conferring on it a providential value, or more precisely, a mandate. It is the same sentiment that would be expressed centuries later, albeit with a different emphasis but with like emotion, by Rutilius Namatianus upon the fall of the empire. This obscure official was navigating the Italian coast from Rome to his native Gaul and, delighted by Rome, found in his "provincial" soul the inspiration to compose a moving farewell to the "city of all cities":

*Listen, most beautiful queen of a world you have made, O Rome, welcomed into the starry heavens, listen, mother of men and gods. We are not far from heaven when we find ourselves in your temples. . . . You scatter your gifts like the rays of the sun. Everywhere that the Ocean surges in a circle. . . . The flaming sands of Libya did not stop you, nor the far land armored in ice repel you. . . . You made a single country out of different peoples, helped him who was without laws become your tributary, as you transformed the men into citizens and made a city from what was formerly but earth.*

This, in effect, is the profound meaning of the Roman empire and its mission in the world. In the history of humankind, there have been more extensive realms, more overwhelming victories, and even more enduring political creations. But there has

**RECONSTRUCTION OF THE ARA PACIS**
The Ara Pacis, built between 13 and 9 B.C. by Augustus in the Campus Martius in Rome, was a large altar located at the center of an almost-square enclosure, approximately 10 meters long on each side. This enclosure, which has been reconstructed over time, is covered by a series of large reliefs that summarize the most important stages in Roman history and celebrate Augustus and his family. The most famous scene *(above)* depicts a procession that includes recognizable portraits of the emperor and the members of his family, the *gens Iulia*.

been no other experience capable of amalgamating profoundly different peoples, civilizations, and cultures into a single entity. These epic deeds were not achieved by one clever, successful individual (although there is no shortage of political and military geniuses in Roman history). Nor did they come about through an unexpected toss of the dice on the table of history (even if the millennial life of the city is marked by numerous sensational and unforeseen turns of events and surprises). Rather, they were achieved through work and sacrifice on the part of millions of ordinary people. Divided on many issues, these people were, nonetheless, united by a shared sense of discipline, by an extremely elevated sense of state and duty, and by an enduring if often unconscious awareness of their mission in the world, which they pursued with tenacity, character, organization, and method. The exceptional qualities of these everyday people illuminate the Roman experience:

Treasures of Rome
*Views of Ancient Rome*, eighteenth-century painting by Paolo Panini.

a fabric of events that inspired the affecting pages of the English historian Edward Gibbon, enchanted Charlemagne and Napoleon, and even now act as a touchstone for every political, military, and civil creation. In order to understand how thoroughly Rome has permeated our universal culture, one need only think of the survival of its terminology in current political systems. Capitol, senate, republic, palace, empire, magistrate, code (to string together at will the first words that come to mind) are all legacies of Rome that have entered into the languages of five continents. Perhaps only one of a hundred people in the United States knows, or cares to know, why the hill of power in Washington is called Capitol Hill. But this lack of knowledge in no way weakens the symbolic ties between the ancient and modern powers. And certainly very few of those who speak of "fascism" are familiar with the Roman lictors' *fasces*, adopted as both a symbol and a name by a modern-day political regime. Nonetheless, it is the memory of ancient Rome that still survives in contemporary political struggles.

In its turn, the solid, imposing political and military structure of the empire was the foundation that gave rise to the great civil, artistic, and cultural creations of the Roman world: baths and trade; the passionate narration of history; the network of roads that linked the different parts of the empire; the affirmation of a culture of citizens; imposing public and private architecture; epic poetry; the rigorous, stoic code of the ruling classes. The dust of history has settled on many of these creations. But what survives is more than sufficient, even now, to guarantee immortality to Rome and the culture it created, to make them a *monumentum aere perennius*, "more enduring than bronze."

# Chronology

| | 800 B.C. | 600 B.C. | 500 B.C. | 400 B.C. | 300 B.C. | 200 B.C. |
|---|---|---|---|---|---|---|
| **ROME AND ITALY** | – Founding of Rome in 753 (according to tradition)<br>– Tarquinius Priscus, 616–579<br>– Growth of the city | – Servius Tullius, 579–534<br>– Reorganization of the tribes, army, and the civil establishment<br>– Tarquinius Superbus, 534–509<br>– Beginning of the Republic, 509<br>– Rome's predominance in Latium | – Latins defeated at Lake Regillius in 499<br>– Incursions of the Sabines, Aequians, and Volscians<br>– Predominance of the patricians<br>– Campania occupied by the Samnites, 420<br>– Siege and conquest of Veii, 405–396 | – Rome sacked by the Gauls, 390<br>– War against the Latins, 340<br>– Dissolution of the Latin League, annexation of Campania to the Roman state, 338<br>– Conquest of Italy, 334–264<br>– Second Samnite War, 327–304 | – Third Samnite War, 298–290<br>– Pyrrhus descends on Italy, 280–275<br>– First Roman coins (c. 280)<br>– First Punic War, 264–241<br>– Gauls invade Italy, 225<br>– Second Punic War, 218–202 | – Trial of the Scipiones, 187<br>– Cato censor, 184<br>– Abolition of direct taxes for Roman citizens, 167<br>– Tribuneship of Tiberius and Gaius Gracchus, 133, 123–122<br>– Marius consul seven times, 107, 104–100, 86<br>– Defeat of the Cimbrians and the Teutons, 102–101 |
| **ART AND ARCHITECTURE** | – Primitive huts on the Palatine<br>– Rich, Eastern-style tombs in Caere, Praeneste, etc.<br>– Beginning of the Roman Forum; first permanent stone buildings in Rome | – Temples of Diana, Fortuna, and Mater Matuta, c. 560<br>– Wall of Servius Tullius<br>– Capitoline Temple of Jupiter, 509<br>– Etruscan funerary paintings | – Temple of Saturn, 497<br>– Temple of Ceres, 493<br>– Temple of Castor and Pollux, 484<br>– Temple of Apollo, 431 | – Rebuilding of Roman walls, 378<br>– Temple C, Largo Argentina, c. 350<br>– Via Appia and Aqua Appia, 312<br>– François tomb, Vulci, c. 320–310 | – Construction of new temples in Rome, 302–272<br>– Production of refined Roman crockery<br>– Tomb of Scipio, c. 280<br>– Circus Flaminius, 221 | – Greek art in Rome<br>– Construction of the Basilica Porcia in the Roman Forum, 184<br>– Basilica Emilia and Ponte Aemilius, 179<br>– Temple of Fortuna, Praeneste, c. 120 |
| **LATIN LITERATURE** | | – First Latin inscriptions, c. 600 | – Laws of the Twelve Tables, 451–450 | | – Appius Claudius Caecus, orator<br>– Livius Andronicus, Nevius, Plautus, Ennius, Cecilius Statius, and Pacuvius, playwrights and poets<br>– Cato, orator, historian, and man of letters | – Terence and Accius, playwrights<br>– Lucilius, satirical poet<br>– Calpurnius Piso and Coelius Antipater, historians<br>– G. Gracchus, L.Crassus and Q. Ortensius, orators |
| **AFRICA, SPAIN, AND THE WESTERN MEDITERRANEAN** | – Founding of Carthage, 814<br>– Phoenician settlements in the western Mediterranean<br>– Beginning of Greek colonization of southern Italy | – Greeks from Phocaea defeated at Battle of Aleria (Corsica) by the Etruscans and the Carthaginians, 535<br>– First treaty between Rome and Carthage, 509 | – Defeat of the Carthaginians at Himera, 480<br>– Hieron defeats the Etruscans at Cuma, 474<br>– Athenians defeated at Syracuse, 413 | – Second treaty between Rome and Carthage, 348<br>– Timoleon pushes the Carthaginians out of Sicily, 344<br>– Agathocles, tyrant of Syracuse (317–289) invades Africa, 310–307 | – Sicily a Roman province, 241<br>– Occupation of Sardinia and Corsica, 238<br>– Romans occupy the Carthaginian territories in Spain | – Third Punic War, 149–146<br>– First war against the slaves in Sicily, 136–132<br>– War against Jugurtha, 112–104<br>– Second war against the slaves in Sicily, 104–102 |
| **GAUL, BRITAIN, AND CENTRAL EUROPE** | – Hallstatt culture | | – La Tène culture<br>– Celtic invasion of northern Italy | The Gauls sack Rome, 390 | – The Gauls invade Macedonia, Greece, and Asia Minor, 279<br>– Invasion of Italy by the Gauls stopped at Telamon, 225 | – Roman conquest of Cisalpine Gaul, 202–191<br>– Narbonne Gaul becomes a Roman province, 121 (?)<br>– Migration of the Cimbrians and the Teutons, 120–100<br>– Roman campaign in Dalmatia, 118–117 |
| **GREECE AND THE ORIENT** | – First Olympiad, 776<br>– Homer, Hesiod, c. 700<br>– Era of Greek colonization (beginning c. 750)<br>– Era of Greek tyrants | – Cyrus the Great establishes the Persian empire, c. 550–530<br>– Domination of Sparta in the Peloponnesus, from c. 560<br>– Pisistratus tyrant of Athens, 546–528 | – Ionian Revolt, 499–494<br>– Persian invasions of Greece, 490, 481–479<br>– Athenian empire, 478–404<br>– Construction of the Parthenon, 447–432<br>– Peloponnesian War, 431–404 | – Philip II makes Macedonia the foremost Greek power, 359–336<br>– Alexander the Great conquers the Persian empire, 333–323<br>– Seleucidian dynasty in Syria and Mesopotamia<br>– Ptolomeic dynasty in Egypt | – Athens occupied by Macedonia, 261<br>– Wars between Rome and Illyria, 229–219 | – Second Macedonian war, 200–197<br>– Syrian war, 191–188<br>– Third Macedonian war, 172–158<br>– Destruction of Corinth, 146 |

| 100 B.C. | 1 A.D. | 100 A.D. | 200 A.D. | 300 A.D. | 400 A.D. |
|---|---|---|---|---|---|
| – Social War, 91–89<br>– Civil War: Sulla dictator, 83–82<br>– Revolt of Spartacus, 73–71<br>– First Triumvirate, 60<br>– Civil War: Caesar dictator, 49–44<br>– Death of Caesar, 44<br>– Second Triumvirate, 43<br>– Reign of Octavian Augustus, 31 B.C.–14 A.D. | – Julio-Claudian dynasty, 27 B.C.–68 A.D.<br>– Rome burns, 64<br>– Flavian dynasty, 69–98<br>– Eruption of Vesuvius, 79 | – Antonine dynasty, 117–193<br>– Trajan, 98–117 | – Severan dynasty, 192–235<br>– Extension of Roman citizenship to all free inhabitants of the province, 212<br>– Usurpation and fragmentation of the imperial office, 235–284<br>– Diocletian establishes the tetrarchy, 293 | – Extensive persecution of Christians, 303–305<br>– Restoration of freedom of worship, 313<br>– Constantine sole emperor, 324–337<br>– Julian attempts to restore paganism, 361–363<br>– "Abolition" of paganism, 382<br>– Division of the empire, 395 | – Transfer of the imperial court to Ravenna, 402<br>– Alaric sacks Rome, 410<br>– Rome plundered by the Vandals, 455<br>– Ousting of the last Roman emperor of the West, 476<br>– Barbarian kings in Ravenna, 476–540 |
| – *Tabularium*, 78<br>– Theater of Pompey, 55<br>– Forum of Caesar, 46<br>– Arch of Augustus, 21<br>– Baths of Agrippa, 19<br>– Theater of Marcellus, 17<br>– *Ara Pacis Augustae*, 9<br>– Forum of Augustus, 2 | – Augustus's building program in Rome<br>– Inauguration of the Coliseum, 79 | – Inauguration of Trajan's Forum, 112<br>– Rebuilding of the Pantheon, 118–128<br>– Hadrian's Villa in Tivoli, 126–134 | – Constructions by Septimius Severus at Leptis Magna<br>– Construction of the Baths of Caracalla in Rome, 216<br>– Aurelian extends the Roman wall, 271 | – Arch of Constantine<br>– Building of churches in Rome, Jerusalem, and Constantinople | – Mosaics in Ravenna churches |
| – Cicero, orator and philosopher<br>– Caesar, historian<br>– Lucretius, poet and philosopher<br>– Sallust and Livy, historians<br>– Catullus, Virgil, Horace, Tibullus, Propertius, and Ovid, poets | – "Silver age" of Latin literature<br>– Seneca, orator, playwright, and philosopher<br>– Persius, Lucan, Martial, poets<br>– Pliny the Elder, naturalist<br>– Pliny the Younger, writer of letters<br>– Tacitus, historian | – Juvenal, poet<br>– Suetonius, historian<br>– Apuleius, writer | – Ulpian and Papinian, jurists<br>– Tertullian, Christian apologist | – Ausonius and Claudian, poets<br>– Lactantius, Christian apologist<br>– Ambrose, Jerome, and Augustine, Christian writers<br>– Simmacus, orator<br>– Ammianus Marcellinus, historian | – Jerome completes the *Vulgate*, c. 404<br>– Orosius, historian<br>– Servius and Macrobius, scholars<br>– Compilation of Theodosian Code, 429–437<br>– Sidonius Apollinaris, poet |
| – Defeat of Pompey in Spain (49), Africa (46), and Munda (45)<br>– Sextus Pompey—controls the western Mediterranean, 40–36<br>– Agrippa conquers northwest Spain, 27–19 | – Annexation of Mauretania | | – Expanded Roman colonization of North Africa | – Beginning of Donatist schism | – Vandals penetrate Spain<br>– Reign of Vandals in Carthage, 439 |
| – Caesar conquers continental Gaul, 58–51; expeditions to Britain, 55–54<br>– Noricum and Rhaetia become provinces, 16–15<br>– Tiberius conquers Pannonia, 12–9 | – Vindice rebellion, 68<br>– Roman occupation of Britain, 43<br>– Reinforcement of the frontier in Germany and in Illyria<br>– Dacian Wars, 86–92 | – Formation of province of Dacia, 107<br>– Wars of Marcus Aurelius against the Marcomanni<br>– Barbarian invasion of Dacia, 167 | – "Empire" of the Gauls, 259–273<br>– Upheaval in Britain (Carausius and Allectus, 287–296)<br>– Trier becomes capital of Gaul<br>– Dacia is ceded to the Goths in 272 | – Entry of Goths into interior of the empire, 376<br>– Battle of Adrianopolis, 378 | – Reign of Goths in southern Gaul<br>– Britain colonized by the Saxons<br>– Burgundians occupy the central Rhone valley<br>– "Empire" of the Huns led by Attila |
| – Mithridatic Wars, 88–84, 83–82, 74–63<br>– Pompey conquers the Orient, 66–63<br>– Pompey defeated at Pharsalus, 48<br>– Brutus and Cassius defeated at Philippi, 42<br>– Antony and Cleopatra defeated at Actium, 31 | – First Jewish rebellion, 66–73<br>– Destruction of the Temple in Jerusalem, 70<br>– Flavius Josephus, Jewish historian | – Second Jewish rebellion (Bar-Kochba), 132–135<br>– Formation of province of Mesopotamia, 165<br>– Plutarch and Pausanius, Greek writers<br>– Neosophism in Greek literature | – Sassanid Dynasty in Persia<br>– Rebellion of Palmyra, 266–272<br>– The Herulians invade Attica and the Peloponnesus in 267<br>– Cassius Dio and Herodian, Greek historians | – Nicene Council<br>– Constantinople becomes the new capital of the empire, 330<br>– Visigoth invasion of Greece, 395<br>– Eunapius, Greek historian | – Invasion of the Huns<br>– Council of Chalcedon assembled in 451<br>– Olympiodorus, Priscus, and Malcus, Greek historians |

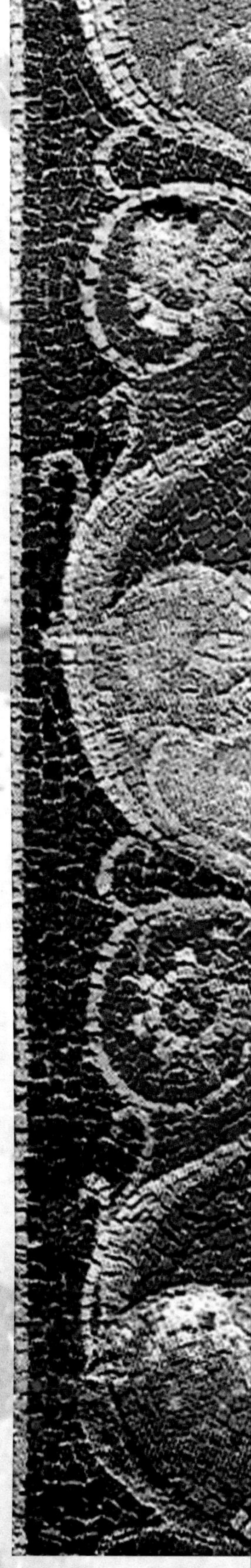

# Italy before Rome

In a lively and varied panorama, indigenous populations interacted and others came from farther afield—each conveying a distinct culture and a different body of knowledge.

At the time Rome was founded, Italy had an extremely diverse political and cultural life. For maximum simplification, one could say that the peninsula was inhabited by two types of populations: "Italic" peoples, who had been settled in the region for some time and whose development had taken place on Italian soil, and those who had come from territories beyond—Etruscans (perhaps), Greeks, Phoenicians, and Celts.

## *Foreign populations*

Greeks and Phoenicians were "old acquaintances." In fact, Mycenaean and Syrian-Palestinian merchants had visited the Tyrrhenian islands and the coasts of Italy as early as the middle of the second millennium B.C. Their regular visits were interrupted or became somewhat rare toward the end of the millennium, however, not to

**Capestrano Warrior**
This famous sculpture in stone with traces of pink paint comes from the necropolis of Capestrano, in the Abruzzi. Dating from the sixth century B.C., it represents an armed warrior with a mask on his face, broad headgear, and perhaps a shield.

**Fully Armed**
This small bronze of a warrior armed with a shield (eighth century B.C.) comes from the Veneto. According to ancient tradition, the Veneti came by sea from Asia Minor and settled in the region that has taken their name.

**Small Sardinian Bronze**
Small bronzes, like the one illustrated below, which represents a votive boat, are of crucial importance for the documentation of Nuraghic society.

be resumed until centuries later, about the eighth century B.C. It was at this point that true colonization began, with Greeks settling along the southern Italian coasts, in the Tyrrhenian islands, and in eastern Sicily, and Phoenicians migrating to western Sicily and Sardinia.

More or less during the same period, various Celtic populations crossed the Alpine passes to penetrate the Po valley. Their presence, verified in this region as early as the sixth century B.C., took on increasing significance. Between these two areas of colonization lay the territory of the Etruscans, whose city-states occupied the land between the Arno and Tiber Rivers, with "expansions" to the north beyond the Apennines and to the south as far as Campania, where the Etruscan town of Capua bordered on the Greek towns of Cuma and *Neapolis*.

## *The Italic Peoples*

These populations mingled with the Italic tribes: the Apulians, Lucanians, Samnites, Latins, Umbrians, Picenes, Ligurians, Veneti, etc., as well as the Siculi and the Sards. Each group had its own characteristics, and there was often much internal differentiation except for a rather strong community tie created by certain beliefs or shared religious centers. There was tremendous variation in settlement types (the Latin city-state, for example, differed from the scattered settlements of the Samnites or the Ligurians). Despite a common Indo-European root, the languages varied widely; for example, an Umbrian could understand a Veneto only with great difficulty. Social conditions differed widely, as well (women occupied an almost servile position in Rome and the Latin world but played a significant role in nearby Etruria).

Relationships between the various Italic populations and between these peoples and foreign colonizers were often stormy but productive in the long run. The Greeks and Phoenicians brought their knowledge of the alphabet to the peninsula, while Greek architecture had considerable influence on Etruscan, and thereby on Roman and Italic, forms. Moreover, beautiful ceramics of Greek production soon became a status symbol, highly appreciated throughout the Italic area, as was the wine that these ceramics were meant to contain.

Roman conquest had an enormous effect on this entire complex and lively mosaic; it unified traditions, languages, customs, and habits. The result was an enormous remixing of structures stratified by centuries, which in the end produced a completely new culture, simultaneously inheriting and surpassing the sources that had come before.

A House for the Deceased
Bronze or terracotta miniatures like this Etruscan example (*above*) from Vulci were used as cinerary urns, particularly toward the end of the late Bronze Age and in the early Iron Age in Etruria and Latium. They allow us to reconstruct the exterior appearance and interior architecture of huts.

### REGION BY REGION

What follows is a summary of the peoples who inhabited the present-day regions of the peninsula, before the founding of Rome.

**Piedmont and Val d'Aosta**
Taurini, Salassi, Lepontii, Ligurians, Victimuli
**Liguria**
Ligurians
**Lombardy**
Camuni, Etruscans, Celts
**The Veneto**
Veneti
**Emilia-Romagna**
Etruscans, Gauls, Senones, Boii, Lingones
**Tuscany**
Etruscans
**Umbria**
Umbrians, Etruscans
**Marches**
Picenes, Senones
**Latium**
Latins, Sabines, Volsci, Ernici, Equifalischi, Capenati
**Abruzzi and Molise**
Samnites, Equii, Marsi, Vestini, Peligni, Pretuzi, Marrucini
**Campania**
Campanians, Lucanians, Sidicini, Opici (Oschi) Publia
**Sardinia**
Sards

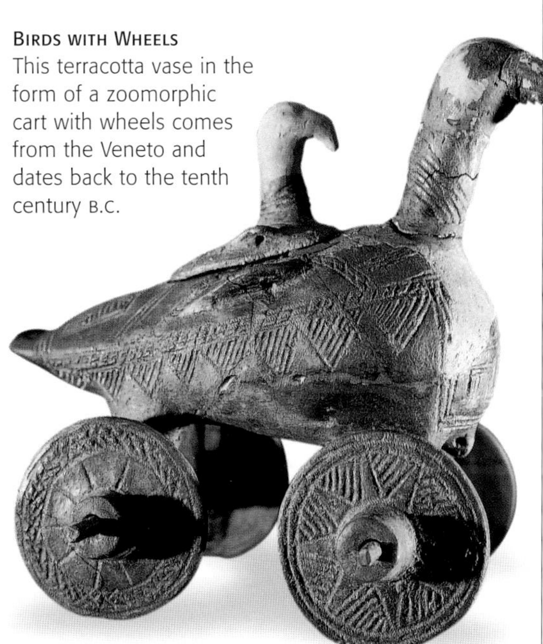

Birds with Wheels
This terracotta vase in the form of a zoomorphic cart with wheels comes from the Veneto and dates back to the tenth century B.C.

# The Age of Kings

Inhabiting a realm between legend and historically documented reality, the era of the kings saw the development of the city of Rome, its initial ascent, and the birth of the myths upon which Roman identity would be founded.

Clearly Rome was not founded on April 21, 753 B.C., as tradition states. Nor was it built in a day. Rather, it resulted from a long formative period, characterized by the growth and union of various prehistoric villages into a larger whole. This *sinecia*, or "coming together to live," probably centered on the Palatine and was "fueled" by trade with Etruscan cities to the north and Greek cities to the south. Indeed, the newly populated area became an important port of call and a stopover for goods that would travel inland, up the Tiber valley. Contacts with more evolved cultures were profitable for the rough Latin community; the Romans learned from the Greeks how to cultivate grapevines and olives, radically changing their primitive economic activity, which had been focused on cattle breeding and sheep farming. From the Etruscans they gained technological, artistic, and religious knowledge.

## *The Myth of the Founder*

According to legend, the history of Rome began with the adventure of two twins, Romulus and Remus. Descended on their mother's side from the Trojan Aeneas and on their father's side from Mars, the god of war, they were raised by a she-wolf after being abandoned in a basket along the banks of the Tiber. They grew up amid the hills of the future city and assumed leadership over a collection of Latin and Sabine tribes, which they decided to unite within a single settlement.

**The Rape of the Sabines**
The episode, depicted here in a 17th-century painting by Pietro da Cortona, took place during the *Consualia* (named for a local god, *Consus*), a celebration specifically instituted by Romulus, to which the Sabine men were invited along with their wives and children. After an apparently friendly welcome, a disturbance was deliberately instigated, during which the Romans abducted young Sabine girls to take as wives.

**Adoptive Mother**
According to legend, the twins Romulus and Remus were nursed by a she-wolf. Many sculptures and reliefs, such as the one illustrated above, record this episode.

### The Seven Kings

The series of kings of Rome and their chronology, according to historical tradition corroborated by historians who lived during the late republican and Augustan period, is as follows:

| | |
|---|---|
| 753–716 B.C. | Romulus |
| 715–672 B.C. | Numa Pompilius |
| 672–640 B.C. | Tullus Hostilius |
| 640–616 B.C. | Ancus Marcius |
| 616–578 B.C. | Tarquinius Priscus |
| 578–534 B.C. | Servius Tullius |
| 534–509 B.C. | Tarquinius Superbus |

**Profile of the Founder**
Romulus, the king of Rome, depicted on the front of a coin minted in 51 B.C.

Each brother laid out the perimeter of a projected city upon a different hill (Romulus on the Palatine, Remus on the Aventine). But Romulus prevailed, after killing his brother who, mocking him, had dared to cross the line he had laid out on the Palatine.

Naturally, things did not really happen in this manner. But although the personalities are legendary, there must be some truth to the story. If nothing else, there is the presence, documented by archeological excavations, of settlements organized on the Palatine about the eighth century B.C., the period traditionally indicated for the founding of Rome.

## *The Italic Kings*

Tradition states that, after Romulus, there were six other kings who governed the city between the eighth and sixth centuries B.C. The first three—Numa Pompilius, Tullus Hostilius, and Ancus Marcius—were said to have belonged to the founders' Latin and Sabine communities, to whose benefit they worked, each according to his own inclinations. Numa Pompilius brought structure to the religious practices of the day, Tullus Hostilius organized the army, and Ancus Marcius led the city to conquer neighboring territories.

## *The Etruscan Kings and the Collapse of Royal Power*

The Sabine and Latin kings are said to have been followed by three sovereigns of Etruscan origin: Tarquinius Priscus, Servius Tullius, and Tarquinius Superbus. They introduced their own culture to Rome, built large public works—from city walls to sewer systems—and modified the power structure in increasingly autocratic fashion to the point where the last king was a veritable tyrant. This aroused the citizens to action and brought about the collapse of royal power. It is difficult to ascertain just how much truth there is to this sequence of events. Some points, however, are clear. At its beginnings, Rome had a form of royal government; this period saw the first of the long string of conquests that would lead to the creation of the empire. Etruscan civilization had a significant impact on this process; it shaped many of the beliefs and political and social structures that then became typically Roman.

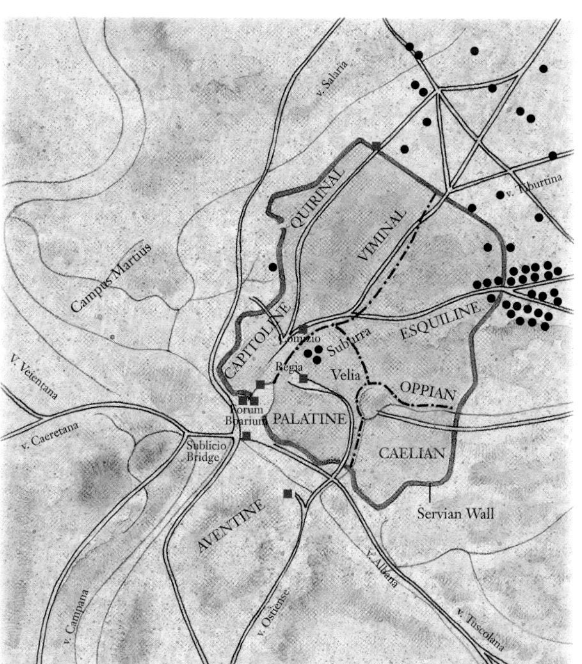


**Rome at the Time of the Tarquin Kings**
A plan of Rome (*left*) during the archaic era shows the city enclosed within the Servian Walls, which divided it into four urban regions, shown by the shaded lines. The dots indicate tombs and the small squares indicate sanctuaries.

**Etruscan Smile**
Contacts with Etruscan cities, particularly Veii, profoundly influenced the customs and cultural life of the early Romans. The Apollo (*at right*), bearing the faint smile typical of Etruscan sculpture, dates from the 5th century B.C. and, along with other statues, would have adorned the roof of a temple in the city of Veii.

# The Birth of the Republic

Toward the end of the sixth century B.C.—the date traditionally given is the year 244 *ab urbe condita*, that is, "from the founding of Rome," corresponding to 509 B.C.—the Romans deposed their seventh king, Tarquinius Superbus, and established a form of republican government.

**The First Consul**
Since the 16th century, the Brutus Capitolinus, a magnificent bronze bust in the Capitoline Museum in Rome, has been identified as Junius Brutus, the first consul of the Republic.

Ancient historiography attributes this development to the people's anger at the rape of a virtuous noblewoman, Lucretia, by the king's son, Sextus Tarquinius—clearly a simplified version of the facts. A revolution of such sweeping significance does not take place suddenly, but rather entails the involvement of much broader social forces and dynamics. One indication of the nature of these forces can be seen in the structure of the government adopted after the fall of the Etruscan king. This was a strongly aristocratic republic, where executive power was entrusted to two consuls who also held supreme military command and who, in cases of extreme danger, could be replaced for a brief period by a dictator. Thus it is likely that the rise of the Republic was the consequence of a coup d'état or in any case a violent rupture of the preceding order at the hands of a certain number of *gentes*, or patrician families. Upon achieving victory, they reserved the right to hold all offices, both new ones, such as the consulate, and old, such as religious posts. During the monarchy, the principal exponents of these *gentes* probably were *patres*—that is, members of the Senate. These were influential figures who controlled and could easily mobilize a great number of citizens who were tied to them by business relationships. It is likely that one reason behind their rebellion against royal power was the growing propensity of the king to reduce their influence in favor of the nascent commercial and artisan classes. In the long run, this policy might have excluded the patricians from the political arena and reduced their class privileges.

### A Revolutionary Change

Tradition attributes to Servius Tullius the revolutionary reform of the army, which decisively influenced the passage from the royal to the republican era. This reform substantially replaced earlier armed forces, which had been subordinate to aristocratic groups, with an army recruited on the basis of the census. Eliminating privileges that derived from membership in the aristocratic class, it allowed all citizens able to provide themselves with military gear to be on equal footing.

**Italic Art**
*Below and right*, two terracottas dating from the fourth century B.C., the work of Italic artists.

### ENEMIES OF THE REPUBLIC

From its beginnings, the Republic had to do battle with the Etruscans, who attempted to reassert their dominion over Rome, and with the Latins, who began to fear the city's plans to expand into Latium. The Latins, in order to contain the nascent power of Rome, had created a league among their major cities, such as Tusculum, Lanuvium, Pometia, and Tivoli. The clash between Rome and the Latin League took place in 499 B.C. with the battle of Lake Regillus. This led to the signing of a treaty, the *foedus Cassianum*, in 493 B.C., whereby the two parties (Latins and Romans) made a commitment to aid each other reciprocally in the case of outside attack.

The fall of the monarchy also brought about substantial changes in religion: Heretofore the king had stood at the apex of the hierarchy. The aristocratic government created a new *rex sacrorum*, who kept the title and ceremonial prerogatives of the monarchy but was confined to an exclusively sacred role exercised under the strict control of the Pontifex Maximus, a political figure and not a priest by profession (one Pontifex Maximus, for example, was Julius Caesar).

## *New Social Classes*

Rome did not develop into a Republic merely because of an uprising of nobles against the monarchy but also because of the pressure of new social figures, who deemed the old monarchic state to be primitive and who found the tool for their ascent in the form of military service.

The most important feature of the authority of the new republican magistrates was *imperium militiae*, military command over an army the core of which was made up of heavy infantry. In fact, the cavalry, composed of patricians under the command of a *magister equitum*, was flanked by infantry "centuries" (groups of one hundred soldiers), made up of commoners who were sufficiently wealthy to buy the required arms for themselves and who were led by a *magister populi*, also known as *dictator*. This revolution, which fused aristocrats and affluent commoners into a single organism, constituted the social foundation of the Republic, symbolized by the very motto that Rome adopted: *S.P.Q.R.*, *Senatus PopulusQue Romanus* (The Senate and the People of Rome).

The republican structure was perfected over the course of the fifth century B.C., when new magistracies were established, such as the praetorship, which was concerned with judicial inquiries, and the quaestura, which was responsible for the administration of the state treasury. All the magistracies had similar terms and structures; magistrates were elected for a single year and were always at least two in number in order to avoid abuses and dishonesty.

**The Lavinium Minerva**
This statue, depicting Minerva, comes from Lavinium, a Latin city considered sacred by the Romans because, according to tradition, it had been founded by Aeneas.

# The Conquest of the Peninsula

The two centuries subsequent to the birth of the Republic were marked by a prolonged war against the peoples of the Italian peninsula, who one by one were forced to bow down before the supremacy of Rome.

**Citizen and Soldier**
Within the framework of the total subordination of the individual to the community, which characterized early Rome, military service was an integral part of *civitas Romana* and did not require sanction by law. Here we see a Latin warrior ready to do battle.

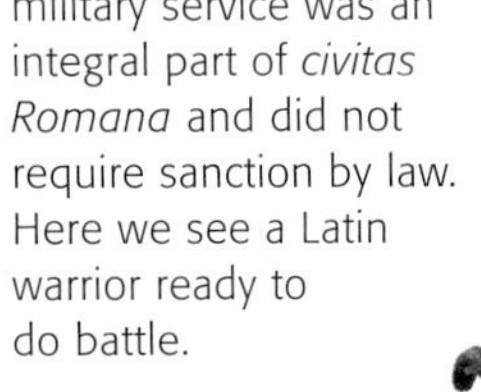

Toward the end of the royal era, Rome had achieved a predominant albeit challenged position over the other cities of Latium. The convulsions resulting from the change in regime threatened this supremacy and forced the city to fight for its very survival. But a series of bitter wars, often conducted with the force of desperation, resulted in the reclaiming of territory by the Romans and then the gradual expansion of their domain. The Latin peoples, whose league barred Rome from progressing southward, were subdued through a series of conflicts that lasted over a century and a half, until they were completely brought under control in 338 B.C. The

**Armored Vehicle**
The first battle between Pyrrhus and the Roman legions took place in Heraclea, in Lucania, in 280 B.C. The elephants of the king of Epirus unleashed panic among the Romans, who suffered extremely serious losses. *Above*, a plate dating from the third century B.C., depicts an elephant equipped for battle.

**The Caudine Forks**
The proverbial episode of the Caudine Forks dates back to the conflict between the Romans and the Samnites. While crossing a narrow wooded gorge near Caudium, the Roman soldiers were lured into a trap by the Samnites. The Romans were then forced to pass, unarmed, beneath a yoke made of three lances (forks) and to be subjected to the derision of the enemy. *Below*, a bas-relief of a Samnite gladiator.

**Humiliation and Revenge**
The Gauls put the city of Rome to fire and sword and forced its inhabitants to barter their freedom in exchange for an extremely high ransom in gold. The dictator Furius Camillus prevented this humiliation, bearing down with his legions on the Gauls and definitively routing them. *Above*, a gilded dagger with sheath, a magnificent example of Celtic art.

### THE CULT OF THE DIOSCURI

The battle between the Romans and Latins at Lake Regillus is connected to the introduction to Rome of the cult of Castor and Pollux, the Dioscuri *(above, in a relief from the Altar of Juturnas in the Roman Forum)*. It is said that two mysterious knights appeared to the troops amid the din of battle and led the Romans to victory. After leaving the battlefield, the two young men reappeared within the walls of Rome and led their horses to drink at the Fountain of Juturnas. They announced to the citizenry that victory had been won over the Latins and then disappeared again into the void. The populace and the authorities elected to build a temple in the Forum, dedicated to the two young knights, the Dioscuri, and this was consecrated in 484 B.C. The legend can be interpreted as the introduction of a myth from Magna Graecia into Roman tradition. In fact, in the Greek centers of southern Italy, Castor and Pollux were considered the guardian deities of the cavalry, which was made up exclusively of members of the aristocracy. The establishment of a cult specific to the nobility might underlie, on an ideological level, the need for reinforcing political power on the part of the Roman aristocratic class at a delicate moment of transition from the monarchy to republican institutions.

conquest in 396 of the large Etruscan city of Veii, which overlooked Rome from the north, allowed the Romans to expand beyond Latium for the first time.

During the fourth century in three extremely bitter wars (entailing many reverses but crowned with victory in the end), the Samnites were subdued, and the fertile lands of Campania were opened for use by Rome. The first half of the third century saw the conquest of the Hellenic cities of Magna Graecia; Taranto, the region's capital, was conquered in 272. Now all of Italy south of the Tiber had come under Roman rule.

## *Enemies from the North and East*

Rome's progression in conquering the Italian peninsula was neither linear nor constant. In 390 B.C., the city had barely recovered from the harsh war against Veii when, over the northern plains, came rolling a wave of Gauls (as the Romans called the Celts). After overwhelming the Roman troops at the River Allia, they besieged and sacked the city, a disaster that was not fatal only because the rest of Latium likewise had been weakened by the Celtic invasion and could not effectively shake off the Roman yoke.

A century later, in 280 B.C., Taranto called upon Pyrrhus, the king of Epirus (present-day Albania), to come to its aid against Rome. Pyrrhus was the first to bring to Italy the methods of war of the Hellenistic kingdoms and introduced the Romans to elephants, a terrible fighting force of the eastern troops. Pyrrhus was victorious, but his troops suffered tremendous losses and he was prevented from taking advantage of his victory (bringing the phrase *Pyrrhic victory* into the language). The Romans lost on the battlefield but knew how to reconfigure their tactics in order to confront their adversaries, and in the end they won the war. By the mid-third century B.C. Rome had become a continental power.

**Consul, Dictator, Farmer**
Lucius Quintus Cincinnatus can be considered the prototype of the ancient Roman, both farmer and man of state. Named consul in 460 B.C., while the struggle between patricians and commoners was raging, he brought calm to both sides and then returned to his farm. Dictator in 458 B.C., he defeated the Equians and the Volscians. Having obtained victory, he refused to be reappointed dictator in order to devote himself once again to his fields. *Right*, a later relief depicting work in the fields.

# The Conflict with Carthage

The conflict between the two great cities lasted nearly 120 years, and its outcome determined the destiny of Rome as a major power.

"To navigate is essential. . . ."
Farmers by origin and vocation, the Romans were forced rapidly to adapt as sailors, both because of the need for food supplies and for military reasons. They were so successful in doing this that they became the lords of the Mediterranean, which they proudly called *Mare Nostrum* (Our Sea). *Above*, a relief showing a Roman ship laden with soldiers.

The pretexts for the conflict were casual and banal, but the reasons that led to a mortal struggle between the two cities were written in the stars. Coexistence between two powers such as Rome and Carthage, the principal players in an inexorable expansion in the Mediterranean region, was impossible. As long as their respective conquests remained separated by buffer-territories, a series of treaties that sanctioned their separate spheres of influence managed to preserve the peace. But when the conquest of Magna Graecia brought the Roman legions into direct contact with the Carthaginian garrisons, outright conflict became only a matter of time. It is no accident that the spark that ignited war—the alliance the Romans made with the Mamertines, mercenaries who were occupying Messina—spread across the straits between Calabria and Sicily, where the two empires faced off. This was the beginning of a far-reaching struggle carried out in three successive wars across more than a century. In the end Carthage was reduced to a salt-strewn field of burned ruins, and Rome assumed hegemony over the entire western Mediterranean.

### ROME AND WAR

The Roman heroic ideal was not aggression for the purposes of conquest but in defense of the state's boundaries and security. According to traditional Roman custom, war was justified exclusively by legitimate defense and had to be subject to specific legal procedures. First of all, it was necessary to solemnly request that the enemy make reparations for wrongs committed, and only in the case of refusal could the dispute move on to weapons. In this manner, war became juridically *bellum iustum piumque* (just and acceptable to the gods). In similar fashion, a conflict could be concluded only by a treaty, which was considered an inviolable moral commitment. During the period of great expansion, which culminated in the Second Punic War, Rome undertook no act of war that was not justified, at least formally, by the need for self-defense or the protection of its allies. Within this framework, the annexation of new territories can be seen as an uninterrupted attempt to make the state's frontiers more secure. To the Roman way of thinking, the fact that this led to the creation of a gigantic empire was secondary.

Roman Imperialism
A marble relief with the personification of Victory, who holds up a trophy.

## *The First Punic War*

The first Punic War, which broke out in 264 B.C., was initiated by the Romans, who landed troops in Sicily; it continued with ups and downs until 241 and concluded with a victory for Rome at the Battle of Mylae. There, Rome demonstrated an unexpected ability for naval as well as land combat. Sicily was expropriated as the first province of the nascent Roman empire, soon followed by Sardinia and Corsica. The victory seemed decisive, with the humiliation of the adversary and its loss of colonies. In reality, this was only the first round.

## *The Second Punic War*

This is known also as "Hannibal's War" because it was begun and conducted substantially by Hannibal Barca, the great Carthaginian general whose father, Hamilcar, had conquered Spain and restored strength to Carthage. The war lasted seventeen years, from 218 to 201 B.C., and was the most terrible and dramatic conflict sustained by Rome in its entire history. Beaten repeatedly, in the Ticino, at Trebbia, at Lake Trasimeno, and then catastrophically at

Cannae, Rome came close to collapse before it succeeded in turning the tide, under the leadership of a brilliant young general, Publius Cornelius Scipio. Scipio's victory took place on African soil, where he inflicted an irreparable defeat upon the enemy at the Battle of Zama.

## *The End*

The Third Punic War was in substance an appendix to the earlier conflict, and at this point there was little parity between the opposing sides on the battlefield. It served Rome's purposes to remove its adversary definitively from its midst and to take over another province, that of Africa, to add to the Italian islands and to Spain, which had already been wrenched from the Carthaginians. Above all, the situation conclusively confirmed Rome's role as the hegemonic power in the Mediterranean.

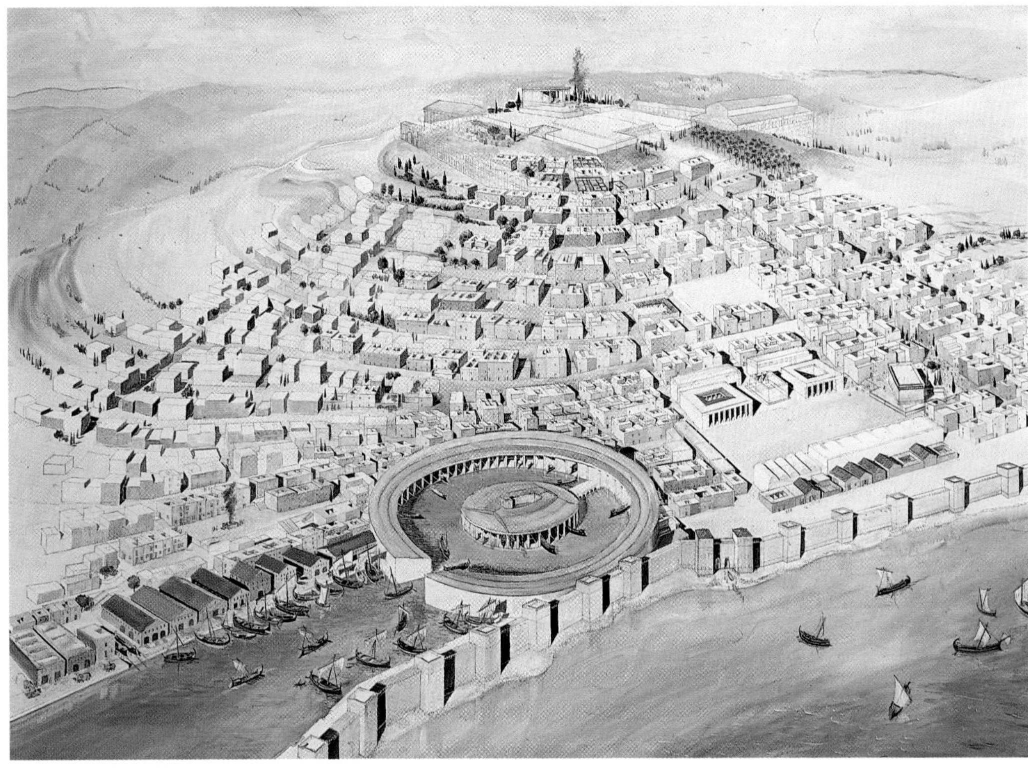

**Double Port**
Carthage, which lay on the Gulf of Tunis, on the north coast of Africa, was a fortified city with broad streets and multistoried houses. There were two ports: a rectangular one was set aside for mercantile ships; a circular one was reserved for the fleet. At the center a dock held the military command post.

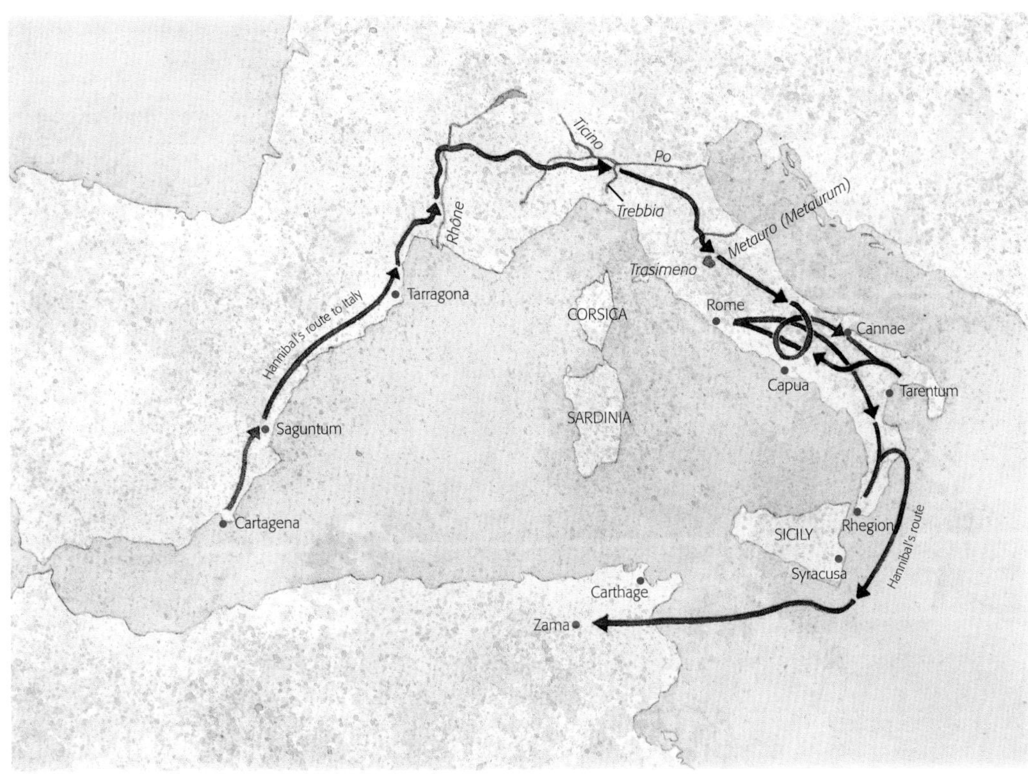


**Sites of the Second Punic War**
The map illustrates the route taken by Hannibal—from Spain to Italy and finally to Africa—and the battle sites of the Second Punic War.

### THE REFORMS OF SCIPIO AFRICANUS

A cultivated and intelligent man, an admirer of Greek culture, the young Publius Cornelius Scipio was treated somewhat diffidently by the Senate, which, not mistakenly, sensed innate gifts of leadership in this offspring of a noble family. He demonstrated his character as a reformer above all in the military field where he introduced innovations in weaponry that proved to be decisive. He made the legions more agile by having them fight in looser formations, and he armed the soldiers with a new sword, the *gladius hispaniensis*, which was longer and more effective than the traditional dagger. This sword remained the most distinctive weapon of the Roman legionnaire.

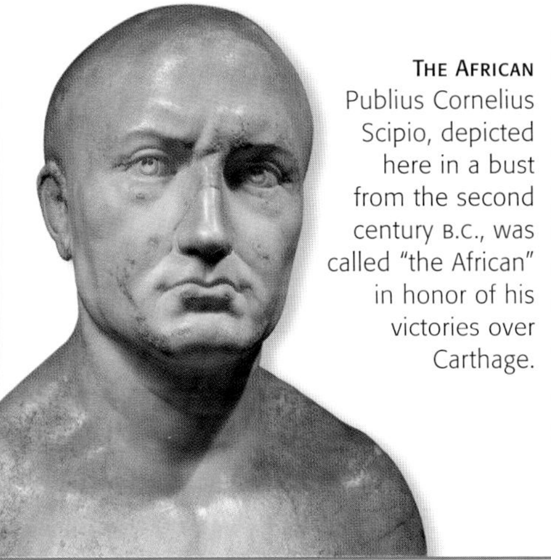

**The African**
Publius Cornelius Scipio, depicted here in a bust from the second century B.C., was called "the African" in honor of his victories over Carthage.

# The Birth of the Empire

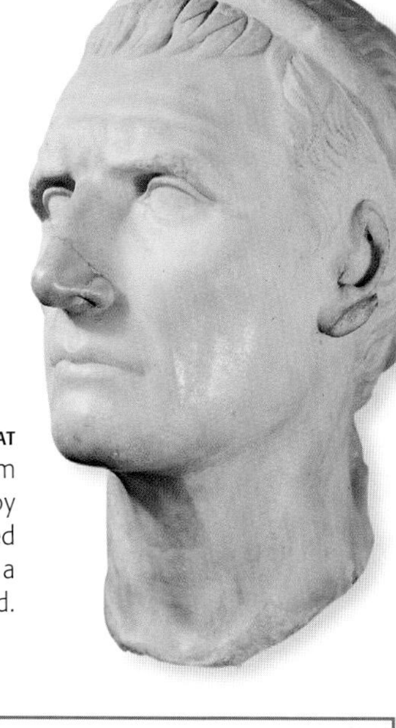

During the second century A.D., Rome extended its dominion to Macedonia, Greece, and Asia Minor; defeated Syria; and consolidated its position in Cisalpine Gaul, Narbonese Gaul, and Spain. It now ruled supreme over the Mediterranean, and the empire was born.

**ANTIOCHUS III, KNOWN AS THE GREAT**
King of Syria from 223 to 186 B.C., Antiochus transformed his kingdom into a power of the first order before suffering a disastrous defeat by the Romans at the Battle of Magnesia. The great sovereign is identified as the subject of this portrait bust, now in the Louvre. It is a masterpiece of portraiture from the mid-Hellenistic period.

Over the course of the Second Punic War, when Rome seemed close to collapse, Philip V of Macedonia entered into a treaty of alliance with Hannibal. Perhaps this was only a sort of counter-action on the part of the Macedonian king in order to deal with someone who seemed likely to rule over Italy. This affront drew Rome fatefully into the eastern sector and forced a series of interventions and wars that, in the end, brought about Rome's domination of Macedonia and, if only from spite, of Greece.

This expansion eastward led in turn to a conflict with Syria, whose king, Antiochus III, had profited from the collapse of Macedonia to expand into Asia Minor. Syria, among other things, made use of Rome's great adversary, Hannibal, as a military advisor. This was something the Romans could not accept, and they were drawn into the complex political situation of the Middle Eastern world.

In all these conflicts, the Roman legions and allies were easily victorious, thanks to their system of command and their tactics, which were greatly superior to those of the Macedonians, Greeks, and Asians. In order to consolidate its victories, however, Rome had to assume the burden of administering the new provinces in addition to those that were being established in the west: Cisalpine Gaul, to protect the Italian peninsula from Celtic invasions; Narbonese Gaul, to assure links with Spain; the interior of Spain, to protect the Iberian coastal strip "inherited" from the Carthaginians. Almost involuntarily, Rome thus found itself at the head of a vast empire.

## BATTLE TACTICS

During the Battle of Cynoscephalae, which ended the war against Philip V, the Romans were left facing phalanxes of Macedonians, who utilized a tactic, adopted earlier by Alexander the Great, fundamental to many Macedonian military successes. As seen in the relief (*below*), this deployment consisted of the alignment of tight rows of infantry armed with very long lances. Once the first line had fallen, the second would lower its lances and take up position. The phalanx broke through the first Roman lines, but the following lines resisted. This allowed reserve Roman troops to move around and defeat the Macedonians. During the decisive battle between the Romans and the Syrians at Magnesia, in December 190 or January 189 B.C., the Syrian side presented a never-before-seen formation, the heart of which was the Macedonian phalanx, which alone had 16,000 men, flanked by armored knights, Cretan archers, Arabian troops on camels, "mowing" carts (with sickles attached to the wheel hubs), and great numbers of elephants. The Roman troops could count on only two legions and their Italic, Pergamen, and Achaean allies, or at most 30,000 men. Yet they were victorious, thanks to superior tactics. In this and other cases, it was the Roman legions' rigid discipline and tactical flexibility that made the difference, for these were characteristics that the Hellenistic and eastern troops could not emulate.

**GREEK PALADINS**
The war against Philip V was Rome's first intervention in grand style into the Aegean region. In order to justify the "descent into the battlefield," the Romans alleged the need to guarantee the freedom of the Greeks against the expansionist desires of the ambitious Macedonian monarchy. *Above*, a Corinthian helmet (fourth century B.C.).

**THE BATTLE OF PYDNA**
In 168 B.C. the Macedonian city of Pydna was the theater for a memorable battle between the Romans, led by the consul Lucius Aemilius Paullus, and the troops of King Perseus, the son of Philip V. The battle ended with the defeat of the Macedonian phalanx, which lost more than 25,000 soldiers. The coin shown here was issued in 71 B.C. to commemorate the victory. It depicts Aemilius Paullus with a trophy and the vanquished Perseus with his sons.

## *The Logic of the Empire*

The birth of the empire was to a large degree a chance occurrence, although Greek thinkers, such as the historian Polybius, saw it as an ineluctable historical scheme, the result of a precise and all-encompassing plan. In any case, it profoundly modified Roman society. External wars provided a broad range of booty and thus became increasingly popular among the lower levels of the Roman and Italic populations, who saw a means of bettering their position in life. *Negotiatores*, Latin and Italic traders, were even more supportive of these wars, which opened up new markets. Roman military chiefs, in their turn, saw in the overseas victories a tool for rapid political advancement at home. They were aware of the Hellenistic concept of the charismatic leader, favored by the gods and destined by nature to command. All this, along with the perception of the benefits of a "war machine" that could overwhelm any adversarial force, pushed Rome, after it had created an empire, to become truly imperialistic and to modify the "isolationist" policies that had heretofore predominated.

### CLASH OF CULTURES

The Macedonian wars placed the Romans in opposition to the Greek world for the first time. They introduced not only the fascinating philosophical concepts, culture, and art of the Greeks but also sexual customs that the Latin world considered unusual. Greek love, which predominantly concerned young men, with couples of *erasti* (lovers, older men) and *eromeni* (the beloved, young men), scandalized the Romans. The phenomenon of the *hetaerae* (courtesans) was perhaps even more difficult to understand. These were, literally, "companions," cultivated women who shared not only the bedchamber with men but also conversations, cultural awareness, and political ideas—something that was unthinkable in Rome.

**A HARSH LESSON**
After entering Rome's sphere of influence, the cities of Greece maintained a certain degree of autonomy at least as long as their domestic conflicts did not force the Romans to intervene with an iron fist. In 146 B.C. a force of 30,000 soldiers under the command of the consul Lucius Mummius defeated the Achaean League at Leucopetra and obliterated Corinth *(left)*, which was sacked without mercy. Julius Caesar refounded the city as a Roman colony in 44 B.C.

# Social Wars and Civil Wars

During the first century B.C., Rome, while victorious abroad, was tormented within its borders by a series of grave problems. Political opponents pushing for the suppression of their adversaries, a bloody social war against the Italic allies, and merciless civil wars between Romans culminated in terrible massacres, as well as slave revolts and plots against the Republic.

All these episodes were echoed by an equal number of upheavals within the political structure, which at this point was clearly not up to the task of managing the political and social problems tied to territorial expansion. At the same time, the government was unable to find the tools necessary to restore continuity.

**The Challenge of the Gracchi**
Improvement of the economic and social conditions of the peasants was central to the political activity of Tiberius and Gaius Gracchus, who attempted to break the aristocrats' monopoly over public land. *Right,* a small-scale reconstruction of a military surveyor at work.

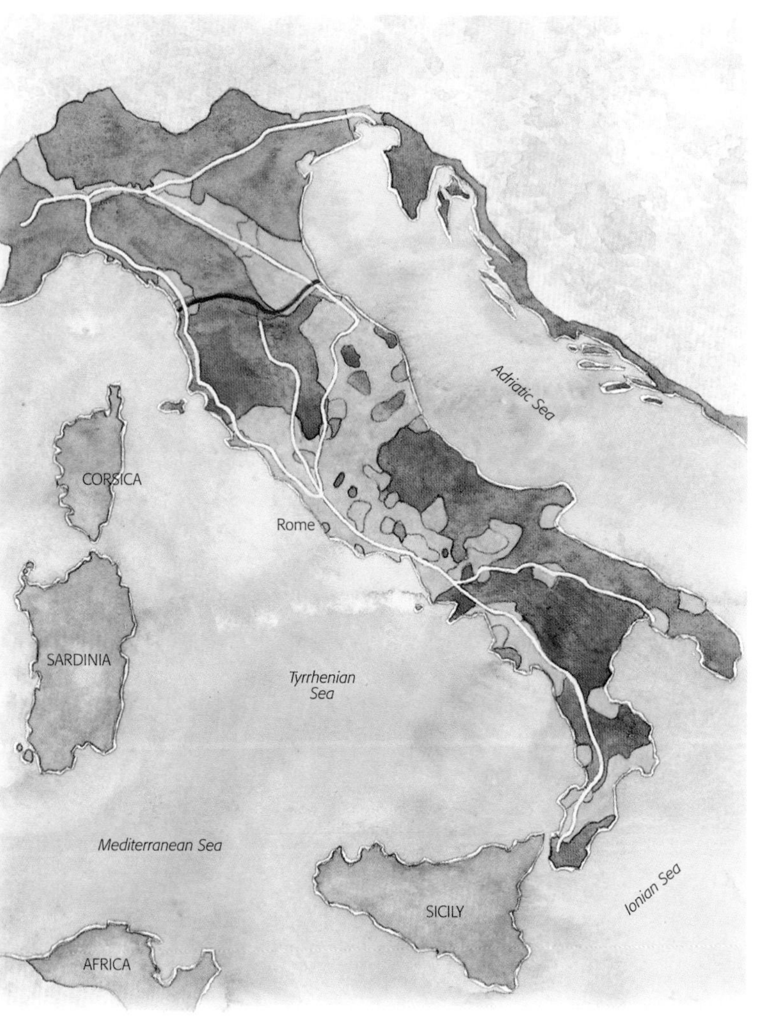


**The Peninsula in 91 B.C.**
The map shows the political organization of Italy before the outbreak of the Social War.

## *The Reforms of the Gracchi*

133–121 B.C.

The victorious wars procured new lands for the state but perilously impoverished the peasant classes that had borne the greatest burden. Two audacious tribunes of the plebs, or commoners, Tiberius and Gaius Gracchus, sought to remedy the situation. They proposed agrarian reforms that attempted to grant public lands to the poor—namely, land expropriated by public domain following various military campaigns. But they encountered fierce opposition among the senatorial class, which leased these lands from the state at ludicrously low prices. First Tiberius and then Gaius Gracchus were killed and their supporters slaughtered.

## *The Revolt of the Allies*

90–88 B.C.

Rome's Italic allies had contributed to the state's victories no less than the peasants. In exchange they expected to be granted Roman citizenship with the greater rights that this entailed. But the Romans wanted nothing to do with this. Despairing of receiving their due, the Italic allies decided to force recognition and unleashed the so-called Social War against Rome. They lost, but in order to defeat them, the city finally had to grant citizenship to the allies that remained loyal and then to all those who bore arms.

## *The Struggle between Generals*

88–80 B.C.

With the reform of the army carried out by Gaius Marius in 107 B.C., Roman soldiers no longer enlisted on the basis of income, as during the time of Servius Tullius, but signed up voluntarily in exchange for a stipend and a promise of land upon discharge. The troops thus began to identify more with their generals than with the state and in the end were used by their military leaders as tools for gaining or preserving power. Gaius Marius and then Lucius Cornelius Sulla exploited them for such ends and created powerful fratricidal struggles among the Romans.

**Stars of the Arena**
Certain gladiators became so famous that they drew crowds of fans and inspired writings such as the following, discovered in Pompeii: "Concealed, your features make maidens sigh." *Above*, a bronze gladiator's helmet dating from the first century A.D.

## *The Slave Revolt*

73–71 B.C.

Led by the gladiator Spartacus, thousands of slaves, wanting to free themselves from their shackles, took advantage of the civil struggles in Rome to rebel and fought fiercely in southern Italy. Although defeated by the Roman legions under Publius Licinius Crassus, they nonetheless landed another heavy blow to the Roman social system.

## *The Conspiracy of Catiline*

63–62 B.C.

The profound crisis of the Republic led an ambitious aristocrat, Lucius Sergius Catiline, to plot to take over power. Thwarted by the consul Marcus Tullius Cicero, the conspiracy exposed the fragility of the Roman political structure.

Lucius Cornelius Sulla

Gaius Marius

**Marius and Sulla**
The ferocious rivalry between these two men, nurtured by jealousy and greed for power, was central to one of the bloodiest and darkest pages in Roman history, which culminated in the establishment of Sulla's dictatorship.

### THE TROOPS OF SPARTACUS

The slave uprising that spread through Italy between 73 and 71 B.C. was the most notable in a series of slave revolts, which ignited hotbeds of rebellion in Sicily and Asia Minor, as well. In comparison to these, however, the revolt in Italy proper was of much greater import. It put Rome in danger and all the Italic peoples in fear. The bloody ferocity of the rebellion was matched by the harshness of the Roman reaction: the six thousand slaves who survived the battle that ended the rebellion were crucified along the Via Appia as a warning to any who might harbor similar ideas. For centuries, that "lesson" prevented slave rebellions within the empire. Spartacus's uprising had no ideological implication; it was simply an expression of the slaves' desire to regain a free way of life without the humiliations and risks of servitude. Nonetheless, in the modern era there have been numerous "spartacist" movements that have turned the gladiator rebel into a mythic figure and a symbol of rebellion against oppression—an image to which the cinema has also fallen prey. *Right*, a relief with a scene of gladiatorial games.

# From Republic to Principate

The first triumvirate, civil war, dictatorship, the second triumvirate, civil war, principality: in the repetition of these upheavals, the glorious Republic died and gave way to the autocratic power of the emperor, based on the strength of the army.

**The Triumph of Octavian**
This cameo depicts an allegory of Octavian's victory over Antony and Cleopatra at Actium in 31 B.C.

In 60 B.C., 693 years from the founding of Rome, during the consulate of Quintus Caecilius Metellus Celer and Lucius Afranius, a treaty was signed that signaled the true, if not official, end of the Republic. The three signers were Publius Licinius Crassus, Gnaeus Pompeius Magnus, and Gaius Julius Caesar, officially three private citizens; the subject of the agreement was the division of power in Rome.

**Mosaic of Peoples**
During the time of Caesar, independent Gaul was inhabited by an array of peoples—the civitate—who were subdivided among territorial cantons. Northern Gaul was inhabited by the Belgae, in particular the Nervians, Treverians, Suessiones, and Bellovaci, characterized by Caesar as being fierce and warlike. Even central Gaul boasted powerful groups, especially the Arvernians, Carnutes, Aedui, and Sequani. Aquitania, the most southern region, was inhabited by ethnic groups of Iberian origin.

## *The First Triumvirate*

Of the three figures who would pass into history as the "first triumvirate," Caesar was the youngest, the least wealthy, and the least famous. He also seemed to be the weakest but instead proved to be the most able, strong, and foresighted. Thanks to the agreement,

### THE GALLIC WARS

"All Gaul is divided into three parts: the first is inhabited by the Belgae, the second by the Aquitani, the third by those who in their own language are called Celts; in ours, Gauls. All these differ from each other in language, customs, and laws." Thus begins the first of the seven books of Caesar's *The Gallic Wars* (*De bello gallico*), published, to use the author's own words, "so that future historians would not be lacking in documentation about such grand undertakings." It was quite a noble goal, although probably the author's intention was principally to give his own version of the events in which he had been a leading figure, thereby anticipating the criticisms of his opponents and defending his actions from distortions and biased interpretations. It was not enough to have subjugated the barbarians; he had to convince public opinion of the value of his choices—a task at which Caesar revealed himself to be a master, just as he had been as a general on the battlefield. For us, the most interesting aspect of *De bello gallico*, at a distance of more than two thousand years, is the fact that Caesar described not only battles and itineraries but also the nature of the peoples he encountered, their lifestyles, institutions, and religions. This all constitutes a patrimony of information that allows us today to reconstruct the features of the ancient and composite civilization of the Gauls.

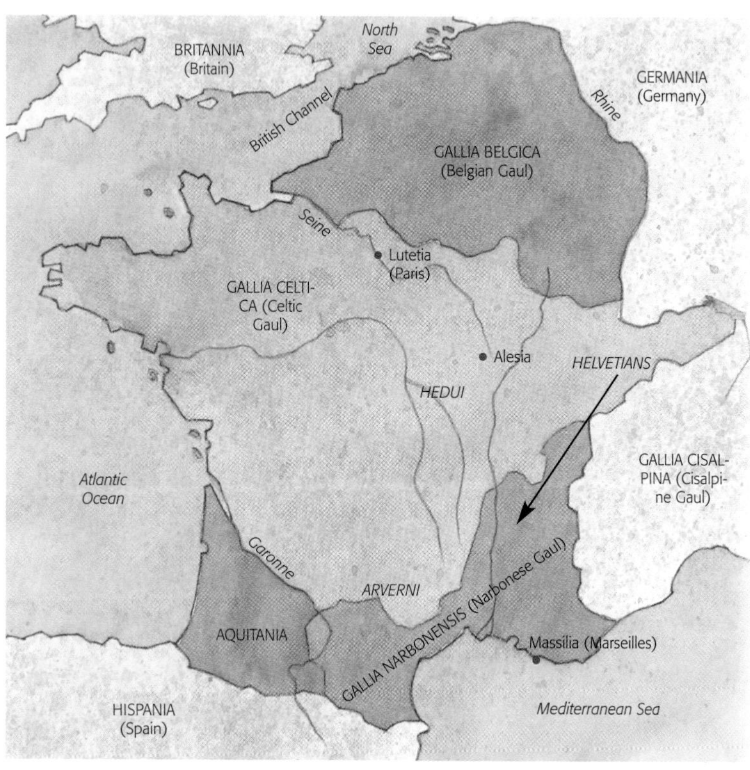


**The Surrender of Vercingetorix**
Vercingetorix, whose name is stamped into this gold coin, led the revolt of the Gauls against Roman occupation in 52 B.C. After some successes, he was surrounded by Caesar's troops at the fortress of Alesia and forced to surrender after a bitter assault.

he became consul in 59 B.C. and was named proconsul in Cisalpine Gaul the following year. He began the conquest of Gaul—an extraordinary operation that enormously enlarged the Roman empire—an epic he himself described in the splendid prose of *De bello gallico*. When Crassus died in the war against the Parthians in 49 B.C., the two surviving generals reached a point of confrontation. Caesar, commanding legions tempered by years of campaigns and venerated by them as an invincible commander, was undoubtedly the stronger. Without excessive effort he won the civil war against Pompey and the senatorial troops that supported him in a decisive battle in 48 B.C. at Pharsalus. For the next four years, until Brutus and the other conspirators put an end to his life, Gaius Julius Caesar was the uncrowned king of Rome, the revered prince victorious who decided the fate of the city and of the entire world. The empire did not yet exist in name, but in fact it was established.

## CAESAR, THE KAISER OF ROME

Caesar (*above, in a bronze bust*) was a brilliant and multitalented personality, one of the greatest political figures, generals, and writers not only in Rome but in all history. Indeed his name became the common appellation for Roman emperors and also a synonym for "sovereign" in many other languages and cultures: *Kaiser* in German and *Czar* in Russian are derived from the name of this famous Roman. Furthermore, from Caesar's family name, *Iulius*, is derived the name for the month of July, when the great man was born.

**CAESAR'S GREAT RIVAL**
Pompey the Great, depicted *(at left)* in a marble bust, was one of most notable figures in Roman public life during the late Republican period. Ambitious and tireless, he achieved much success in the military arena, thanks above all to his organizational abilities.

## *The Second Triumvirate*

Caesar died without legitimate offspring. His heir was a grandnephew, Gaius Octavius, whom Caesar had adopted as his son. After his adoption, the young man assumed the name Gaius Julius Caesar Octavianus. When he was barely nineteen years old, Octavian signed an agreement (the "second triumvirate") with Marc Antony and Marcus Aemelius Lepidus, the two other "pretenders" to Caesar's legacy. Like Caesar before him, Octavian seemed the weakest of the three. Marc Antony had everything: military fame, control over the wealth of the eastern provinces, the support of Egypt and its sovereign, Cleopatra. Nonetheless, it was Octavian who prevailed and in the end defeated Antony's Roman-Egyptian fleet at Actium in 31 B.C., crushing his rival, who committed suicide. Caesar's grandnephew held the destiny of the empire in his hands, and he was recognized as *princeps*, uncontested lord. Gaius Julius Caesar Octavianus became Augustus, the enlarger of the Roman empire and the founder of a power that would endure five centuries.

**PORTRAIT OF MARC ANTONY**
When Caesar's will revealed that the dictator had named his adopted son, Octavian, as his heir, Marc Antony went to war to contest Caesar's decision. Eventually, Marc Antony and Octavian reached an agreement that led to the second triumvirate.

# From Principate to Monarchy

During the first century B.C., a system was developed that, while formally maintaining the Republican constitution, concentrated all powers in the hands of a *princeps* who had to answer to no one.

When Julius Caesar, the conqueror of the Gauls and the head of a victorious and well-trained army, crossed the Rubicon, he initiated civil war against Pompey and the Senate—the crucial moment of rupture with the ancient republican system. The defeat and death of Pompey, in fact, gave Caesar full powers in Rome. Persuaded of the need to reform the state, he began a grand legislative project, to establish an enlightened monarchy. The conspirators' dagger, which took Caesar's life on the Ides of March in 44 B.C., brought these plans to a halt. After the victory at Actium, Octavian resumed his famous uncle's plan. He created a system in which power was concentrated in the hands of a single *princeps* who united in himself the prerogatives of the major republican offices, including the religious. What the Romans had sought to avoid for many centuries finally came to pass, as a necessary epilogue to nearly a century of long and disastrous civil wars.

## *The Mechanism of Power*

The legal foundation of the system was the recognition in the *princeps* of a *potestas* based on *consensum universorum*, that is, exceptional power based on the consent of the entire population—power that came to include oversight of the traditional republican magistracies, the proconsular imperium for the

**A Man of Quality**
Claudius, depicted here as Jupiter, was a wise and farsighted emperor. Thanks to a clear vision of the empire's prospects, he made important decisions, such as the extension of citizenship to the provinces.

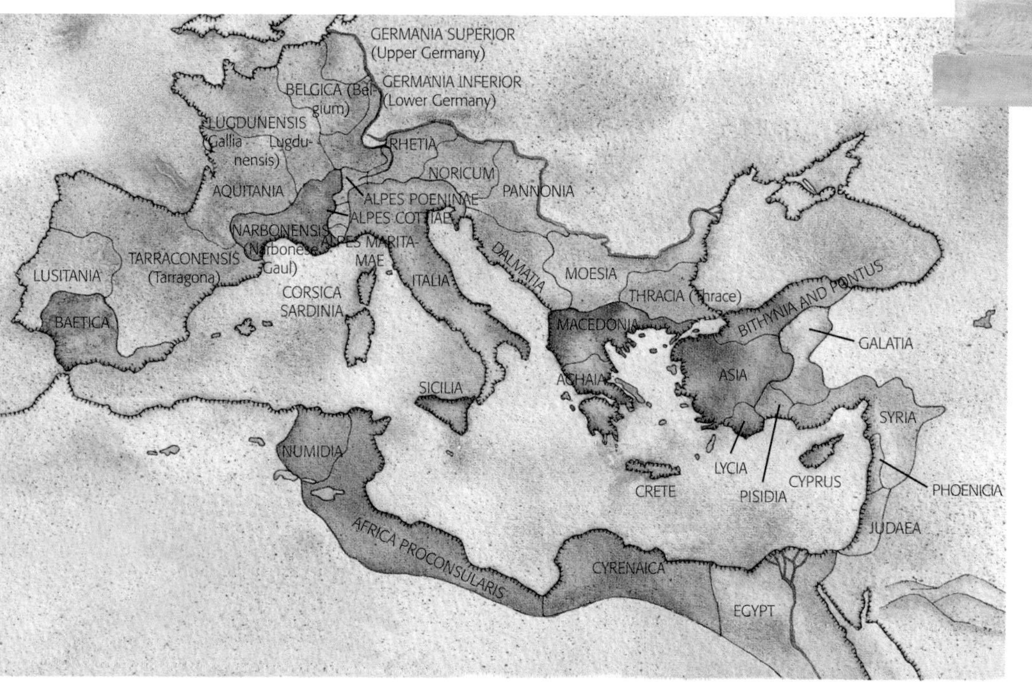


**From Germany to Egypt**
The map shows the empire upon the death of Augustus. Beyond Italy, it included the imperial provinces, directly dependent on the emperor because they were considered less secure, and the senatorial provinces, now pacified. Moesia, conquered under Augustus, was elevated to the status of a province by his successor, Tiberius.

Imperial provinces

Senatorial provinces

| THE JULIO-CLAUDIAN DYNASTY | |
|---|---|
| 27 B.C.–14 A.D. | Augustus |
| 14–37 A.D. | Tiberius |
| 37–41 A.D. | Caligula |
| 41–54 A.D. | Claudius |
| 54–68 A.D. | Nero |

**Augustus Pontifex**
The statue (*below*) depicts Augustus as *pontifex maximus,* an office that the *princeps* did not attain until 12 B.C., because the former triumvir Lepidus, *pontifex* since 44, had been granted this post for life. From Augustus to Gratian (A.D. 375), the emperors held the position of *pontifex maximus*.

**Augustus's Heir**
Front of a gold coin of Tiberius (*above*) from the first century A.D. During the imperial era the front of such coins always had a portrait of the emperor or members of the royal family, who were granted the right of effigy.

### AUGUSTUS AT THE CENTER OF CONTROL

In 27 B.C., Augustus was confirmed in the post of consul, which he had held since 31 B.C., with certain prerogatives, such as the right to convene the Senate and to present proposals with priority over other magistrates. At the same time he was granted the *imperium proconsulare* and the title *Augustus*. The *imperium proconsulare*, considered *maius* (greater) with regard to the other military heads, allowed him to exercise supreme command over all imperial provinces even without being proconsul. Augustus proclaimed him "choice of the augurs"—in other words, predestined to lead. With the *tribunicia potestas* (23 B.C.) Augustus was able set himself up as the patron of the common people, keeping them from supporting various powerful factions. He also acquired the right both to convene Senate and plebs and to have his decisions voted on as plebiscites, with the weight of law, as well as the right to issue an unrescindable veto of laws proposed by other magistrates. Finally, in 12 B.C. he assumed the post of *pontifex maximus* and thereby united in his person civil, military, and religious power.

imperial provinces (those that required a military command), and the granting of *tribunicia potestas*, the power and inviolability of the commoners' tribunes. Formally the old offices still existed, but in practice the *princeps* assumed them or subordinated them to his control.

## *Autocratic Degeneration*

With Augustus, the substance of imperial power was still cloaked in republican form. But under his successors, who ascended to the heights of power through dynastic succession, the contours of the empire began to change. Power became increasingly autocratic; the role of the army—in particular the praetorians, the military body that had been established to defend the prince and that was, against all republican norms, stationed in the city of Rome itself—became ever more important, while the Senate's power decreased. The administration of the state became more and more despotic until there was a veritable reign of terror under Nero, the last member of the Julio-Claudian dynasty. The principality had now given way to a monarchy tinged with an Eastern character, which finally provoked a rebellion on the part of the military commanders. They defeated Nero and then faced off against each other in a civil war to establish who among them should ascend the throne. Meanwhile, again from the East and spreading through the empire, came a new religion and worldview that would totally transform (and in part assimilate) the ancient Roman order.

**Insane and Cruel**
The ruler commemorated on this coin is Nero, offspring of the first marriage of Agrippina Minor, the last wife of Claudius. Nero became emperor at only seventeen years of age; but, after a good beginning, his rule degenerated into madness and bloodshed.

# The Brilliance of the Empire

The Flavian dynasty retraced the course of the Julio-Claudian reign in an even briefer period of time: the first emperor placed on the throne by arms; the second, an excellent administrator; the third, a dissolute autocrat killed in an uprising. But the long series of emperors that followed made the second century A.D. the golden age of the empire.

When Nero died, the four generals who had brought about his fall fought among themselves for the imperial throne. The one who emerged victorious, Titus Flavius Vespasian, the first emperor to come from the ranks of the Italic middle classes, proved to be an energetic and wise sovereign. His two sons followed him; the first, Titus, timid and well liked, reigned for only two years; the second, Domitian, aggressive, authoritarian, and dissolute, was assassinated by conspirators with the complicity of the Senate.

## *Flavian Monuments*

The Flavians were assiduous builders. Vespasian undertook the reconstruction of Rome, still devastated by the fire in A.D. 64 during Nero's reign. Vespasian also initiated the construction of the Flavian Amphitheater, the Coliseum (which, occupying the site of the artificial lake created by Nero in conjunction with his royal palace, the *Domus Aurea*, symbolically signaled the restoration of the area to the citizens of Rome). Vespasian's son Titus was able to do little more than inaugurate the amphitheater, given the brevity of his reign, ravaged by the tremendous eruption of Vesuvius in A.D. 79. Domitian, however, engaged in such an extensive policy of public works that he depleted not only the public treasury but also his own personal wealth.

The New Man
Vespasian was the first emperor who did not come from a noble family. His ascent to the throne marked an important change and demonstrated that it was possible to achieve the highest state office without belonging to the traditional ruling class.

Marcus Aurelius
The only imperial equestrian statue in gilded bronze that is still intact is this renowned portrayal of Marcus Aurelius. Erected after the victory over the Sarmatians in 176, it depicts the emperor dressed in a tunic and extending his right arm in a gesture of reconciliation.

DOMITIAN'S GAMES
Domitian loved gladiatorial games and combat. In 86 he had a stadium built for athletic competitions, where the Piazza Navona now stands. It was 275 meters long and 106 meters wide, and the two superimposed tiers held approximately 30,000 spectators.

TRAJAN'S LEGACY
The Trajan Markets *(above)* were part of Trajan's Forum, a gigantic and monumental complex built between the Capitoline and Quirinal hills.

A BELOVED EMPEROR
Titus, whose profile is stamped into this coin, was a wise sovereign, balanced and attentive to the needs of his subjects, and indeed was characterized as the "love and delight of humankind."

| THE FLAVIANS, NERVA, TRAJAN, THE ANTONINES | |
|---|---|
| 69–79 | Vespasian |
| 79–81 | Titus |
| 81–96 | Domitian |
| 96–98 | Nerva |
| 97–117 | Trajan (97–98 with Nerva) |
| 117–138 | Hadrian |
| 138–161 | Antoninus Pius |
| 161–180 | Marcus Aurelius (161–169 with Lucius Verus) |
| 180–192 | Commodus |

## *Emperors by Adoption*

After the death of Domitian, the Senate succeeded in imposing a new way of choosing the emperor: by senatorial nomination and by adoption.

Marcus Cocceius Nerva, who had been elected by the Senate, adopted his successor, Marcus Ulpius Trajan, an advocate of the senatorial aristocracy of Spanish origin; and he had the Senate ratify his appointment.

This practice, also followed by Nerva's successors, made it possible to avoid, with a series of cautious choices, the worst defect of the dynastic structure—namely, the passing on of power to an inept or despotic son, unsuitable for the office.

The results proved excellent and, thanks in part to the long period of domestic tranquillity guaranteed by the system, granted the empire an efficient administration and widespread prosperity. As a result, the provinces were merged with Italy and a truly universal Roman civilization was created, which embraced the entire Mediterranean basin.

Unfortunately, the tradition was broken by one of the most beloved, moderate, and intelligent emperors in Roman history, Marcus Aurelius. Rather than choosing his successor through a prudent adoption, he left the throne to his son, Commodus, who was utterly unsuited to the role. Despotic, surrounded by corrupt courtiers, and unpopular with the senatorial aristocracy, the new sovereign reopened the doors to disasters of dynastic successions and began a cycle of disorders, regicides, and violence that precipitated the Roman world into chaos.

# Autocratic Eccentricity and Anarchy

After the long series of "enlightened" emperors selected by adoption, the resumption of the dynastic principle, military crises, and the concomitant economic crisis shook the structure of the empire to its foundation.

This was the beginning of a period of instability that sometimes degenerated into outright anarchy, threatened the unified state with dissolution, and made the third century A.D. the most tormented era of the entire imperial period.

## *A New Dynasty*

The ascent to the throne of Commodus marked a watershed in the history of the Roman empire. The renunciation of the principle of adoption, which allowed the selection of the most suitable candidate for the post, and the policy of conflict with the Senate, begun by the sovereign, created a domestic crisis for the empire. At the same time, growing waves of barbarians pressing at the borders, the inadequacy of the "lin-ear" system of fortifications that defended

**Amidst Concubines and Gladiators**
The emperor Commodus, shown here in a youthful portrait, reigned as a despot for twelve years before being killed by a gladiator during a palace plot. He detested military life and loved carousing. He passed his nights in taverns and brothels in the company of sinister personalities, whom he sometimes elevated to the rank of advisers. He also loved circus games in which he himself participated, arousing the disapproval of the Senate.

**Triumphal Arch**
Erected in 203 in the western part of the Roman Forum, the arch of Septimius Severus commemorates the emperor's triumph over the Parthians.

**Fratricide**
*Below*, the front of a golden coin of Caracalla with the emperor's effigy. The sons of Septimius Severus—Caracalla and Geta—succeeded their father. Caracalla lost no time in clearing his brother out of the way by having Geta killed. A cruel and despotic sovereign, Caracalla was, according to some historians, obsessed by the myth and figure of Alexander the Great in whose footsteps he dreamed of following.

| THE SEVERAN DYNASTY | |
|---|---|
| 193 | Elvius Pertinax |
| 193 | Didius Julianus |
| 193–211 | Septimius Severus |
| 211–217 | Caracalla (211–212 with Geta) |
| 217–218 | Macrinus |
| 218–222 | Elagabalus |
| 222 235 | Severus Alexander |

**Hand-to-Hand Combat**
This marble relief from the so-called Amendola sarcophagus depicts battle scenes between Romans and barbarians.

the frontiers and forced excessive dispersion and pernicious immobilization of the troops, and the economic crisis caused by increasing military expenses created a situation of grave and imminent danger. The murder of the emperor in a plot and the ascent to the throne of a new dynasty in the person of an eminent military leader, Septimius Severus, stemmed but did not resolve the crisis, which re-exploded during the reign of Septimius's son, Caracalla. Despite the expansion of the tax base, achieved through the historic granting of Roman citizenship to all residents of the empire (A.D. 212), the economic crisis, triggered by the vertiginous growth of military expenses, became increasingly serious. In reaction, imperial power became more and more despotic and based on force rather than consensus: a tyranny tempered by repeated regicides.

## *Political and Military Anarchy*

Not even the last member of the Severan dynasty, Severus Alexander, escaped this tragic scenario; he was killed by his soldiers (A.D. 235), upon whom he had imposed excessively harsh discipline. The empire entered an era of devastating political and military anarchy, and the fifty years that followed were among Rome's darkest. There were rebellions, disputes among generals—there were years marked by five and even six emperors—and defeats abroad (one emperor, Valerian, was captured by the Persians). Incursions by the barbarians penetrated ever deeper (Rome had to be enclosed by walls, something that had not been seen since the times of the early kings) and the provinces progressively broke away. All this seemed to lead to only one outcome: the dissolution of the empire.

**Prisoner of the Persians**
In the year 260 an unprecedented event occurred: a Roman emperor was captured by the enemy. It happened to Valerian; and it was Shapur I, the Sassanian king, who inflicted this humiliation, after the battle of Edessa. In this relief from Naqsh-I-Rustam (Iran), the emperor surrenders to Shapur.

### THE NEW MILITARY STRUCTURE OF THE EMPIRE

The crisis of the third century put to a harsh test the defensive devices and war apparatus of the Romans. These previously had been oriented to conquest but progressively assumed a defensive aspect, needed to safeguard the geographical unity of the empire and to protect its inhabitants, whose legal status had gone from "subjects" to "citizens." On the eastern front, along the line of the Euphrates River, the Sassanian dynasty, which ruled Persia, loomed threateningly. The Goths, as well as the Carpathians, so-called because of their postings along the Black Sea and the lower Danube, represented a serious threat for Asia Minor, the northern Aegean, and the Balkan peninsula. The Iazyges and the Roxolani pushed along the middle Danube sector, the Sarmatians and the Alamanni along the Rhine. In mid-century there was an added danger from the sea, and Germanic and Celtic populations inflicted heavy defeats upon the Roman fleet, which until that moment had ruled the waves.

This situation also brought about a profound modification of Roman military structure. As far back as the early imperial age, the need to patrol the borders had led to the development of light-cavalry divisions, the only ones that, in case of danger, could rapidly reach threatened areas. The clash with the barbarian populations of the steppes, who were extremely skilled in combat on horseback, led to the creation and use of heavy-cavalry divisions, as well. The legions, the crux of the Roman war machine, also were strengthened through the creation of infantry divisions equipped with lances, suitable for blocking the Germanic cavalry.

# Reorganization of the Empire

**Nicomedia**
Diocletian built his imperial residence in Nicomedia (present-day Izmit, in Turkey). This marble portrait of the emperor comes from that Roman city.

At the end of the third century, the emperor Diocletian succeeded in arresting the dissolution of the empire but at an extremely high price: the bureaucratization and total and merciless militarization of the state, and its division into geographic-political units that were administratively autonomous and destined to split apart.

Diocletian's ascension as emperor, 17 September 284, seemed like the rerun of a hackneyed plot: the rebellion of the legions in part of the empire, the ephemeral rise to power of their commander, grand intentions soon frustrated by a new military rebellion. Gaius Aurelius Valerius Diocletianus, however, who assumed the throne with the name Diocletian, was destined to endure. His reign (284–305) was among the longest of any Roman emperor and one of the most accomplished. His reforms, bolstered by an enormous sense of duty, an unshakable faith in the grandeur and universal mission of Rome, iron determination, and a huge and unremitting capacity for work, had a profound impact on every sector of life in the empire.

## *Reform of the State*

The crux of the reorganization of the state carried out by Diocletian was the grouping of the empire into two parts, each ruled by an emperor with the title *Augustus*.

Diocletian took for himself the eastern portion, which included Illyria, Greece,

**Power Shifts**
The map shows the situation of the empire under Diocletian with the new imperial residences located in more decentralized positions with regard to Rome.



**Milan**
Among the very few remains of Roman *Mediolanum* are the columns of the portico of the basilica of San Lorenzo, precious testimony of what was, for nearly a century, the capital of the empire.

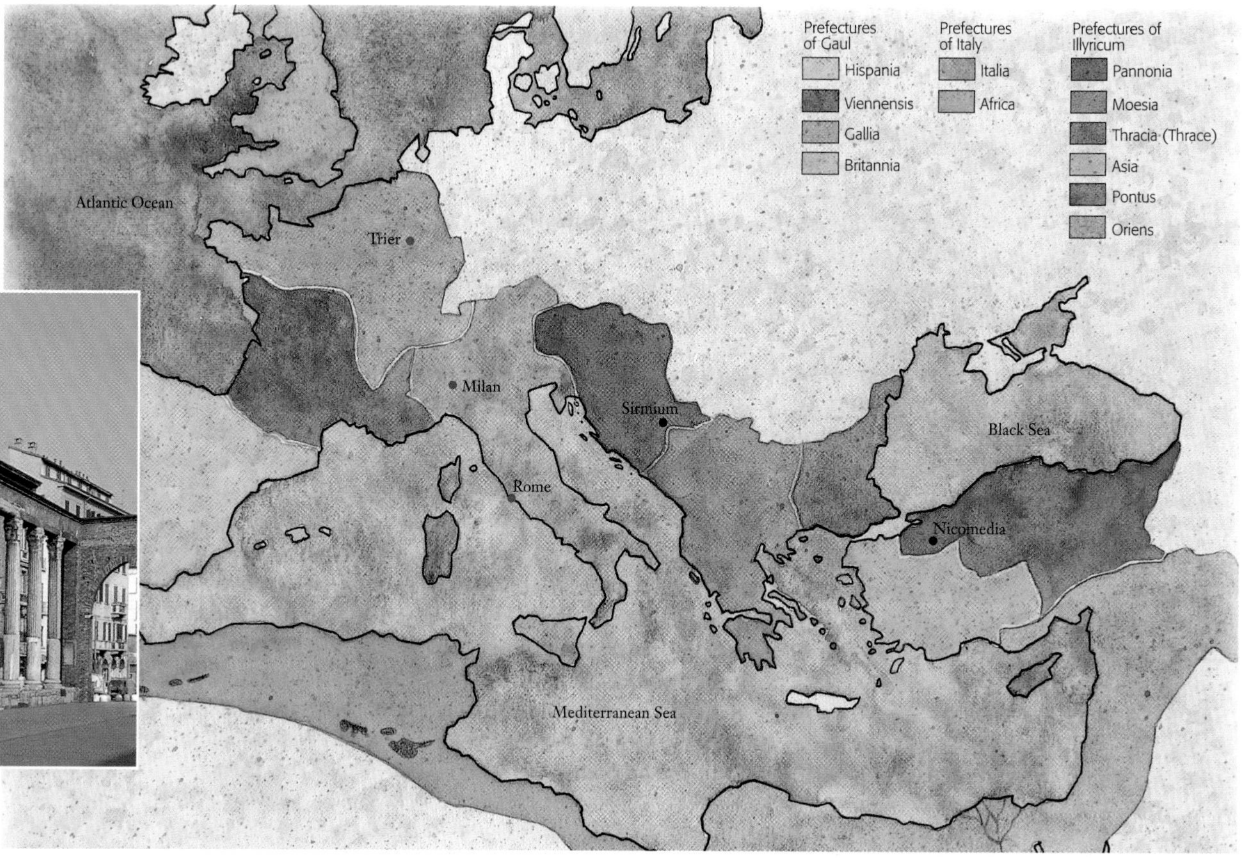

Pannonia, Asia Minor, Syria, and Egypt. He took an able colleague, Maximian, into partnership as the second Augustus and entrusted him with the western portion of the empire, including Italy, Gaul, Britain, Spain, and northern Africa. In turn, each Augustus was to have a subordinate Caesar, appointed to govern part of the territory and designated to succeed him in case of death or abdication.

This reorganization of powers corresponds to a shift of the capitals of the various sovereigns toward the frontiers. Diocletian established himself in Nicomedia in Asia Minor, Maximian in Milan. The two Caesars, Constantius and Galerius, established themselves in Trier and Sirmius (present-day Serbia), respectively. Thus in each frontier area, someone would be nearby and directly responsible, able to repel any attacks, instead of relying on a distant and overwhelmed emperor, always late in learning about events.

With this organization of the power structure came a systematic internal reorganization of the empire that rigidified its social configuration in a strongly hierarchical manner and subjected the productive sector to a stifling "planned economy" system, strictly regulated and controlled, with extremely onerous taxes. The provinces were fragmented into smaller units, each headed by a civil officer and a military commander who controlled by turns and were too weak to oppose the central power. The defense of the borders was totally reorganized through the construction of an uninterrupted series of ramparts reinforced by strategically placed fortresses, which were further provided with other lines of defense, capable of hemming in and containing any breaches. The short-term results were brilliant. External enemies were put to rout, domestic rebellions were cut short, and order was re-established. After twenty years of rule, Diocletian was able to withdraw to the palace he had built in his native city (present-day Split), confident that he had restored the empire and put it on track to survive at length. But this was simply a sort of "plaster cast," an extremely rigid cage that masked the problems within. The overall system of succession to power was destined to fail, the economy to lose vitality, defense to become increasingly precarious and costly, and the various regions to separate into autonomous blocks. Soon, Diocletian's successor, Constantine, would fundamentally change the very concept of the empire and Roman society, bringing about legalization of the Christian religion against which emperors had fought for 250 years, and definitively shifting the capital of the empire away from the city that had been its source and cradle.

**The Purple**
Otto II of Saxony, elected Holy Roman Emperor in 973, is depicted in this miniature with the symbols of power introduced in the Roman era: purple robes, a scepter, and a globe.

## COURT PROTOCOL

Diocletian introduced a complex court protocol that recalled rather closely a practice followed for centuries at the royal Persian court. The ritual of *adoratio*, public adoration on the part of subjects, typically Eastern in origin, was one of the most significant and ostentatious features and entailed, among other things, the obligation to kneel down in the presence of the sovereign. Every event that involved the emperor and his family in person, such as ascent to the throne or the birth of a son and even every simple appearance in a public place, was celebrated with pomp and solemnity. The *adventus*, the arrival of the emperor in a city, was considered a true divine "epiphany" and was greeted as an extraordinary event. On such occasions, spectacles and banquets for the people were organized, and lavish gifts were distributed to the troops. The purple of the emperor's robes became an exclusive symbol of imperial power. Its unlawful use was severely punished by law, even with death, because it was considered an attempt to usurp power.

The "imperial purple" par excellence was a red cloak, fastened at the right shoulder by a golden pin decorated with precious gems. Beneath, a silk tunic was worn, edged in gold, held at the waist by a wide purple belt. The scepter and the globe, respectively symbols of absolute power and the universe, along with processional arms—cuirass, helmet, and sword—completed the external display that symbolized the absolute power embodied by the emperor.

**Diocletian's Native City**
View of the Roman ruins of Salona, the native city of Diocletian. The emperor returned here in 305, after his abdication, and died here in 313.

# The Christian Empire

With the reign of Constantine, the Christian religion emerged from the catacombs and existed side by side with the imperial power in a symbiosis that completely changed the very structure of Roman society and the life of the empire.

The "tetrarchy" devised by Diocletian did not function for long. From its failure and the resulting long civil struggles, Constantine—the son of Maximian's Caesar—emerged victorious. His success, however, had a price for the empire: the recognition of the freedom of worship of the Christians, who had effectively supported the new sovereign. The Edict of Milan in 313 definitively sanctioned this recognition, which allowed the Christians to come out of hiding and gave their faith a powerful boost, despite the attempt by Constantine's nephew, Julian, to reinvigorate the ancient pagan religion.

The affirmation of the new faith favored the other great change made by Constantine: the transfer of the capital to a completely new city, created on the Bosphorus where the old Greek city of Byzantium stood. It was given the name of the emperor: Constantinople. Rome, the city of the ancient gods, was abandoned, although the empire continued to be called "Roman." For more than a millennium,

**Sun Worship**

The conversion of Constantine to Christianity was much slower than the story that has been handed down by the Church fathers. The emperor was a worshiper of the cult of the sun and had been educated in this faith by his father, Constantius Chlorus. It was only when he was about to die that Constantine decided to be baptized. This sculptural group from Rome depicts Mithras, often interpreted as a sun god, killing a bull.

## QUEEN AND SAINT

Helena, the mother of the emperor Constantine, is a figure of great importance. A woman of extremely humble origins (perhaps an innkeeper or even a servant at an inn), she was an early convert to Christianity. In 326 or 327 she made a long voyage to the Holy Land where, according to tradition, she found on Calvary the cross of Christ's suffering and had it brought back to Rome. To preserve and honor the relic, she erected a monumental basilica, Santa Croce in Gerusalemme, located close to the Aurelian Wall, not far from the Lateran. Her remains were placed in a magnificent porphyry sarcophagus (*below*), now in the Vatican Museums.

**Reduced Budget**
In the years when the Arch of Constantine *(right)* was built, Rome was losing its role as world leader, and the funds for its architectural prestige were greatly reduced. Thus, in order to decorate the arch, portions were taken from pre-existing monuments dedicated to Trajan, Marcus Aurelius, Domitian, Hadrian, and Commodus.

**Constantine's Daughters**
One of the best examples of Roman mosaic art is found in the church of Santa Costanza in Rome. The building was erected at the beginning of the fourth century as a mausoleum for Costantia *(below, detail)* and Helena, the daughters of Constantine.

until 1453 when the emperor Constantine XII fell defending Constantinople against attack by the Turks, that city would be home to the "Roman" emperors.

## *A New Legitimacy*

The Christian religion soon went from being "recognized" to becoming "official": a step that was formalized by the emperor Theodosius in 380, but which had already begun under Constantine. Empire and religion now had a relationship of complete symbiosis. One legitimized the other, and vice versa, creating a tradition that would be renewed in the Middle Ages. At the beginning, the emperors occupied the highest position, intervening as Constantine did in doctrinal disputes and in the organization of the Church. This rapidly reversed. St. Ambrose, for example, was in a position to recall and to censor the actions of the sovereign. A new and more enduring power, destined to outlive the authority of Rome and to continue its tradition, was now at the gates.

### THE SPREAD OF CHRISTIANITY

At the beginning of the Constantinian era, the spread of Christianity in the empire was quite varied. Three principal areas can be identified:

- The area of greatest diffusion, including Asia Minor (above all, Phrygia, Bythnia, and Pontus, as far as the Caucasus), Armenia, the regions to the west of the Euphrates River, Thrace, the islands of the Aegean, Cyprus, and the area around Edessa.
- Areas where Christianity spread but to a lesser degree than other religions: Greece, Macedonia, Syria, certain cities of Palestine, Egypt, Proconsular Africa and Numidia, Rome and adjacent areas, the coast of southern Italy and Sicily, Spain, and Gaul, as far as the Massif Central.
- Areas where the process of evangelization was just beginning: Palestine, parts of Arabia and Pannonia, Cyrenaica, Libya, and Mauretania.

Isolated communities existed along the northern coast of the Black Sea, in northern Gaul, along the Rhine River, in Rhaetia, in Noricum, and in the British Isles.

# Invasions and Collapse

It became increasingly difficult for an empire divided and rocked by continuous military revolts to control the barbarian tribes that were pushing against the borders at the Rhine and the Danube Rivers. At the beginning of the fifth century, defenses collapsed and the invaders spread through the land.

Since the second half of the third century, the empire had found itself subject to growing pressure at its frontiers. The population of the Germanic tribes, which for some time had settled along the borders of the empire, had increased greatly, and the space available to them was proportionally restricted. Between the end of the fourth century and the beginning of the fifth, these tribes—pushed from behind by the Huns and encouraged by the manifest weakness of the Roman world which was shaken by military revolts, religious divisions, and increasingly relentless taxation—pressed with growing frequency inside the borders and finally completely upset the balance of the empire.

## *The Collapse of Defenses*

Frequently, faced with a fait accompli, the emperors "legitimized" these invasions, granted the barbarians the status of *foederati*, or allies, and used them to fight alongside the imperial troops to defend

**Peaceful Invasion**
In 376 the Goths, under pressure from the Huns, asked to be allowed within the borders of the eastern empire and settled in Thrace. *Above*, a bronze Gothic plaque.

**The Weapons of the Barbarians**
The iron swords of the barbarian troops were between 80 and 90 centimeters long. The bronze hilts were polished or embossed to provide a better grip.

**Ravenna, Mausoleum of Galla Placidia**
In 402–403 Honorius, the emperor of the West, moved the imperial seat from Milan to Ravenna. Until mid-century, Galla Placidia, the sister of Honorius and the mother of his successor (Valentian III), held de facto power in the city and in Italy. The interior of her mausoleum *(right)* is covered with splendid mosaics.

## THE LAMENT OF ST. JEROME

"Words fail me, I am choked by sobs and can no longer dictate. The city that had dominated the entire world has fallen… the head of the world is cut off and in the ruins of a single city, the entire world has perished." These were the words of St. Jerome upon receiving news of that earthshaking event, the sack of Rome by the Goths.

occupied territory. This policy was often successful. For example, in 451 the help of the Goths was fundamental in pushing back the Huns led by Attila. The Roman world came under ever more barbarian influence, however, entrusting the empire's defense precisely to those from whom it should have been defended. In any case, the process of assimilation of the barbarians would have taken time, which is exactly what was lacking. Often the "allied" tribes, having penetrated imperial territory, took to brigandage and war with the Roman troops. Even worse, they were often victorious. In 378, at Hadrianopolis, the Visigoths who had gathered in the empire inflicted a searing defeat on the imperial troops, who abandoned the emperor himself, Valentian, on the battlefield. In 410 Rome was sacked by the Visigoths; in 455 the Vandals repeated the humiliation. In 452 the march across Italy by Attila's Huns was halted only by the intervention of Pope Leo the Great. The capital of the Western Roman Empire, the weaker of the two halves into which, since the time of Diocletian, the empire had been divided administratively (and since 395, politically and militarily, as well), was moved to Ravenna, where the protecting marshes fulfilled a role that was now beyond the capacity of the Roman army.

**Visigoth Votive Cross** Among the artistic expressions of the so-called barbarian peoples, goldsmithing assumed particular significance. This gold cross is mounted with precious gems and quartzes.

**The Last General** Flavius Stilcho (c. 360–408) was the last great Roman commander. In 402 he defeated the Visigoths, led by Alaric, at Pollentia, and in 406 he annihilated a horde of invaders under the command of Radagaisus. The general, depicted with his family in this ivory relief, was a *semibarbarus* in that he was the son of a Vandal father and a Roman mother.

## *The End*

What lived on in Ravenna, however, was only a simulacrum of the empire. In 476, Odoacer, a Germanic chieftain, deposed the last emperor, who by a cruel joke of fate bore the names of the founders of Rome and the empire, Romulus Augustulus (but was also Germanic on his father's side). This was the final blow. The glorious empire of Rome, at least in the West, was over. It continued for over a thousand years in the East but with a different language, religion, and traditions. The era of barbarian reign had begun.

## MONTESQUIEU'S OPINION

"Here in a word is the story of the Romans. With their principles they conquered all peoples, but obtaining this, the Republic could not hold. And so it needed to change governments, and principles contrary to the traditional ones caused the decline of their grandeur." In the *Considerations of the Causes of the Greatness of the Romans and Their Decline*, written in 1734, Baron Montesquieu had no doubts: it was the loss of freedom and the transformation of the active citizen into a subject that caused Rome's decline.

# Rome after Rome

Over the centuries, the millennial history of Rome, the greatness of its empire, and the wonder of its monuments have inspired and fascinated thinkers, artists, statesmen, sovereigns, and generals. Even today, European culture is an offspring of Rome.

More than a thousand years: such is the duration of Rome's history. The imperial period alone covers more than five centuries, and its events involve three continents. The legacy of this extremely long period is so vast and engaging that it is difficult to delineate its characteristics, even summarily. For example, one has only to consider the history of the law and institutions to understand how deeply Rome has affected modern societies. The study of how the myth of the Eternal City developed and was nurtured constitutes in itself a line of research that is extremely productive for social, institutional, political, and cultural history.

Throughout European culture, the imminent presence of Rome is conclusive: "I was aware of the affairs of Rome before I had any notion of those of my own house. I knew the Campidoglio and its plan before I knew the Louvre, and the Tiber before I knew the Seine. . . . The view of places we know to have been frequented by illustrious men moves us even more than hearing the story of their undertakings or reading their writings."—French writer Michel Eyquem de Montaigne (1533–1592)

## *Books and Voyages*

Within the framework of European cultural tradition, the rediscovery of Roman civilization came about from two major sources. The first was literature: the works of Cicero, Tacitus, Livy, Virgil, Horace, Caesar, and other Latin authors, handed down through the Middle Ages. The second source was the

**The Re-founder of the Empire**
Detail of the sarcophagus of Charlemagne in the Palatine Chapel of the palace in Aachen.

**The Coliseum according to Canaletto**
Giovanni Antonio Canàl, better known as Canaletto (1697–1768), stayed in Rome for a productive period during his career as a painter and engraver.

**Rome and Regime**
View of the Palace of Culture and Work in EUR (Rome). Fascism was the most recent but not the only regime to be inspired by the Roman empire, the unsurpassed symbol of universal domination.

arts, particularly architecture. Beginning in the Renaissance, the consuming fascination with ancient ruins aroused passion in masses of artists, religious figures, and men of knowledge, who felt duty-bound to travel to Italy to commune with these famous monuments. Finding themselves in places where history had unfolded gave rise to an incomparable emotion that enabled them to face with patience, if not outright cheer, the inconveniences of modern Rome—about which, broad and biting critiques exist.

Beginning in the seventeenth century, a trip to Italy with a principal stop in Rome was considered a fundamental stage in the education of the European ruling classes. The Grand Tour, as it was called, was a voyage of education and initiation, a "rite of passage" that gave life and depth to academic ideas. At the same time, it constituted the common educational foundation for the elite class of the Old World, an experience that all these people shared and that was fundamental to their culture.

## *To Each His Own*

From this rich and glorious past, visitors and scholars from time to time celebrated, according to the period and to their own personal inclinations, the grand tradition of either the Republic or the empire. There is no doubt that in time the latter had many more followers than the former, but the Republic also had its moments of glory—for example, between the eleventh and thirteenth centuries, contemporary with the development of municipalities in Italy, or during the French Revolution. However, it was the imperial tradition that prevailed, from Charlemagne, who re-established the Roman empire; to Napoleon, who took it as a model for his own projects and their accompanying settings; to Fascism, which often revived the imperial idea with involuntarily comical results. In Europe and not only there—one thinks, for example, of the United States, where the capital was reproposed as the "fourth Rome"—the face of power is still that of the Caesars.

**Emperor Napoleon**
Napoleon Bonaparte on the throne with the symbols of imperial power in a portrait by Jean-Auguste-Dominique Ingres (1780–1867).

**The Rediscovery of Rome**
This painting by Claude Gellée, known as Le Lorrain (1600–1682), depicts the Campo Vaccino (or cow field) in Rome. The artist showed great sensitivity to the lure of the city's ruins.

### THE TWO ROMES

The appreciation and emotion stirred by the history and monuments of ancient Rome often are accompanied, above all in the comments of visitors from the north, by annoyance, if not outright contempt, for the reality of Rome in their own day. "Newcomer who in Rome looks for Rome, and nothing of Rome appears to you there," reads a couplet from the sixteenth century, translated throughout Europe. "No Roman, if indeed truly a Roman, will ever kill a rat without leaving a registered account of the event," wrote the English playwright Thomas Nasche during roughly the same years (who, moreover, must have seen very few Romans, inasmuch as he was never in Italy). In 1796 a German man of letters, Karl Ludwig Fernow, wrote, "Just as ancient Rome contains everything that is most beautiful and noble that the human spirit has ever created in the happiest days of its flowering, modern Rome contains without doubt what is most unworthy, shameful and inauspicious that human foolishness has ever devised." The Romans can only console themselves with Goethe, a better judge of the city (and greater writer) than Fernow.

# The Revival of Forms

During the Middle Ages, classical buildings often were open-air quarries from which one might take, at little cost, previously worked building materials. With the Renaissance these buildings became venerable vestiges that provided inspiration for creating greater architecture—a process the effects of which are still felt today.

The collapse of the empire and the consequent demographic decline made available an enormous quantity of buildings that could be drawn upon to create new structures. Despite laws that sought to halt these depredations, Rome and other cities of the empire became vast quarries: People took capitals, architraves, columns, slabs of roofing and flooring, friezes, steps, and anything that might be put to use or, often, broken down to make lime. With time, the architectural, proportional, and symbolic notions that were fundamental to the ancient buildings were lost. Thus reuse became increasingly casual and "primitive": column shafts mounted upside down, capitals out of proportion to the supporting columns or used as holy water stoups, sarcophagi adapted as baptismal fonts, ceiling coffers used as façade decoration, and so on.

In different proportions, less evident but in any case widespread, the same fate befell gems, cameos, and other objects of use, in other words, the lesser arts. Often, to pieces known to be rare or prestigious in origin were attributed magical meanings or miraculous powers. Thus the remains of an empire served to confer prestige on reigns born from its ashes.

**Carolingian Residence** This marble fragment *(above)*, depicting a winged victory, comes from Charlemagne's residence in Ingelheim, which was built over the remains of a grand Roman villa. When, in 777, Charlemagne decided to rebuild it, he issued a precise order: favor the use of marble rather than wood in order to imitate ancient imperial residences.

## TRAFFIC IN MARBLES

In the Middle Ages, traffic in ancient marbles became a true "business." In Rome, as in the principal cities of the empire, workshops of marble-workers and furnaces for making lime multiplied in number. These profitable activities probably were the prerogative of just a few families, who handed down the profession over generations. Beginning in the eighth century, the right to issue authorizations for the despoiling of ancient buildings was held by the Pope: clear proof of the importance, above all economic, of this new industry, which was perhaps most remunerative during the early Middle Ages. Roman marbles were much coveted, not only in Italy; in the Carolingian era they reached the most northern regions of Europe. According to tradition, the marble columns and capitals of the Palatine Chapel in Aachen *(right)* came from Rome and Ravenna at Charlemagne's behest and with the pontiff's consent. Ancient pagan statues were also much in demand and, suitably remodeled to look like saints, were considered actual relics. Precious marbles were transported on carts or boats, generally of enormous size, given the proportions and significant weight of the materials.

**Imperial Seat** Charlemagne's throne stands at the center of the Palatine Chapel in Aachen.

## *The Rediscovery*

With humanism and then again with the Renaissance, which marked its artistic flowering, the vestiges of ancient monuments were seen as inspirational models for a rational art, tied to codified rules of proportion and not to the arbitrary "Gothic." The theory of the architectural orders—Doric, Ionic, Corinthian—was reconstructed and perfected on the basis of surviving (and now carefully studied) Roman buildings, and these orders were used to "frame" and give proportion to new buildings. The rediscovery of the forms of ancient art totally altered the history of architecture and the figurative arts. The Gothic style was abandoned, and a classically derived art was born that has persisted to the present. For centuries, Italy, the cradle of this movement, assumed the role of guide for the entire Western world. The monuments of Rome returned to live again in the hearts and drawings of designers everywhere: the last but not the least legacy of Roman civilization.

THE BATHS IN BATH
In the first century A.D., the Romans built present-day Bath at *Aquae Sulis*, in southern England. This was a grand hot springs facility with a profusion of sculptures and mosaics. Many decorative elements were utilized in later periods, such as the statue in the foreground of the photograph *(above)*.

MEDIEVAL CROSS AND ROMAN CAMEO
Shown in this detail of a gold and gem-studded medieval cross is its central cameo with a profile of Augustus.

### THE PILLAGING OF THE PANTHEON

Considered a masterpiece of Roman architecture, the Pantheon was erected in Rome by Marcus Vipsanius Agrippa in 27 B.C. in honor of all the gods. It was restored by Domitian and has come down to us in its present form through a reconstruction executed by Hadrian in A.D. 130. Its colossal dimensions are striking: The height of the dome, 43.4 meters, is equal to the diameter of the base. The sixteen columns on the façade are 14 meters high *(above)*. The coffered dome had an exterior facing of bronze roofing tiles that were taken away by the Byzantine emperor Constans II. Later, Pope Urban VIII (1623–1644) removed the remaining bronze structures from the porch and used them to create the baldachin in St. Peter's.

# The Capital of the Empire

Magnificence and complexity without limits: this is the face of the Urbs, the "city" par excellence—Rome, the largest capital of the ancient world.

**Imperial Rome**
This model of imperial Rome shows part of the city with the Circus Maximus in the foreground and, in the background, the Coliseum. At this time the city probably had over one million inhabitants.

If ever there were a people who organized and planned, it was the Romans. They imposed a rigid geometric law not only on the cities they established throughout half the world, from Scotland to Mesopotamia and from Romania to Morocco, but also on the farmland that extended around these cities, rigorously subdivided in a checkered formation through the practice of "centuriation." Yet the capital of this extremely orderly and well-organized empire was a monument to improvisation and irrationality, if not chaos.

The fault—more than with the hurried rebuilding after the Gallic invasion, as Roman historians maintained—seems to lie in the way in which the city was established. This occurred not on the basis of a unified foundation or a regular urban plan but rather through *sinecia*, that is, through a union of the various communities that arose on the hills on the left bank of the Tiber and that clearly had no inkling of the luminous destiny of their creation. Then rapid military conquests gave the city a universal role to which its urban layout was frighteningly unequal.

A plan for reorganization and beautification of the city began only with Augustus, so that it was said that the emperor "had found the Urbs made of bricks and had left it made of marble." Nero, after the disastrous fire of A.D. 64, which burned down a good portion of the city, started a vast program of urban renewal and rebuilding, which was soon interrupted

**Model of the Capitol**
Although it was the smallest of the seven hills of Rome, the Capitoline soon became the city's stronghold, symbol, and the affirmation of the capital's eternal duration.

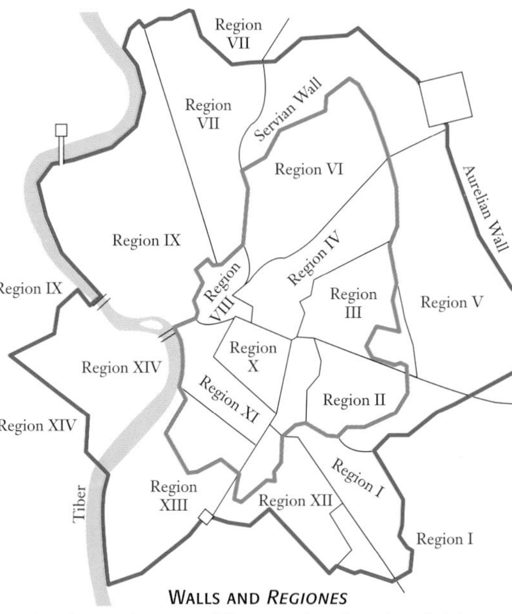


**Walls and *Regiones***
A schematic map of Rome, showing the division of the urban territory into 14 *regiones* (regions), which correspond roughly to present-day districts, and the Servian and Aurelian walls.

## THE FORUM OF CAESAR

About 54 B.C., Caesar fully developed the idea of building, next to the ancient Roman forum—laden with memories and evocations but narrow and disorganized—a new, rational forum, to be financed with the spoils from his campaigns in Gaul. The chief problem for the dictator was not to conceive and finance the project but to bring to completion the complex series of expropriations necessary for freeing up the land (an undertaking that employed a host of lawyers, including Cicero). Many administrative functions formerly carried out in the republican forum were meant to be transferred to the new space (with the indirect benefit of shifting the center of gravity of power to a place that glorified the *gens Iulia*). But the new forum also accommodated activities not foreseen by the founder: amorous encounters that, at least according to the poet Ovid in his *Ars amandi*, took place beneath the forum's porticos under the protection of Venus. The forum of Caesar was for the most part exceeded in size and sumptuousness by later imperial forums, but without it, these later projects probably never would have been realized.

PORTICO OF THE FORUM OF CAESAR
The construction of the forum was financed with revenue from the spoils of war collected principally in Gaul.

THE PORT OF ROME
Founded by Ancus Marcius at the mouth of the Tiber, Ostia became the port of call for Rome from the time of Augustus on. Goods coming from every corner of the empire were stored in warehouses *(horrea)*, such as those in the photograph.

by his death. The grandiose face of Rome, the remains of which still make an impression on visitors, is in large part the work of the great emperors of the second century A.D., who created the complex of forums that made up the center of the city and expanded the small palace on the Palatine into an immense structure occupying the entire hill. Their successors erected many of the monuments now and forever associated with the grandeur of Rome, from the baths of Caracalla to the basilica of Maxentius.

The fruit of their centuries-long work was a city of extraordinary monumentality and beauty, which nonetheless could never completely correct the disorganized layout inherited from its origins and largely the result of chance.

## *One Center, Two Circumferences*

The center of the city (and of the entire world) was the Roman forum, later extended by the imperial forums. This extraordinary and monumental grouping, wedged between the Palatine, Capitoline, Quirinal, and Viminal hills, was where the heart of Rome beat. Here were the most sacred temples, the senatorial curia, and the city's most ancient and venerated remains, its most significant symbolic sites. The encircling masonry city walls gave organization, if not order, to this immense urban agglomeration—in the imperial era the largest in the entire ancient world. The first wall, conventionally attributed to King Servius Tullius, enclosed the original hills of Rome. The second, erected toward the end of the third century A.D. by Emperor Aurelian, surrounded the inhabited area as it existed at the time (also crossing over the Tiber in the area of the Tiber Island). The urban fabric was divided up into 14 *regiones*, or districts, on the basis of an administrative reorganization that dated from the time of Augustus. Outside the walls, the urban periphery extended for kilometers with its dense series of tombs, mausoleums, rural villas, postal stations, stables, and suburban estates clustered around the consular roads that branched out from the city gates and led as far as the empire's borders. For centuries, this empire was the greatest and most glorious ever witnessed by humankind.

# The Cities of the North

Gradually as the Roman legions ventured out into the lands north of the Mediterranean, they brought laws, order, development, and a familiarity with urban life and its advantages, which found expression in new, large, rational cities, built according to Latin criteria.

The first colony created by the Romans outside the peninsula was *Narbo*, founded in 118 B.C. along the banks of a wide coastal lagoon (now filled in) along the Via Domitia, the consular road that linked Roman Italy with the Spanish territories. Narbo played a critical role in many crucial events in Roman history. It was a forward base during the campaigns against the Cimbri and the Teutons, and it was a fundamental cornerstone during Caesar's conquest of Gaul (and was refounded by Caesar himself in 45 B.C. as *Colonia Iulia Narbo Martius Decumanorum* and repopulated by veterans of the celebrated Tenth Legion). Under Augustus it became the capital of the maritime province of Gaul, which assumed the name Narbonese Gaul. Later, it lost some importance, but in any case it remained one of the major cities of Gaul until the end of the empire.

**Cologne on the Rhine**
This tower *(right)* is what remains of the circle of walls, almost four kilometers long, that surrounded Cologne in Roman times.

## *The Capital on the Rhine*

Trier, probably founded by Augustus about 16 A.D. but raised to the rank of colony by Claudius with the name *Augusta Treverorum*, was for centuries the city behind the front lines for the legions operating along the Rhine. Then, in the third century, it became the capital of *Imperium*

**Provincial Metropolises**
Under Augustus the cities of Narbonese Gaul were the object of massive planning and building projects. Arles and Nîmes, in particular, had public buildings that almost rivaled those of Rome in monumentality and elegance. *Below*, the amphitheater in Arles.

**Porta Nigra**
The principal surviving Roman monument in Trier is the Porta Nigra *(above)*, which owes its name to the color, taken on over the centuries, of the large blocks of sandstone from which it is built.

*Galliarum* (the administrative authority for Gaul), and, under the reign of Diocletian, Caesar's headquarters in the West. At that time it was one of the largest cities in the empire, extending over an area of almost three hundred hectares, enclosed by an impressive band of walls (of which the spectacular Porta Nigra remains, one of the largest constructions of this type left from Roman times). Everything in this city was on a colossal scale, from the imperial baths, which covered over three and one-half hectares, to the gigantic *horrea*, the granaries that held the provisions for the Rhine legions. Its decline began early in the fifth century, when Stilicho recalled to Italy the legions that still defended the Rhine, in practice abandoning the northern frontier. Thus after four centuries, Rome lost its outpost in the north.

**Along the Via Domitia**
Narbonne was traversed by the Via Domitia, an important artery that linked Italy to Spain. The photograph shows a stretch of the road that was discovered in the center of the city.

### THE GLASSWORK OF COLOGNE

In antiquity, Cologne was famous throughout the empire for its glasswork: little bottles for perfumes and unguents, glasses, and, above all, bowls with decorations in relief and bottles with square bases, known as "bottles of Mercury." Some pieces were obtained through glassblowing; others, such as the bowls, with the use of a mold. They were so valued that they were exported throughout the empire and even beyond its borders. This commercial success anticipated the equally resounding fame of another celebrated local product, "cologne water." Developed as a medicine in the early eighteenth century by a Cologne resident of Italian origin, this became the male perfume par excellence.

**Made in Cologne**
This little flask in blown glass (second century A.D.) is a true work of art.

## *City of the Empress*

The present-day German city of Cologne was founded about 39–38 B.C., when the Roman general Marcus Agrippa, the son-in-law of Augustus, quartered the Ubii tribe there; the new settlement was called *Oppidum Ubiorum*, fortress of the Ubii. Imperial intentions were for this to become the capital city of a new Roman province that extended from the Rhine River to the Elbe. But the defeat of Varus forced the Romans to withdraw along the Rhine, giving up their plans for expansion. However, this lull did not affect the city. Agrippina the Younger, the daughter of the imperial prince Germanicus and wife of Claudius, had been born there and always retained affection for the place. She raised it to the rank of colony with the name *Colonia Claudia ara Agrippinensium*. She encouraged the city's development as a Roman stronghold to defend the northern *limes* (border). In fact, in A.D. 80, Cologne became the capital of a province, *Germania inferior*. As long as the Romans succeeded in holding the Rhine frontier, for which Cologne was the pivotal point, the city prospered. The collapse of the imperial borders, however, led to its eclipse although not its disappearance. Today Cologne, known as Köln in German, is one of the most important cities in Germany.

# Guarded by the Volcano

The two Campanian cities of Pompeii and Herculaneum, buried suddenly by the eruption of Vesuvius in A.D. 79 and rediscovered in the eighteenth century, provide us with a vivid and fascinating image of two prosperous Roman provincial centers from the first century.

**Everyday Life**
The ruins of Pompeii have given us not only great works of art, such as sculptures, frescoes, and mosaics, but also many utilitarian objects, such as this dish with eggs. These have allowed us to reconstruct the everyday life of the inhabitants of the Campanian city.

Pompeii, with most of its inhabitants, was wiped out in a few moments. Streets, houses, and monuments remained sealed for centuries beneath a blanket of volcanic ash and stone several meters thick. Thus vanished a settlement rich in history. Its origins dated back to the fifth and sixth centuries B.C., and, prior to being a flourishing Roman city, Pompeii had been an important center for the Etruscans and the Samnites. It was during the Samnite era that the city assumed its definitive shape with a rectangular city-block layout based on the perpendicular intersection of streets, the forum surrounded by the major religious and administrative buildings near the southern walls, and the residential quarters in the northern part. When the eruption occurred that finally buried the city, Pompeii was just recovering from a violent earthquake that had struck in A.D. 62. The new catastrophe thus found a city in the midst of reconstruction, and excavations have been able to bring to light even minute and curious details of city life, those that usually have been lost in archeological sites.

## *Herculaneum*

Initially, the volcanic eruption buried Pompeii and Stabia beneath ash and stone. Nearby Herculaneum, however, was in large part spared these destructive agents. A few days later, however, it was suddenly inundated by a sea of mud that then solidified, "sealing" the city with everything it contained. Even the upper stories of houses were preserved along with some of the organic material found there, from wood structures to papyruses and other perishable objects, which in Pompeii had been consumed by the great heat of the eruption. This type of catastrophe, disastrous for the inhabitants, was providential for us, for today we have nearly intact buildings and a large quantity of household goods through the study of which even the

**The Baths**
*Above*, the vestibule of the baths of Herculaneum, illuminated by a skylight that rests on four columns.

### THE DISCOVERY OF HERCULANEUM

The history of the discovery and excavations of Herculaneum is one of the most tormented and disastrous in archeology. The first chance discovery, in the early eighteenth century, led to a series of campaigns conducted by the Prince d'Elboeuf, who attempted to pilfer the statues from the ancient theater. Beginning in 1738, official excavations were conducted under the aegis of Charles III of Bourbon. However, these were not open-air excavations, and traces of the city were reached through deep tunnels in the tufa with the sole goal of enriching the collections of the nearby Royal Villa in Portici. Throughout the nineteenth century, work was continually resumed and interrupted. It was only in 1927 that regular campaigns began, carried out with modern criteria and continuing until the present. Thus far, much of the southern quarter has been uncovered, two bath structures, a large gymnasium, a suburban sacred area, and part of the forum quarter. In recent years, excavations have resumed in the most celebrated building in the city, the Villa dei Papiri.

**The Heart of the City**
*Above*, the remains of the forum of Pompeii with the Arch of Triumph and the entrance to the covered market *(macellum)*.

**Mosaic of Alexander the Great**
This mosaic, considered one of the masterpieces of ancient art, was discovered in the House of the Faun in Pompeii in 1831. Made up of approximately one million tiles, it depicts the battle of Issus, fought between Alexander the Great and Darius III of Persia.

**Death by Asphyxiation**
Cast of an inhabitant of Pompeii, surprised by the fatal rain of volcanic stone and ash.

## THE FINAL HOURS OF POMPEII

The agony of the Pompeians, surprised by the sudden and deadly rain of volcanic stone and gas spewed from the volcano, was terrible. When the bodies of the inhabitants who were mown down in the streets decomposed, they left a series of cavities in the surrounding volcanic material, which had solidified. Thus, by injecting plaster into the spaces, archeologists have managed to obtain a dramatic and moving gallery of "statues" of people and animals killed by the eruption and then "reconstructed" in the poses they had at the moment of death.

smallest details of life from another time can be reconstructed.

Herculaneum had been an Etruscan, Oscan, and Samnite city before it entered the Roman orbit at the beginning of the third century B.C. after the Social War (in which it participated on the side of the rebels fighting against Roman hegemony). It reached the high rank of *municipium*, populated by Roman settlers. At the time of the eruption, it had become fully integrated into the Roman world and was well known as an elegant vacation spot. While less extensive than the excavations at Pompeii, those at Herculaneum reveal an even more intact city with its paved streets, porticoed façades of houses resting on pillars, baths, public buildings, a splendid theater, and ample and comfortable noble residences.

# The Role of Africa

The Roman occupation of northwestern Africa, corresponding to present-day Libya and the Maghreb (Morocco, Algeria, and Tunisia), was relatively slow and laborious. For a long time after the destruction of Carthage, Rome governed the region through protectorate systems, which entrusted the administration to various local realms.

Later, with the creation of the African provinces, a great urban civilization was born that was capable of taking advantage of the opportunities offered by maritime trade and by a territory considerably richer and more fertile than it is today.

## *Leptis Magna: Splendor Beneath the Sands*

Buried beneath a mantle of sand up to twelve meters deep, the ruins of Leptis Magna, the native city of Emperor Septimius Severus, were saved from pillage and now reveal the splendid face of a Roman African city of the first order. It was established on the Libyan coasts as a Punic settlement, but after the fall of Carthage, it came under the political influence of the kingdom of Numidia and the intellectual influence of nearby Alexandria. Leptis Magna (the adjective distinguishes it from another Leptis, less important and therefore known as Leptis Minor) was a major settlement in the Roman African world. Already extensive and flourishing in the second and first centuries B.C., the city was favored by

### PORT OF MARBLES

Leptis Magna was the preferred port of call for building materials (marble, above all) and works of art (especially sculpture) used to embellish the Roman cities of Africa. Most of the marble—and probably many of the stonecutters who worked on site—came from the quarries of Proconnesus in Asia Minor. The material arrived at Leptis Magna in semifinished form or even blocks and then was finished on the site. Columns were an exception and arrived in Africa already carved. Sculpture, at least in part, was produced in the city; only those of greatest value arrived already finished from Greece, Italy, or Asia Minor. Thanks to this traffic, during the middle imperial period Leptis Magna had more monuments than any other settlement in the entire North African area.

**Medusa's Head**
*Above*, an architectural detail from the forum in Leptis Magna.

**Forest of Columns**
*Below*, the theater of Leptis Magna, built in the Severan era.

**Mosaic Art**
This mosaic from the second century A.D., depicting Venus astride a centaur, came from a private residence in Timgad.

**Arch of Trajan**
This is the best-preserved monument in Timgad. Its name comes from an inscription that commemorates the founding of the city by Trajan. In reality the arch is later, dating from the time of the Antonines or the Severans.

Augustus, who reorganized its urban plan, and by Septimius Severus. Its large port, which covered an area of over ten hectares, was famous; and, during imperial times, it was a collection point for great quantities of Italian and Asian marbles. These were used in large part for monuments in African cities, which lacked building material of this type. Partially damaged by various earthquakes, the city never recovered from the devastation of the last quake, which also caused a disastrous flood, due to the rupture of a dike. It was finally abandoned and buried by the sands. Rediscovered in part in the seventeenth century, it owed its definitive rebirth to the Italian archeological missions of the 1920s.

## *City of Trajan*

Built about A.D. 100 at the behest of Trajan, Timgad—*Colonia Marciana Traiana Thamugadi* in Latin—was one of the major urban centers in the region, a metropolis celebrated throughout the Mediterranean world for its splendor. It was constructed by the legate Munatius Gallus at the foot of the Algerian mountains, where the coastal road branches off toward the interior. With a regular *insulae* (city block) layout, typical of newly founded Roman cities, it had a forum near the intersection of the main axes. The great development of the colony led to an impressive expansion of the city, also encouraged by the tearing down of the walls and by the creation of a new monumental center, west of the original city core. During this expansion—which peaked in the Severan era—the large triumphal arch that still dominates the ruins of Timgad probably was built. However, the complex system of trade and farming that made possible the city's prosperity did not survive the Vandal invasion of the fifth century, and then the Arab invasion of the seventh century brought about its decline.

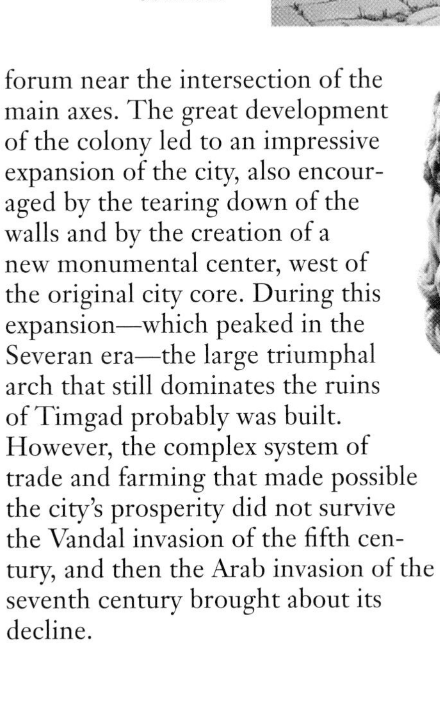

**African Emperor**
Septimius Severus *(right)* was born in Leptis Magna in 145 and returned there as emperor between 202 and 203, during a long voyage in Africa, then one of the most prosperous provinces.

# The Crossroads of the East

Trade with the East, important at any time, became truly vital for the economy of the Roman world between the second and fifth centuries. Centers that functioned as crossroads for this flow of travelers and goods, such as Dura Europos, Gerasa, and Palmyra, became large and prosperous cities, among the liveliest and proudest of the empire.

**River Sentinel**
The city of Dura Europos was built along the bank of the Euphrates. The acropolis was situated on a peak above the river, and on its slopes the city spread out, divided into regular blocks by rectangular streets.

Dura Europos, founded by a Seleucid general upon the remains of an older settlement, was the Roman port on the Euphrates. It was fundamental to the control of commercial and military traffic that took place along the banks of the great river. A crossroad for goods and people, it boasted a blend of Greek, Parthian (it had long been a part of the Parthian empire), and Roman architectural models. Its period of greatest brilliance was under the reigns of Septimius Severus and Caracalla in the third century A.D. At that time, a strong garrison resided there under the command of the *dux ripae*, the general who supervised the restless river frontier. The city's glorious era ended with its conquest by the Sassanids in 256 A.D.; and it is only in modern times that this "Pompeii of the desert," as it was called, re-emerged from the sands.

## *Jewel of the Desert*

Gerasa—present-day Jerash in Jordan, some forty kilometers from Amman—is one of the most suggestive archeological sites in the East. First founded in the Bronze Age, along the valley of a stream that supplied the most precious desert commodity—water—it reconciled its Nabathean cultural beginnings with

**A Theatrical Beauty**
Built about the mid-second century A.D., the theater of Palmyra is one of the most beautiful of antiquity. The lower level of the stage *(right)* is particularly well preserved with its façade with columns that spread over three exedrae.

**The Colonnaded Road of Palmyra**
This triple arch, built in the Severan era, led into a colonnaded road 1,100 meters long, which included the central street, 11 meters wide, and two covered and porticoed side streets, each 6 meters wide.

**The Oval Piazza**
The Oval Piazza *(left)*, its form unequaled in antiquity, is one of the most fascinating and mysterious places in Gerasa. In the shape of an irregular ellipse with axes respectively 90 and 80 meters long, it is surrounded by a colonnade. Its practical function has yet to be clarified.

**The Columns of Artemis**
The greatest sanctuary in Gerasa was the Temple of Artemis, a divinity comparable to the great Eastern goddess, Ishtar. The building was erected at the height of the city's economic power, in the second century A.D.

Hellenistic and then Roman influences. It was a grand city with two theaters and colossal and unique monuments, such as the great Oval Piazza and the Temple of Artemis, the tutelary divinity. Gerasa reached its culmination in the second century A.D., when its merchants dominated the caravan routes and the new road laid out by the Romans between Damascus and the port of Aqaba on the Red Sea. It survived, almost unscathed, the crisis that struck the western portion of the empire and passed under Byzantine rule. It was sacked, first by the Sassanids and then by the Arabs, but the final blow was a series of earthquakes that devastated the city in the eighth century.

## *Imperial Oasis*

Palmyra, built around an oasis in the Syrian desert, was for centuries one of the greatest caravan centers of the East. Its merchants traveled as far as the borders of India and even China and penetrated the Arabian desert. Meanwhile, its rulers managed skillfully to steer a middle course between the Romans and the Parthians, while remaining independent of both. The situation changed in the third century, when the Parthians were replaced by the Sassanids. Their rigid policy of closed trade strangled commerce in the city and forced it to depend increasingly on the Roman empire to the point of assimilation. This situation in turn provoked the rebellion of a great sovereign, Queen Zenobia (one of the most notable women in antiquity), and harsh Roman repression at the hands of Emperor Aurelian. This was a blow from which Palmyra never recovered, although it continued to struggle along at least until the ninth century, first under Byzantine, then Arab rule.

### THE POMPEII OF THE DESERT

Dura Europos was given this designation by archeologists not only because of the state of preservation of its ruins but, above all, because—like the Vesuvian city—it constitutes a great museum of wall paintings. In fact, a series of fortunate conditions (particularly the dry desert climate) have allowed the preservation of perishable materials almost always lost elsewhere. These include textile and leather fragments and, most important, numerous documents written on papyrus and parchment. Many bas-reliefs *(see example below)* and paintings also are preserved, both of a decorative nature and with historical-religious subjects. These decorated the walls of both public and private buildings. Just as in Pompeii, there is also a series of graffiti related to the everyday life of the citizens.

# The Frontier of the Empire

Few monuments in history have been as clearly significant as the ramparts of Hadrian and Antoninus Pius—the Roman fortifications that divided the romanized lands of Britain from the wild territories of Scotland. On one side was Rome, with its order and civilization; on the other, the tumultuous and rebellious world of the unshakable Celtic tribes.

**Roman Art in Britain**
This bronze head with a ceremonial helmet, which can be dated to the second century A.D., was found near London.

For a long time, Rome had an offensive mentality, bent on conquest. The fortifications, of which its legions made ample and wise use, were field structures, temporary instruments of protection during respites or for winter camps, or used as bases for maneuvers during wartime operations. Between the first and second centuries A.D., however, this mentality changed. The empire had become ever larger and the forces to protect it increasingly costly to maintain. The impetus toward conquest subsided, and emperors began thinking more about how to defend what had been annexed than about conquering other lands and other populations difficult to absorb.

**The Northern *Limes* of the Empire**
The map shows the borders of Roman Britain under Hadrian and Antoninus Pius.

Wall of Antoninus Pius

Hadrian's Wall

**Corbridge, Northumberland**
*Below*, Hadrian's Wall near Corbridge. In the foreground, the foundations of the military encampment structures.

## *A* Vallum *along the* Limes

Then there emerged the concept of the *limes*, a boundary between romanized lands, to be defended, and wild lands, inhabited by barbarian populations not worth subduing. For much of its extent, this boundary was marked by large rivers—the Rhine, the

Danube, the Euphrates—or deserts—such as those in Arabia, Syria, and Africa—obstacles that in themselves constituted an effective barrier. Where such natural defenses were lacking, large fortification projects were undertaken, intended as a potentially impenetrable barrier against incursions by hostile tribes.

Among these fortifications, none was as impressive, emblematic, or militarily and architecturally coherent as the ramparts marking the border of the Roman empire in Britain. Roman penetration of the island, after initial successes, was arrested along the borders of Wales and Scotland. The former gradually could be integrated, at least formally, into the Roman world. The latter was considerably more difficult and costly to conquer. Thus the emperor Hadrian, after having inspected the territory in about 121 and 122, gave up pushing northward and decided to build a permanent frontier barrier "to separate the Romans from the barbarians." At the point where Britain narrowed, between the Tyne and Solway Rivers, for a distance of eighty Roman miles, arose a formidable barrier—an imposing example of the empire's defensive engineering. First, along the entire length of the isthmus a *vallum* was excavated, a large ditch that clearly separated romanized Britain from the northern lands. Then a continuous wall was erected behind the ditch. It was approximately 4.5 meters tall and functioned as a patrol path and as a barrier against all penetration. At regular intervals, numerous forts (about seventeen) were set up, each accommodating a garrison sufficient to defend a stretch of the frontier. Crenellated towers and "citadels" for emergency troops completed the project. An accessible side road allowed easy communications between all installations and permitted the troops to be brought quickly toward threatened sectors. Approximately twenty years later, the emperor Antoninus Pius decided to "rationalize" this frontier, shifting the barrier about 120 kilometers farther north, where the coasts of Britain were so much closer to each other that the length of the rampart could be cut in half, thus saving troops. Solid frontier fortresses also were erected to protect this new defensive line, such as the one at Newstead. However, this forward *limes* proved too difficult to hold, due to the turbulence of the populations to the north and south of it. Well before the end of the second century, the Roman troops had already fallen back to Hadrian's wall, which for three centuries was the boundary between Roman civilization and Celtic turbulence.

A STRETCH OF THE WALL
The emperor Hadrian ordered the construction of a *vallum* to protect the fertile and civilized regions of southern Britain from attacks by the warlike tribes to the north.

# A Palace in the Form of a City

The dream of glory of Diocletian, the simple Dalmatian soldier who became one of the greatest emperors of Rome, is preserved in a testimony of solid stone: the city-palace of Split, a striking illustration of the Roman world's desire to dominate and instill order.

Diocletian was one of the very few Roman emperors who abandoned the throne to withdraw to private life. For his voluntary exile, he chose a spit of land that extended into the Adriatic Sea, a few kilometers from his native city of Salonae (present-day Split) in Dalmatia. There he built a colossal palace-fortress where he remained from the time of his abdication in A.D. 305 until his death in 313. This imposing complex, built of limestone blocks from the nearby island of Brazza, occupied an area approximately 190 by 160 meters, and it was modeled on the classical form of the *castra*, the Roman military encampments. It was rectangular, reinforced along its entire perimeter by towers (square or octagonal), divided into four regular sections by colonnaded streets that marked out the *cardo* and the *decumanus*. The latter separated the southern portion of the palace, occupied by buildings set aside for official use and by Diocletian's residence, from the northern portion, which contained the "service" spaces. The *cardo*, just beyond the intersection, led to a colonnaded piazza, the so-called peristyle (perhaps an outdoor hall for religious rituals and imperial ceremonies), still perfectly preserved. From here it continued southward as an underground road, ending at the base of the palace, facing the sea, where an entrance led to a wharf.

The most impressive architectural element of all was the dramatic arched loggia that ran along the side of the complex that faced the sea. Here, where fortifications like those on the sides facing inland were not needed, the retired emperor had a monumental covered walkway from which to view the broad expanse of sea. The palace also included Diocletian's mausoleum—a sturdy octagonal construction on the exterior; circular with niches on the interior. Later, during the Middle Ages, it was transformed into a cathedral (which caused it to be preserved).

The architectural design of the palace at Split is an anomaly among royal residences from late antiquity, which generally are open in form and laid out in such a way that the landscape can be enjoyed (within the Roman world, one need only think of Hadrian's Villa in Tivoli). At Split, however, the inspiration of the military encampments is obvious, in a deliberate, strong

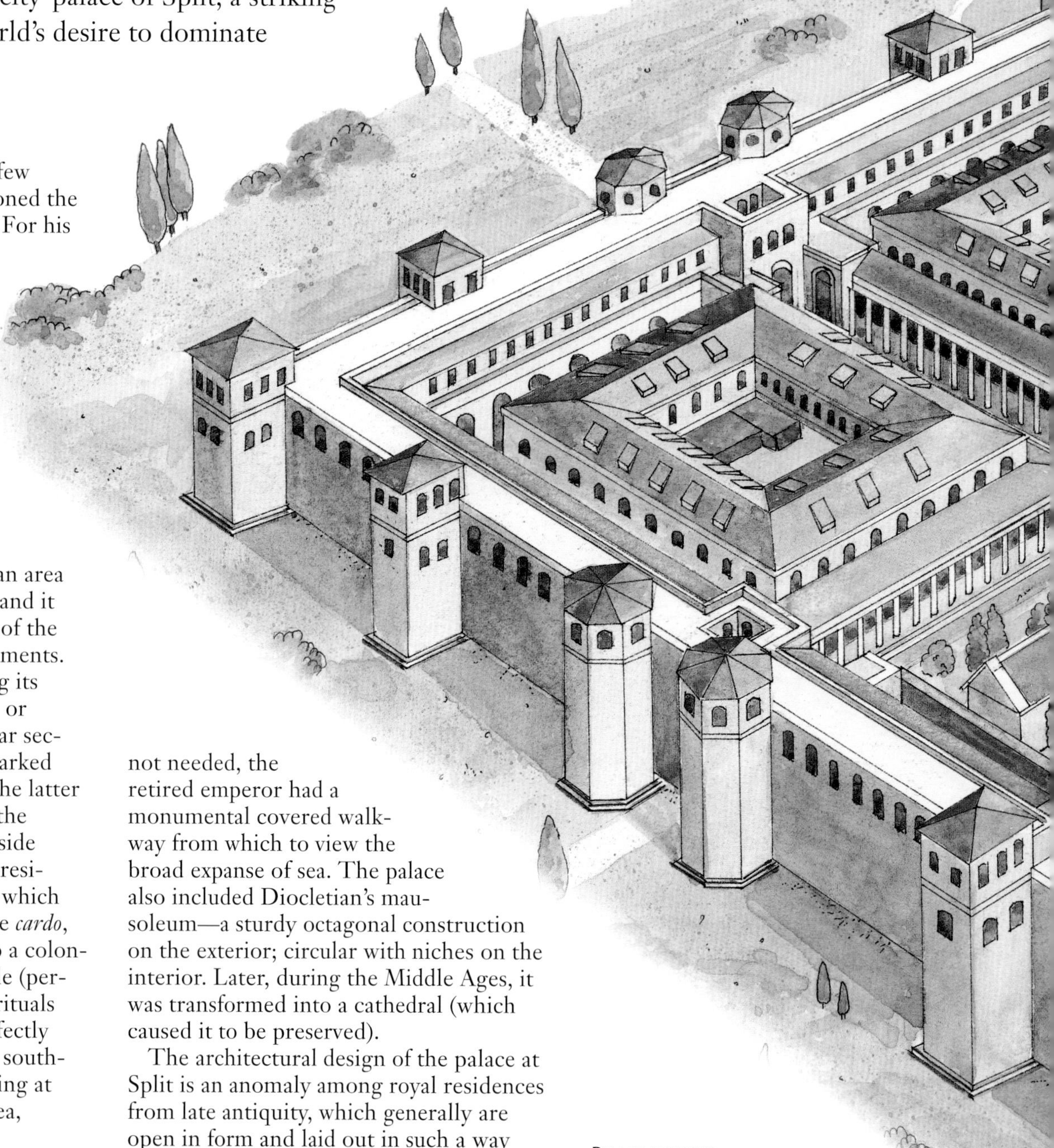

**Palace-fortress**
A reconstruction of Diocletian's palace, seen from the southwest corner. The spectacular loggia on the south side, opening directly to the sea, was equipped with a wharf.

**GREAT ORGANIZER**
During his reign (A.D. 284–305), Diocletian, portrayed on the coin *(left)*, showed a tremendous capacity for organization and an infallible ability in his choice of collaborators.

**THE MAUSOLEUM**
The mausoleum *(above)* was preserved because it was transformed into a cathedral during the Middle Ages. The structure, a sort of octagonal tower, is surrounded by a colonnade, it too octagonal.

**THE PERISTYLE**
Perfectly preserved, the peristyle of Diocletian's palace *(above)* was perhaps an open-air hall for religious rituals and imperial ceremonies.

reference to the emperor's military origins. This massive plan and fortified appearance were backed up by an exceptional technical and construction effort. The buildings were made from square blocks of stone and not from concrete (the *opus coementicium* used for buildings at the time), and the architecture was abundantly embellished with sculptures in precious marble. To guarantee the water supply, an imposing and entirely new aqueduct was built, which brought water from the Ladro River to the palace. It was an encampment solidified in stone, but one worthy of an emperor.

When, in the seventh century, Avar and Slavic tribes devastated Salonae, the inhabitants who survived took refuge behind the walls of the imperial residence, which were used once again to hold off the assaults of invaders.

Thus the ancient palace became the core of a new city, which reflects in its name, *Spalato* (Split), its derivation from a palace (*ex palatio*).

# Passing the Mantle

**Constantinople in Ravenna**
*Above*, floor mosaics depicting Constantinople, originally from the basilica of San Giovanni Evangelista in Ravenna.

Gradually, as pressure from the barbarians at the borders became stronger and more oppressive, the emperors had to spend increasing lengths of time at the frontiers, and they sought to establish a capital closer to the site of military operations. Milan fulfilled this function for nearly a century, then Constantinople, and then Ravenna, during the final years of the Western empire.

After vanquishing his last rival, Licinius, in A.D. 324, Constantine undertook the construction of a new capital for the empire, a "second Rome." He chose the site of ancient Byzantium on the Bosphorus, straddling Europe and Asia and near the most threatened frontiers along the Danube and adjacent to the Parthian kingdom. The city, founded with a ritual that recalled the mythical birth of Rome, received a completely new layout and a solid encircling wall (which, reinforced over time by various emperors, guaranteed the capital's defense for a millennium). The ports were totally rebuilt. From them the imperial fleet would dominate the Mediterranean for centuries to come. The new capital, named Constantinople, was "inaugurated" on 11 May 330, with celebrations that lasted forty days. About a hundred years would be needed, however, to bring Constantine's plan to completion. In any event, the city prospered; and, as capital of the eastern and most wealthy and stable portion of the empire, it endured until 1453: one of the most long-lived political and urban planning creations in human history and an absolute cornerstone of civilization.

**The Walls of Constantinople**
During the first half of the fifth century, the emperor Theodosius erected an imposing enclosing wall to protect Constantinople. A broad trench encircled the outside of the wall, and the wall itself was studded with towers such as those in the photo.

### THE SECOND ROME

When Constantine *(below)* issued a decree forcing his imperial subjects to recognize Constantinople as the "second Rome," the inhabitants of the original city were dismayed. Until that moment, no city had even dared compare itself to the Urbs, the city par excellence. But Constantine's ambitious plan entailed not so much the downgrading of the ancient capital as the pursuit of a concept that he held dear: renewal. The profound significance of the "second Rome" thus was to be connected to a Christian idea, transformed by the emperor into a political program of "second birth" and rebirth to new life of the imperial organism and its capital. Thus Constantinople replaced the old Rome and initiated a historical cycle that was meant to involve (and save) the entire Roman world.

## *The Last Bulwark*

While the capital of the Eastern empire flourished, the seat of the Western empire was moved from Milan to Ravenna. The latter site was chosen not for its proximity to the frontiers but for the defenses insured by the surrounding marshes and for the access to the sea, dominated by Byzantine ships. The city was the capital of an ever-weaker empire, torn by internal dissent, with much of its territory now occupied, more or less permanently, by barbarian tribes, "allies" in name but, in fact, their own masters. However, the residual resources of the great organism that had been Rome were still sufficient to turn Ravenna into a splendid city of art with sumptuous monuments and great refinement. It continued to prosper, even after the collapse of the Western empire; and under Byzantine rule in the sixth century, it reached the height of its splendor. The great number of monumental projects created during those centuries—the mausoleum of Galla Placidia, the basilicas of Sant'Apollinare Nuovo and Sant'Apollinare in Classe, the mausoleum of Theodoric, the stupendous San Vitale with its octagonal structure containing an interior ambulatory typical of imperial churches—make Ravenna one of Europe's art capitals.

**Byzantine Art**
*Above,* the apse of the basilica of San Vitale in Ravenna. The church is decorated with splendid mosaics in Byzantine style. The detail here *(left)* depicts a group of Roman nobles adorned with jewels.

### THE INNKEEPERS OF RAVENNA

Before becoming the last capital of the Western empire, thanks to its strategic position Ravenna had been a large base for the Roman fleet since the time of Augustus. Sailors guaranteed the city's vigor and prosperity, but they were not repaid in kind. The poor quality wine served in its taverns seems to have been proverbial in the Roman world. The poet Martial proclaimed, in one of his epigrams, that if he had been a native of Ravenna, he would have preferred a cistern of water to a vineyard—for, in fact, the water would have brought a much higher price on the market. He exaggerated still further that an astute innkeeper in Ravenna had once played a good joke on him: "I asked for watered-down wine, and he served me the pure stuff." But sailors, we know, are hearty drinkers.

# The Founders: Aeneas and Romulus

A legendary hero, inherited from Greek culture, and a founder-king, semi-divine in nature: these are the figures that Roman tradition places at the roots of its history.

## *Aeneas, the Fugitive*

Aeneas, the son of the Trojan king Anchises and the goddess Aphrodite, is a figure from Greek mythology, one of the protagonists in the Trojan War, praised in the poems of Homer. In the *Iliad*, he appears as a good and balanced hero, the strongest and wisest of the Trojans after Hector. His mother (who intervened twice to save him from the spears of Diomedes and Achilles) entrusted him with the task of establishing a new Troy after the destruction of the glorious city. Roman mythology—perhaps through the mediation of Etruscan culture—reprises these elements but modifies them for its own purposes. Thus the "new Troy" is no longer located in the Greek world; it is identified as Alba Longa on Italic soil, which dates its establishment to Ascanius, the son of Aeneas. In his new country, Ascanius took the name of Iulus, and his descendents included the founders of Rome, Romulus and Remus. The myth, in the consolidated version known to all, derives from Virgil's poem, the *Aeneid*, written during the reign of Augustus to celebrate the *gens Iulia*, but it circulated throughout the Italic world for centuries. The principal story was gradually elaborated with secondary episodes, such as the story of Dido and Aeneas. The hero had abandoned the queen of Carthage, who was hopelessly in love with him, in order to pursue his mission. This led to the queen's suicide and thus gave "historical" justification to the conflict between Rome and Carthage. All these tales, taken together, make up one of the greatest mythological creations in Roman culture.

## *Romulus, the Founder of the Urbs*

The legendary figure of Romulus, inserted in turn into the broader epic of Aeneas and his descendents, gave a solid "rational"

**Etruscan Milk**
The celebrated symbol of the city of Rome is a "fake." In fact, the Capitoline she-wolf is an Etruscan bronze, while the two twins, Romulus and Remus, were added in the sixteenth century by the sculptor Antonio Pollaiolo.

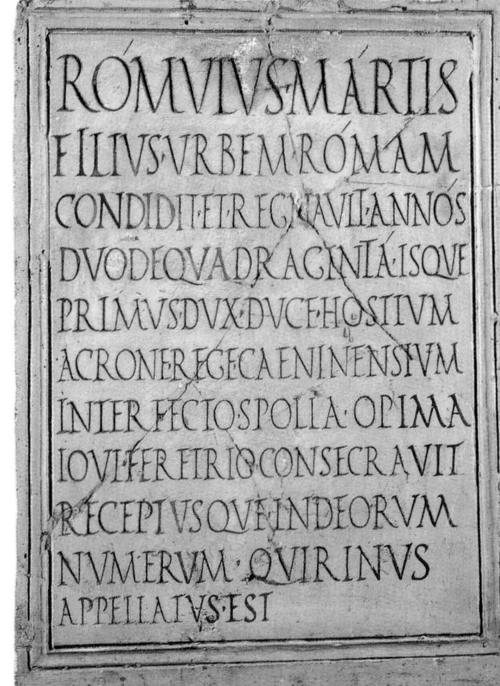


**Official Document**
The inscription on this tablet, discovered in Rome, begins with the following words: "Romulus, son of Mars, founded the city of Rome . . ."

guise to the birth and destiny of Rome and offered a suitable explanation for many aspects of the city's complex mythical-religious history. Roman historians already viewed the details with great skepticism. There must be some element of truth, however, within the vast complex of fantastical tales surrounding the founder of the Urbs: born of the royal stock of Alba Longa; descended from a she-wolf; became king of Rome after killing his brother; and finally, with the name Quirinus, took his place among the gods. Thus, for example, the traditional chronology for the founding of Rome, fixed by the ancients in the mid-eighth century B.C., coincides with archeological discoveries on the Palatine, where early settlements of huts date back precisely to that period. Whatever doubts there may be about the details, the ancient Romans considered many of the deeds attributed to Romulus to be verified historical facts that formed the basis of their national identity. These included the institution of the Senate at the encounter with the Sabines, which led to the abduction of the women of that nearby tribe, and finally, through the intercession of these same women, to the alliance between the two lines. From the name assumed by Romulus as a god, they proudly bore the collective name of the Quirites, reserved solely for Roman citizens of ancient origin.

**Romulus's Father**
This statue of Mars, the god of war *(left),* is part of a marble group from the time of Hadrian (A.D. 120–140).

## ILLUSTRIOUS ANCESTORS

Romulus and Remus were considered sons of Mars, the god of war, and, as descendents of the royal house of Alba Longa, boasted descent from Iulus, the son of Aeneas, and through him from the goddess Venus (the greek goddess Aphrodite). The *gens Iulia*, which also claimed descent from the kings of Alba Longa, took special pains to promote the legends of Aeneas and Romulus, both of whom were considered progenitors. Both also were celebrated by Caesar and Augustus with the erection of a temple to Venus Genetrix and with statues in their forums.

**The Wounded Hero**
The fresco *(left)* from Herculaneum depicts the wounded Aeneas. Next to him is his son Ascanius, the founder of Alba Longa and progenitor of the *gens Iulia*.

**The Final Labor of Aeneas**
Virgil's poem the *Aeneid*, dedicated to the Trojan hero, concludes with the duel between Aeneas and Turnus, the king of the Rutuli. By defeating his rival, who was betrothed to Lavinia, the daughter of the Latin king, Aeneas could marry her and become the designated successor to the kingdom of Latium. *Right, Aeneas Defeats Turnus*, detail of a painting by Luca Giordano (1632–1705).

# Fathers of the Country:
# Camillus and Scipio

One is a half-legendary figure, the other a general, a man of politics, and an intellectual fully illuminated by the light of history; both are "founding fathers" of republican Rome.

The figure of Camillus is fixed in history in the theatrical pose handed down by Latin hagiography, bursting forth tempestuously on the stage as Roman tribute is being paid to Brennus, the king of the Gauls, who had devastated Rome. Camillus is said to have proclaimed contemptuously, "*Non auro sed ferro recuperanda est patria*" ("not gold but iron [weapons] will save our country"). His initiative satisfied Quirite pride, galvanized the defeated Roman legions, and led them to victory against the invaders. As a result, Camillus was recognized as the "second founder" of Rome. The person behind this stereotyped and perhaps not utterly truthful image was much more complex. Camillus was a skillful

**The Conquest of Veii**
Situated on the west bank of the Tiber, only 20 kilometers from Rome, Veii was one of the principal Etruscan cities. Furius Camillus employed a specific strategy that took the city by storm. He dug a tunnel beneath the city walls for a group of soldiers to penetrate the city and open the gates to the Roman troops. *Above*, terracotta head of a young boy, originally from Veii (fifth century B.C.).

**The Influence of Greece**
Scipio's era was characterized by the "discovery" of the Greek world, its culture, and its works of art. The more traditionalist wing of the Senate, led by Cato, considered this contamination to be a potential danger for the integrity of Roman customs. *Left*, Aphrodite Bathing, a Roman copy of a Greek original (third century B.C.).

**A Leader's Charisma**
Without holding specific offices, Scipio Africanus *(right)* had an influence in Rome equal to that of a king, indeed to such a degree that republican structures could be seen as insufficiently able to resist strong political personalities.

man of politics, capable of attaining the office of consul some six times. He was also an astute and decisive general who guided Rome to its first clear victory against a great Etruscan city, Veii; and he was a charismatic figure, able to appease conflict with the mere majesty of his presence. He was, however, the subject of gossip, alleged to have pocketed much of the immense booty from the sacking of Veii. Moreover, he was said to have dared to compare himself to Jupiter Optimus Maximus, the supreme divinity of the Roman pantheon. This accusation earned him the punishment of exile, and only the emergency of an invasion by the Gauls brought him back to Rome. In Roman memory, his merits surpassed any sins he may have committed if it is true that a statue of him was erected in the forum (an extraordinary event for the time) and that public opinion put him on an equal plane with Romulus.

## *An Innovative General and Greek-influenced Intellectual*

With the exception of Julius Caesar, the supreme genius in war, politics, and literature, Rome's greatest general was Publius Cornelius Scipio. He knew how to take in hand the legions who were demoralized from brutal defeats inflicted by another "champion" of the art of war, Hannibal, the Carthaginian. Scipio led the Romans to victory on various fronts. The decisive battle of Zama (202 B.C.), which brought an end to the Second Punic War, earned him the appellation *Africanus*, which has been passed down through history.

Scipio did not succeed only in war. He was also a great aristocrat, a proud member of a family around whom all Roman politics gravitated. He was an intellectual with an extensive and lively education, who introduced Rome to the ideas, language, and culture of the Greek world. This policy, destined to become traditional for his family, sowed the seeds for classical culture as we know it, a fusion of Greek thought and Roman pragmatism. Scipio's pro-Hellenism drew the ire of the traditionalist wing in the Senate, which unleashed a relentless campaign of accusations against the great general. His detractors besmirched his image and cast doubt upon his honesty, forcing him to undergo a public trial. Indignant and embittered, the brilliant general who had been victorious over Hannibal withdrew to his villa at Liternum in Campania, where he resided until his death.

**Scene of Pillage**
Relief from an urn, depicting the sacking of a temple by Gallic warriors (fourth century B.C.).

**The Final Resting Place**
The oldest sarcophagus in the tomb of the Scipio family *(right)* belongs to Lucius Scipio Barbatus.

### THE TOMB OF THE SCIPIO FAMILY

Along the Via Appia, shortly before the Porta San Sebastiano, is the Scipio family tomb, preserved nearly in its entirety thanks to the family's immense fame, which made this a celebrated and much visited monument, even in ancient times. The *gens Cornelia*, to which the Scipio family belonged, was the only one of the great Roman families to practice burial instead of cremation. Thus numerous sarcophagi, arranged in burial niches cut into the tufa stone, were preserved. The interesting inscriptions on these sarcophagi cast the members of this grand dynasty in a moving and humane light. One of simplest of the epitaphs is well known: "This stone encloses wisdom and many virtues and a brief life. To attain the greatest honors he who lies here lacked life, not merit."

# The Gracchi and Marius and Sulla

While Rome expanded outward eventually to dominate the entire Mediterranean basin, it was troubled by increasingly ferocious domestic disputes in part a result of the large changes brought about by conquests.

This turbulent scenario was the backdrop for various figures—the Gracchi, Gaius Marius, Lucius Cornelius Sulla—who in turn attempted to impose on Roman society not only their rule but also their personal views of life.

## *Revolutionary Aristocrats*

Tiberius Sempronius Gracchus and his brother, Gaius, came from one of the grand aristocratic families in the city. Their mother, Cornelia, was the daughter of Scipio Africanus. Their tutors (chosen by

**Personal Army**
Marius and Sulla availed themselves of what were effectively personal armies, which they supported through the income from military campaigns. *Above*, a bas-relief depicting two fighting legionnaires.

**The Exploitation of *Ager Publicus***
The *ager publicus*, made up of lands confiscated from conquered peoples, was set aside in part for pastureland and in part for farming. *Left*, a mosaic with rural scenes, originally from Caesarea.

their mother, since their father had died when the two brothers were still young) were two of the most famous Greek intellectuals of the period, the orator Diophanes of Mytilene and the philosopher Blessius of Cuma. Despite a life of privilege, the Gracchi were not blind to the defects of the society in which they lived. The greatest problem was the progressive disappearance of the class of small landowners, the backbone of the army, whose numbers had been reduced by continuous wars and who were crushed by competition from estates farmed with slave labor. This situation pushed Tiberius Gracchus to stand as a candidate in 133 B.C. for the tribunate of the plebs and, once elected, to propose an effective law for agrarian reform that called for the distribution to less prosperous citizens of plots of *ager publicus*—namely, the immense patrimony of state lands. Until then, these lands had been leased at low prices to members of the great senatorial families. The law was blocked in every way by the conservative classes, which in the end planned and carried out the murder of Tiberius. Ten years later, his brother, Gaius, took up the struggle. He ran for election to the tribunate, again proposed agrarian reform, and led the fight with a toughness and lack of bias that Tiberius had not displayed. Unfortunately, the outcome was similar and ended with the death of the second Gracchus, who chose to commit suicide rather than surrender to his adversaries. The problem remained, however, and the path of the Gracchi would be forged in the future by other great political men, such as Marius and Caesar.

IN FAVOR OF THE LESS WEALTHY CLASSES
The concerns of Gaius Gracchus went beyond agrarian reform. Among other things, he promulgated a grain law, which instituted the monthly sale of grain to the poor at a reduced price, and a military law that forced the state to provide all equipment gratis to the soldiers. *Above*, a pillar inscribed with the laws of the Gracchi (second century B.C.).

## *An Army of Conscripts for Political Power*

At the beginning of the first century B.C., violence had come to play a permanent role in Roman political struggles. It was only a question of time before the most devastating tool, the army, was brought into play. This step was taken by Gaius Marius, an extremely skillful general who came from Arpinium in Latium. There were decreasing numbers of small landowners who had been the traditional source for army recruits, so to fill the ranks of his legions, Marius opened the military to *capita censi*, that is, non-landholding citizens, who were attracted to military life by the prospects of careers and spoils. This new army, reorganized structurally and tactically as well, proved to be invincible. It was a force, however, that was no longer faithful to the Republic but rather to the general on whom it depended for its maintenance during service and for the assignment of lands upon discharge. Marius also used this army to combat his political adversaries from the aristocratic class, for the first time guiding Roman legions against the state. In his turn Lucius Cornelius Sulla, Marius's second lieutenant, became an implacable foe and an exponent of the aristocratic party. Sulla employed the troops recruited for campaigns in the East as a tool to combat the followers of Marius and to establish his rule over Rome, sanctioned by his being named dictator. Roman democracy now had come to an end, and Julius Caesar, the nephew of Marius, would reap the benefits.

A LEGIONNAIRE'S EQUIPMENT
This bronze helmet from the late republican era bears an inscription with the names of two legionnaires and their respective centuries.

THE TRIUMPH OF SULLA
This coin of Sulla probably depicts the dictator himself in a quadriga in triumph. After becoming the sole ruler of Rome, Sulla wrote the notorious "lists of proscription" that sent thousands of his political adversaries to their death.

### "THEY FIGHT AND DIE FOR THE WEALTH OF A FEW"

The sad conditions of the poor classes in Rome are described to great effect in this passage in a discourse by Tiberius Gracchus, reported (and perhaps embellished) by Plutarch: "Beasts in Italy have their dens and each of these has its own bed and its own refuge; while those who fight and die for Italy are granted nothing but air and sunlight, they have neither home nor shelter and are forced to roam with their children and wives. They fight and die for the wealth of a few."

# The Founders of the Empire: Caesar and Augustus

About the mid-first century B.C., the Republic suffered from factional clashes, social crises, and personal ambitions. Then there emerged one of the greatest men in history, Gaius Julius Caesar, who sketched the outlines for a new structure, destined to prevail over Roman society for centuries to come: the principate, to which Caesar's nephew and heir, Octavian Augustus, gave continuity, solidity, and foundation.

**Caesar's Appearance**
This is the "human side" of Caesar, according to Suetonius: "It is said that he was tall in stature, fair of complexion, well proportioned and of robust constitution . . . . He did not tolerate being bald, particularly because he was aware that this provoked the teasing of his adversaries."

Gaius Julius Caesar, a man of irony and aristocratic good taste, probably would have turned up his nose when, after his murder at the hands of Brutus and the other conspirators, his adoptive heir, Gaius Julius Caesar Octavianus, decorated himself with the title *Divi filius*: son of a god, ascended to the heavens. However, Julius Caesar carried out so many successful and often "impossible" projects during his life (100–44 B.C.) that his divine origin seemed possible. He was born to a line that, though impoverished over time, traced its origins back to the kings of Alba Longa and, through them, to Aeneas and the goddess Venus. He succeeded, step by step, with genius and will, in making the entire history of the world revolve around him. Pleasure-seeking spendthrift and impenitent philanderer, refined and even squeamish aristocrat, he also was a courageous soldier and an inspired and brilliant general, a gifted writer, a political man of supreme abilities, without prejudices and at the same time practical. He attained the office of Pontifex Maximus, conquered Gaul, landed in Britain, defeated Pompey in a civil war, and was considered an

**Imperial Privilege**
This coin with the portrait of Julius Caesar was the first Roman coin with the effigy of a living person.

**The Ides of March**
Caesar was killed on 15 March 44 B.C. by 23 stab wounds, only one of which was mortal. The dictator fell backwards at the feet of the statue of Pompey, inside the Curia he had had built precisely to protect him from his one-time enemy. The episode is evoked in this painting by Vincenzo Camuccini (1771–1844).

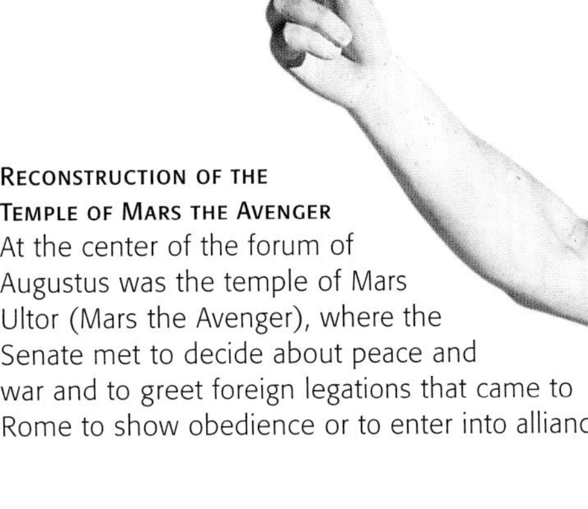

**Reconstruction of the Temple of Mars the Avenger**
At the center of the forum of Augustus was the temple of Mars Ultor (Mars the Avenger), where the Senate met to decide about peace and war and to greet foreign legations that came to Rome to show obedience or to enter into alliances.

invincible commander. In only a few years, he left his mark in every field from urban planning to calendar reform. Bringing him down required the dagger of the man whom he loved as a son (which he may have been), Brutus. Nonetheless, his work went on, for Caesar had laid out the path to be followed: the Republic and its one-year officeholders, incapable of governing a realm larger than present-day Europe, were to be replaced by an imperial power that could plan and bring to completion coherent and wide-ranging designs.

## *The Timid Autocrat*

He had been named adoptive son and heir by his great-uncle Julius Caesar, who lacked direct descendents. When Caesar was brought down by the conspirators, Gaius Octavius—now Gaius Julius Caesar Octavianus—was only eighteen years old. He was susceptible to illness and timid and frail in appearance. Despite the prestigious adoption, he seemed the least talented and important of the three men who shared power (the others were Marc Antony and Aemilius Lepidus). Yet he managed to emerge as the final victor, defeating the fleet of Marc Antony and Cleopatra, the queen of Egypt, at Actium in 31 B.C. The imperial history of Rome began at that moment. Indeed, Octavian laid the foundations for the political structure that was destined to govern the Mediterranean world for half a millennium: an autocracy strongly based on military power and exalted by the deification of the *princeps*. He instituted many things that would influence subsequent eras: the praetorian guard, which protected the person of the sovereign; a permanent and totally professional army; a bureaucracy based on freed slaves, replacing one ruled by senatorial appointment; the systematic use of the arts as tools to celebrate and legitimize power. He gave strength to Caesar's improvisations. There is no doubt that the title *Augustus*, "the venerable one" (although we perhaps would say *the highest* or *the great*) was amply earned.

### AN ENTIRELY NEW ROME

Augustus exercised enormous influence over not only the political life of Rome but its architecture, as well. He had many public and religious monuments erected, and he opened piazzas and built theaters and the first permanent baths in the capital. These structures all bore the stamp of an elegant and severe classicism that was the "trademark" of imperial architecture. Even building materials changed; travertine, tufa, and terracotta were replaced by refined Apuan marble (called *lunense* marble at the time, because it was quarried near the city of Luna).

**The Wife of Augustus**
A basalt head of Livia, the third wife of Augustus, who played a crucial role alongside both her husband and her son, the emperor Tiberius, by whom she was deified after her death (A.D. 29).

**Armed for War**
While he did not demonstrate any great aptitude for the art of war, Augustus, depicted here dressed as a commander, introduced important military reforms. These included a permanent army, which did not change in appearance until the mid-third century A.D.

# The Euphoria of Power: Messalina and Nero

The rise and fall of the Julio-Claudian dynasty followed a course destined to become almost a ritual for the great Roman imperial families: an enlightened and tolerant regime, gradually replaced by an autocracy increasingly unrestrained in power games and private behavior, finally provoking a reaction by the army.

**Treacherous Kinsmen**
Agrippina the Younger *(above)*, the fourth wife of Claudius, allegedly rid herself of her husband using the standard weapon of court intrigues, poison. She then placed her son Nero on the throne, but he, unable to bear her guardianship, had her killed by a hired assassin.

Valeria Messalina, while still very young, became the third wife of Claudius, the fourth emperor in the Julio-Claudian dynasty. Extremely beautiful, intelligent, and bold, she had immense influence over her elderly and timid consort, who could refuse her nothing.

Messalina took great advantage of her situation: She persecuted innocent citizens with the sole goal of taking over their wealth, carried on amorous relationships that were increasingly unbridled and insolently conspicuous, and even entered into a marriage-farce with a young man, Gaius Silius, whose only obvious unique attribute was being "the handsomest man in the empire." This, the final straw, forced the emperor to react; and he ordered both his wife and her lover to be put to death.

Messalina was replaced by another very young wife, Agrippina, who was her predecessor's equal in scandal and political intrigue. Indeed, she poisoned her aged husband in order to smooth the ascent to the throne for her favorite son, Nero. Nonetheless, it was Messalina who passed into history as the archetype of the scandalous and dissolute empress.

**Messalina's Children**
The marriage between Messalina and Claudius produced two children, Octavia and Britannicus. Octavia, the unhappy wife of Nero, would be unjustly accused of adultery; Britannicus would lose his life in the first of a series of brutal crimes ordered by Nero. *Right*, allegorical portraits of Messalina and Britannicus.

**Head of Nero**
This bronze head of Nero came from Cilicia (first century A.D.). The emperor was even eccentric in the way he wore his hair, which was longer than usual, sometimes with curly ringlets, graduated in length.

**The Martyrdom of Peter and Paul**
Peter and Paul, depicted here in a fresco from the catacombs of San Gennaro in Naples, were among the victims of Nero's ruthless persecution, although the precise date and manner of their martyrdoms are not easily reconstructed. Some sources mention A.D. 64 for Peter, others place both martyrs in 67. Tertullian simply mentions crucifixion for Peter; later writers describe an upside down crucifixion for Peter, the prince of the apostles, and decapitation for Paul.

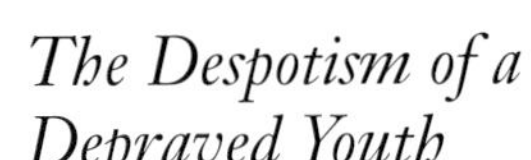

## *The Despotism of a Depraved Youth*

The early years of Nero's reign (A.D. 54–68) were characterized by a balanced and efficient government under the direction of two excellent associates, the praetorian prefect Afranius Burrus and the philosopher Lucius Anneus Seneca. After Burrus died in A.D. 62 and Seneca withdrew to private life, the situation rapidly deteriorated. The emperor's first wife, Octavia, who was exiled and then murdered, was replaced by Poppaea. In the public sphere, the new praetorian prefect, Tigellinus, acquired a squalid reputation. There were summary trials, confiscation of property, plots, both actual and presumed, that ended in bloodshed, and a ferocious persecution of Christians, who were held responsible for the disastrous fire that devastated much of Rome in A.D. 64. In the military realm, things went no better with setbacks in Armenia, rebellions in Britain, and a violent Jewish uprising in Palestine. Then in A.D. 68, the legions of Gaul and Spain revolted. The revolt of Julius Vindex in Gaul was repressed, but that of Sulpicius Galba and Salvius Otho in the Iberian Peninsula was successful. Nero, abandoned by all, was killed by a slave. The glorious dynasty of Julius Caesar, the first to command the Roman empire, was over.

**An Emperor Out of Tune**
Music, poetry, and theater were Nero's true passions. From the time he was a boy, he composed verses and as emperor he practiced singing—where it seems he was hopeless—and studied the cithara to the point of exhaustion. This sculpture depicts Apollo playing the cithara.

### THE GREAT PERSECUTION

During Nero's reign, the first great persecution of the Christians took place. They were not a well-liked minority but, until that time, had been broadly tolerated within the empire. Nero's reasons probably were incidental. The emperor had been accused (almost certainly wrongly) of being responsible for the catastrophic fire of A.D. 64, and, needing to find a scapegoat against whom the accusations could be directed, he chose this small and scorned sect. The persecution was one of merciless and brutal cruelty. According to an account by the historian Tacitus, the Christians were "covered with the skins of wild beasts and were torn to pieces by dogs and burned alive at sunset with torches. Nero offered his gardens for this spectacle, as if it were a circus game; and, dressed as a charioteer, he mixed with the commoners or sat upon a chariot."

# The Philosopher Emperors: Hadrian and Marcus Aurelius

Balanced in the exercise of power, cultivated, and appreciative of the arts, literature, and philosophy—at the same time, able and sometimes ruthless generals—the emperors chosen "by adoption" in the second century represent the apex of imperial Rome.

Some historical sources maintain that Trajan was quite hesitant to name his young relative Hadrian as heir and successor, given their rather different views in many areas. In fact, as soon as Hadrian ascended the throne, he abandoned Assyria, Mesopotamia, and Armenia, the three eastern provinces annexed by Trajan, which had brought the empire to its greatest extent. This was a clear manifestation of Hadrian's desire to "maintain peace throughout the world." His rejection of the expansionist policies of his predecessor brought great disappointment to the military and merchant classes. In contrast, he devoted himself to a new policy of travel throughout all the provinces of the immense Roman realm in order to know firsthand the problems and possibilities and to resolve, on the spot wherever possible, questions that were pending. This activity found expressive resonance in the stupendous villa the emperor constructed near Tivoli, where he had his architects reproduce the buildings that had most impressed him during his wanderings.

Hadrian was a contradictory and complex personality: a lover of Greece but proud supporter of Roman superiority; a cunning and curious patron but also an experienced general; a sage expert in the workings of the empire's bureaucratic "machine" but impatient with any delays; a passionate lover (both hetero- and homosexual: he erected a splendid city along the Nile in memory of his favorite, Antinous) and a not insignificant writer of verse. He is responsible for one of the most touching and serene poetic meditations on death: "*Animula vagula blandula, hospes comesque corporis, quae nunc abibis in loca* . . . ." (Tender vagabond soul, body's guest and companion, in which places you are never more to go . . . .). His reign was not without shadows but nonetheless represents one of the high points of Roman civilization.

**Hadrian, Tireless Voyager**
From 121 to 134 (with a brief interruption in 127 to return to Rome), Hadrian, depicted here in a marble bust, traveled uninterruptedly throughout the empire. Everywhere he went, he left demonstrations of his favor, public works, and administrative innovations.

**Chronicle of War**
The Antonine Column was erected to record the victories of Marcus Aurelius over the Sarmatians and the Marcomanni. Its long spiral-shaped frieze begins with the passage of the Roman troops along the Danube and unfolds in a crescendo of battle scenes, speeches by the emperor, destruction of houses, executions of prisoners, and the subduing of barbarians.

## *Marcus Aurelius: a Philosopher on the Throne*

"The best reign of all time": thus did the era of Marcus Aurelius (A.D. 161–180) go down in history. He was a cultivated emperor, wise, balanced, and competent, who considered philosophy his profession and ruling an unwelcome task. Yet it was precisely during this enlightened period that many historians see the beginning of the empire's decline.

After fifty years of peace, extremely serious problems exploded along the frontiers. They threatened to obliterate the eastern and Danube borders and forced the emperor into a series of exhausting military campaigns. Legionnaires returning from the campaign against the Parthians were the unwitting vehicle for a plague that spread throughout the empire. According to some historians, this scourge destroyed the population and caused a chain reaction of consequences. Production went into free fall, earnings tumbled, there was a lack of recruits for the army, and lands were abandoned and left uncultivated. While the decimated legions attempted to hold off the Germanic invasions on the Danube front, the troops in the east rebelled and proclaimed their commander, Avidius Cassius, emperor. When Marcus Aurelius died in Vienna in March of 180, he left his successor an empire shaken to its foundations.

SACRIFICE TO THE GODS
This relief represents Marcus Aurelius making a sacrifice in front of the temple of Jupiter. Despite professions of tolerance, the emperor was not merciful toward the Christians, who refused to render homage to the gods, an act that was equivalent to the repudiation of the Roman state.

THE EMPEROR'S MEMOIRS
Marcus Aurelius, depicted here in a gold bust, has left us a precious legacy, *Meditations,* a literary work, in which, along with autobiography, a rigorous moral code emerges, one to which the emperor sought to adhere throughout his life.

### THE AGE OF GREAT MONUMENTS

Hadrian and Marcus Aurelius left behind some of Roman history's most famous monuments: Hadrian's Villa in Tivoli, Hadrian's tomb in Rome (the core of the present-day Castel Sant'Angelo), the equestrian statue of Marcus Aurelius (later placed by Michelangelo in the Campidoglio piazza), the Antonine Column (erected by Marcus Aurelius in honor of his father, Antoninus Pius) in the Piazza Colonna Antonina in Rome, opposite the Chigi palace. These are a testament to the second century, a splendid period for Roman art and especially architecture, which reached the apex of its technical prowess and expressive possibilities.

THE BRIDGE AND CASTEL SANT'ANGELO
In A.D. 134 Hadrian opened the Elian bridge over the Tiber, which linked his mausoleum to the city of Rome. The bridge still exists, although in reworked form, and is called the Sant'Angelo, the same name as the castle built over the mausoleum structure.

# The Division of the Empire: Diocletian and Constantine

To save the empire from ruin, Diocletian made a drastic decision: to divide his immense territory into two sections. His successor, Constantine, went even further, removing Rome from its privileged position as capital.

Diocletian's transformation of the imperial structure was radical. In order to be able to defend the borders effectively and at the same time deal with external crises, he decided to share the throne with his loyal friend Maximian, to whom he entrusted control of the West, while he took charge of the East. Together, the two sovereigns succeeded in restoring order in a short time. They wiped out bands of outlaws (*bagaudae*) that were infesting the provinces, put a stop to Frankish and Saxon pirates, and strengthened the eastern frontiers. Immediately thereafter, the structure of the empire was reorganized with a new system of succession to the throne, based on designated heirs (*caesari*), who in their time would be succeeded by titular sovereigns (*augusti*), and a ruthless and rigid stratification of classes and professions.

**A Winning Idea**
Understanding that Rome's domains were too vast to be governed by a single monarch, Diocletian fell back on a tetrarchy (from the Greek "government of four") with good reason. With an emperor ready to intervene in every corner of the empire, encroachments became all but impossible. *Left*, detail of a sculptural group depicting two of the tetrarchs.

**The Imperial Diadem**
Constantine wears the imperial diadem in this detail of a mosaic from the church of Hagia Sophia in Istanbul, ancient Constantinople.

**Colossal Head of Constantine**
Upon the death of Diocletian, six pretenders quarreled over the empire: Maximian, Maxentius, Licinius, Galerius, Maximinius, and Constantine, who ruled over the western provinces. The latter prevailed, after the decisive battle fought against Maxentius at the Milvian Bridge near Rome on 28 October 312.

## The Emperor's Gems

The use of gems, which, by their gleam and multicolored reflections, encircled with splendor the figure of the sovereign, was extremely widespread during Diocletian's reign. With irony it was said that the emperor attempted to inlay even his shoes with gems, something considered infamous, worthy of dissolute sovereigns such as Heliogabalus. The introduction of the diadem as a distinctive symbol is also connected with Diocletian and his presumed vanity (which in reality was a somewhat more political desire to exalt the imperial office, placing it outside the range of common people). Originally, the diadem was a simple white band that encircled the foreheads of Hellenistic sovereigns, but now it was transformed into a precious ornament gold and gems.

**Tomb of a Christian**
This fragment of a sepulchral slab, which can be dated between the late third and early fourth centuries, depicts a famous episode from the New Testament, the multiplication of the loaves of bread.

This forced the inhabitants to furnish the state with taxes and tributes, even to the detriment of their economic freedom and civil liberties. There also was a complete reorganization of defense with the creation of *limites*, fortified and impenetrable borders along the entire perimeter of the empire. An unsparing struggle was waged against the Christian religion, considered to be a divisive element in the state structure. If the "cure" imposed by Diocletian was not sufficient to resolve the empire's problems, it at least permitted its survival for many more decades.

## *The Capitulation to Christianity*

The complicated system of succession set in place by Diocletian did not function. Upon the emperor's retirement, a struggle immediately broke out among his designated successors. Constantine emerged the victor: an emperor destined to remain on the throne for a full quarter century, introducing changes to the empire that would endure even into the distant future.

The Christians, who had supported Constantine, received complete freedom of worship in 313, as well as a rapidly growing role in state affairs. Rome was abandoned as the capital in favor of a "new Rome," erected on the Bosphorus, straddling Europe and Asia. This was Constantinople, where the imperial court settled in 330 and which, for over a millennium, handed down the Roman imperial tradition.

**Sant'Apollinare in Classe**
Built in the sixth century, the basilica of Sant'Apollinare in Classe at the gates of Ravenna has the typical structure of early Christian churches. *In the photo*, the central nave and apse.

### THE BIRTH OF THE CHRISTIAN BASILICA

Thanks to the freedom of worship granted by Constantine, the Christians had the opportunity to build their churches in peace; until that time they had been hidden from the sight of non-adherents. A problem arose: how, in a short period of time, to give canonical form to a religious building. Thus the *basilica* came into being, a construction that changed the name (and, in part, the form) of the homonymous pagan creations, which, however, were used essentially as judicial halls. The typical paleo-Christian basilica, such as those designed during the time of Constantine, was a rectangular building with three naves (five, in exceptional cases) with the entrance on one of the short sides and an exedra (or apse) at the other short side. The roof was extremely simple, with trusses instead of the vaulted system typical of imperial constructions. Leading up to the building was a spacious four-sided portico reserved for the catechumens, or the uninitiated.

# Julian the Apostate and Galla Placidia

While still strong and extensive, the empire in the fourth century had entered its phase of decline, which became irreversible in the following century. Great figures still emerged, however, such as Julian and the imperial princess Galla Placidia.

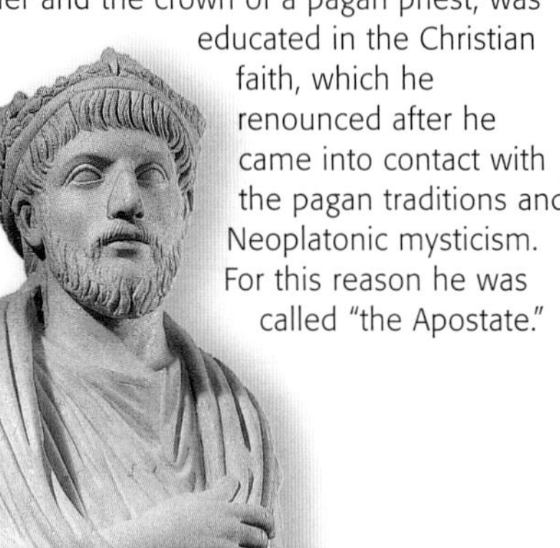

**Julian's Renunciation**
Julian, depicted here in the toga of a Greek philosopher and the crown of a pagan priest, was educated in the Christian faith, which he renounced after he came into contact with the pagan traditions and Neoplatonic mysticism. For this reason he was called "the Apostate."

Julian, who ascended the throne by acclamation of the Gallic legions in A.D. 360, was an emperor at the level of the great sovereigns of the second century—Trajan, Hadrian, and Marcus Aurelius—upon whom he sought to model his activities. He initiated pervasive legislative, fiscal, and economic reforms of the state; and only the brevity of his reign prevented him from realizing them. He is known almost solely, however, for his attempt to restore the ancient pagan religion, which earned him the epithet *Apostate* by which he is generally known. This attempt was countered with resistance on the part of the Eastern empire, now profoundly Christianized. Had Julian not suffered a brutal death during a campaign against the Persians in 363, he might have met with some success in restoring paganism partly because of his ability to borrow various elements of Christian practice—such as the system of alms and charity—putting them at the service of his own ideas. Julian was the last emperor who attempted to maintain a connection with the classical tradition of Rome.

**Empress of the Romans**
The profile of Galla Placidia is stamped onto this Byzantine coin, mounted as a pendant.

**Pagan Basilicas**
This decorative panel was part of the basilica attached to the house of the consul Junius Bassus, built in the fourth century at the summit of the Esquiline hill in Rome. The last representatives of Rome's pagan aristocracy gathered at such places.

## *A Princess in the Storm*

Galla Placidia, the daughter of the great emperor Theodosius, unintentionally played a leading role in the collapse of the Western empire. Born about 388, she was educated in Rome, where she was still living in 410, when the city was sacked by the Goths, led by Alaric. When the Goths abandoned the devastated city, they took the princess with them as a prisoner. For years Galla Placidia, a sort of deluxe hostage, followed the wanderings of the barbarian horde, until her marriage to Ataulf, the brother-in-law of Alaric. This brought peace to both the ferociously adversarial Roman and Gothic peoples and to the young woman, initiating a union that was embodied in the couple's son, baptized Theodosius like his grandfather. The death of her young son and her husband (treacherously assassinated), both within a short time, turned her once again into a prisoner. She was able to return among the Romans, to the court of Ravenna, only after a considerable ransom in wheat had been paid.

### THE LAST ROMAN OR THE FIRST BYZANTINE STRUCTURE

The mausoleum of Galla Placidia in Ravenna *(above)* is a small cruciform structure, extremely simple and bare on the outside, of exposed brick. The interior, in contrast, is a triumph of color and ornamentation, made even more evocative by the light that filters through alabaster slabs placed in the windows. The contrast between exterior and interior in this example of late Roman architecture clearly and splendidly anticipates the characteristics of future Byzantine architecture.

Unfortunately, she was compelled to enter into marriage with the ambitious general Constantius, for whom she felt deep revulsion. Two children were born to this marriage, Honoria and Valentinian III, the future emperor. But Galla Placidia experienced little happiness. Increasingly closed off in the imperial palace in Ravenna, she found comfort in the Christian faith and in religious readings. A cultivated, intelligent, and sensitive woman, she was overwhelmed by the times, which turned her into a pawn on the political chessboard. Yet it was this fragile princess, increasingly engrossed in matters of the spirit, who, for nearly a quarter century, defended the dynasty in the person of her heir, Valentinian. Meanwhile, the centuries-old empire collapsed around her under invasions by the Suevians, Vandals, Parthians, Franks, and Huns. She died in Rome in 450, a final symbol of a fading world.

**CHRIST THE GOOD SHEPHERD**
This mosaic, placed above the entrance door of the mausoleum of Galla Placidia, is a masterpiece of ancient art. The perspective and the delicate colors create the illusion that objects disappear into a mysterious distance, while the face of Christ, surrounded by a gold halo, dominates the entire scene.

# One Triad and Many Gods

Rome did not have a "religion" as we understand the term today—namely, a hierarchical and codified structure of beliefs and divinities. Rather, there was a totality of complex rituals, often extremely ancient and varied in origin.

**Seated on the Throne**
The Capitoline Triad consisted of Jupiter, Juno, and Minerva. The most widespread iconography showed the three divinities seated on separate thrones with Jupiter at the center in a predominant position. *Above*, the Capitoline Triad, from the excavations of the Roman fortress of *Scarbantia*, present-day Sopron in Hungary.

Traditional Roman paganism, instead of creating forms of mysticism or fideistic attitudes, which were foreign to the Latin mentality, tended to scrupulously "regiment" the contractual relationship of giving and receiving that Romans had with their gods. Rather than adoration toward divinities, the ancient Quirites had a holy fear of their wrath, which could be unleashed by a forgotten or neglected or incorrectly executed ritual. Thus they felt an obligation to punctiliously uphold their part of the contract, rendering to the gods the honors due them. In exchange, they expected the divinities to protect devout believers or at least not to harm them through unexpected caprices.

**The Capitoline Triad of Sufetula**
*Above*, the tripartite temple dedicated to the Capitoline Triad of ancient Sufetula in Tunisia. Structures such as this were built in the cities of Italy and later in every corner of the empire, so that conquered peoples gradually assimilated Roman civil and religious institutions.

**Public Sacrifice**
Fragment of a relief from Rome, which depicts the preparations for a sacrifice to the gods.

## SIMONIDES' DOUBT

A passage in Cicero's dialogue *De natura deorum* (On the Nature of the Gods) is indicative of the Roman attitude toward religion. One of the characters, who holds an important priestly office, tells this anecdote: "It is said of Simonides that, having been asked by the tyrant Hieron to explain the nature of divinity, he requested one day to think about it. But the following day, faced with the same request, he asked for two days. And so on, continuing to request ever-longer extensions. Hieron wanted to know the reason for his behavior. And Simonides responded: "The longer I think about it, the more obscure the question becomes for me."

## *The Capitoline Triad*

The fulcrum of this complex system was the so-called Capitoline Triad, the divine threesome comprising Jupiter, Juno, and Minerva. In the triple-cella temple on the Capitoline—and then repeated with infinite variations in every Roman colony—the Triad had its own principal sanctuary. The dominant god of the Triad was Jupiter, who was described by the two adjectives *Optimus* and *Maximus*, "Best" and "Greatest" of all the gods. The Triad was surrounded by hundreds of lesser divinities that the faithful could worship. These minor divinities had extremely intricate and often variable reciprocal relationships, in part because of the tendency—typical of ancient paganism, particularly the Roman variety—to identify divinities of other peoples with local ones and vice versa.

THE ELYSIAN FIELDS
Fresco from the third century, depicting the Elysian Fields, the celestial world in which, according to Greek and Roman mythology, the select passed into a new existence after death, sheltered from illness and other difficulties.

This made the Roman pantheon an open and tolerant system with implications that were more civil—that is, tied to daily life—than religious in a modern sense. Significantly, traditional Roman priestly offices were assigned by election like ordinary public offices. The idea of an autonomous religious structure, devoted exclusively to the service of a god, was inconceivable to the inhabitants of the Urbs.

## *The Stance of Intellectuals*

The shortcomings of such a lack of emotional participation were soon noted by intellectuals, who in fact had a complex and at times ambiguous stance toward traditional religion. Officially, they professed the greatest respect for the divinities and their cults. But in private or in their daily behavior, they often derided these same practices and exposed their formalism and vacuity. They looked more to philosophy than religion to give their lives ethical substance and depth of feeling. Epicureanism and Stoicism, philosophical doctrines of Greek origin that had profound moral significance, were the true religion of the Roman upper classes.

GREEK ANCESTORS
Ancient sources mention that the image of Jupiter seated on the throne, here in a relief from the first century A.D., was introduced to Rome during the time of Sulla. The model was Zeus of Olympia, a work by the great Athenian sculptor Pheidias.

# Important Cults

A peculiar characteristic of the Roman religious system was the capacity for renewal and adaptation to political and social changes.

After the period of expansion in Italy, the Romans assimilated a great many foreign beliefs and divinities. Other cults were established, deifying abstract virtues (*Concordia*, *Fides*, *Virtus*). Moreover, the empire introduced the deification of human beings, particularly in the case of emperors after their deaths. This adaptability served greatly to strengthen conquered peoples' loyalty to Rome. It also had an unexpected effect, however, opening the door to the "importation" of new cults that were somewhat less easily integrated into the traditional context.

## *Eastern Religions*

In the republican period, the Roman state, staggering beneath defeats suffered at the hands of Hannibal and needing to bolster the faith of its citizens, introduced to Rome the cult of the goddess Cybele, which was Hittite in origin. She was the *Magna Mater* (Great Mother), mistress of nature, whose numerous rites marked much of the Roman religious calendar.

With the advent of the empire, her cult became increasingly evident. Under the Flavians, the cult of Isis and other Egyptian

### THE CULT OF THE GREAT MOTHER

Despite certain aspects that were bloody and aberrant for the Roman mentality, such as the self-castration of priests, the cult of the Great Mother, Cybele, was quite ingrained in Rome and found expression in numerous festivals celebrated with great pomp. For example there was the *Megalensia* (from *Megale Meter*, the Greek name for the Great Mother) in April, and the *Hilaria*, March 25, which celebrated the resurrection of Cybele's consort, Attis. In the imperial period, the *taurobolium* was introduced—the sacrifice of a bull whose testicles were cut off while the blood of the victim ran beneath the sacrificial altar, where the faithful received a sort of baptism of blood. This rite, which perhaps came into being as a symbolic castration that would have allowed a Roman citizen to become a priest of the goddess while avoiding castration, later became a simple initiation ceremony for the faithful. The cult of Cybele endured at length; and, in the fourth century A.D., it still had a strong presence in many parts of the empire.

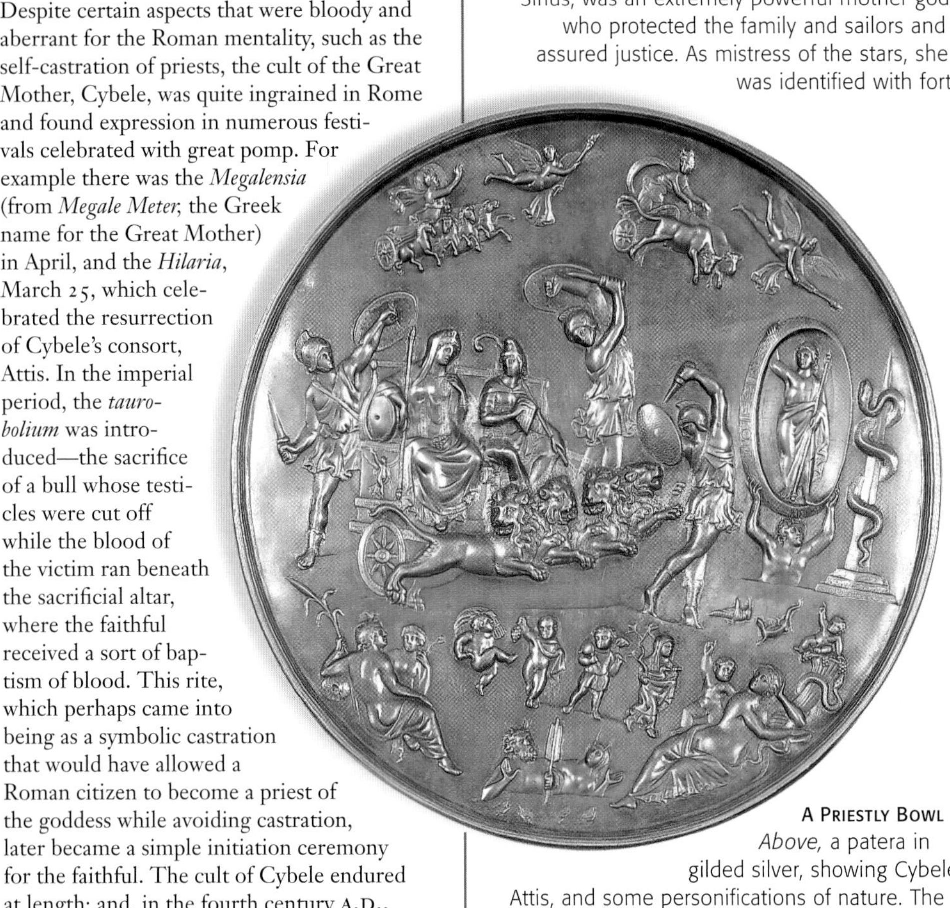

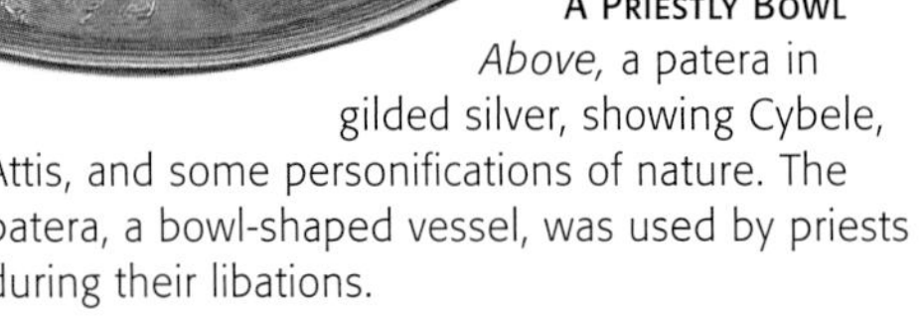

**A Priestly Bowl**
*Above*, a patera in gilded silver, showing Cybele, Attis, and some personifications of nature. The patera, a bowl-shaped vessel, was used by priests during their libations.

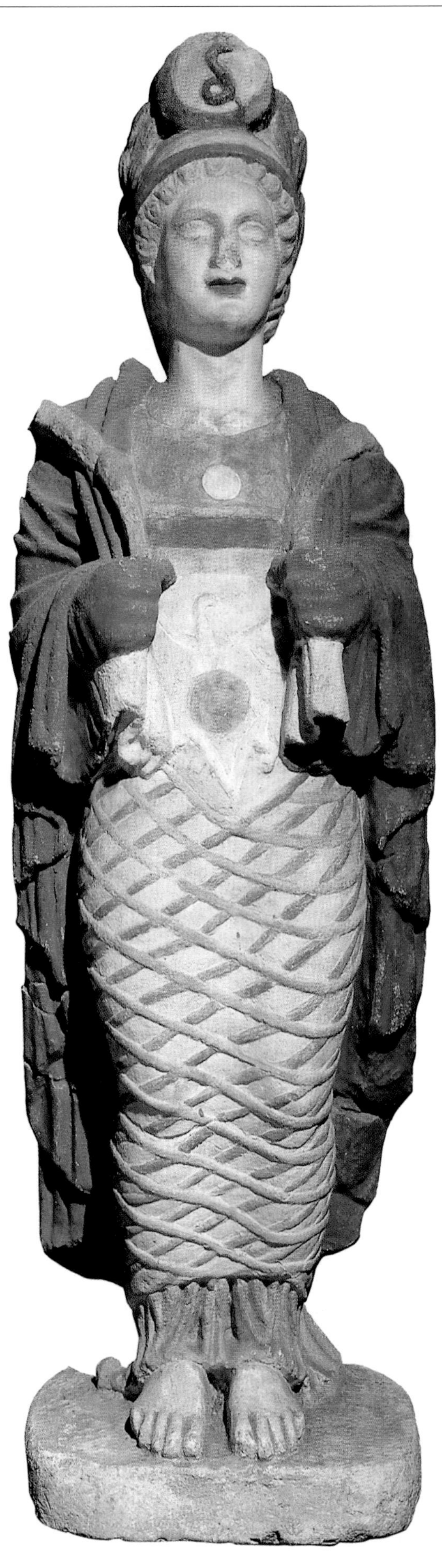

**Isis, the Great Protector**
Isis *(right)*, identified with the moon and with Sirius, was an extremely powerful mother goddess who protected the family and sailors and who assured justice. As mistress of the stars, she also was identified with fortune.

divinities assumed great significance and counted the very members of the imperial family among their devotees. Commodus declared himself a follower not only of Isis but of Mithras, as well. Heliogabalus and Aurelianus introduced the adoration of eastern solar divinities (respectively, the god Elagabal of Emesa [Homs] and the god Malachbel of Palmyra, renamed *Sol Invictus* in Rome).

Between the late first century and early second century A.D., the cult of Mithras spread throughout the empire. This was a religion of mysteries, particularly ingrained among the soldiers of the legions.

## *The Dethronement of the Gods*

All these cults had two dangerous characteristics. First, they came from very distant geographic and cultural worlds and had difficulty blending in with Latin practicality and rationalism. (One need only think of the cult of Cybele, which called for the self-castration of its priests, a requirement that long blocked access to the priestly ranks by Roman citizens, who were prohibited by law from engaging in such practices.) Secondly, they appealed to the deepest and most emotional aspects of the human spirit, and this made their followers potentially uncontrollable in situations where civic duties and religious beliefs might come into conflict. This implication proved devastating with Christianity, which, in addition to the aforementioned traits, had the added pretext of being not "a" religion but "the" religion and which turned the rejection of any other cult into the very symbol of faithfulness to its god. This was an explosive conviction for a multi-ethnic and multicultural empire such as Rome's.

A SUBVERSIVE RELIGION
When Christianity began to spread to Rome, people gossiped that the followers of the new cult were meeting in secret places to indulge in orgies and incest. But even those who did not believe such accusations considered the Christians to be enemies of the empire, for their writings spoke of the advent of a new realm. *Left*, detail of a fresco from the Catacombs of the Giordani in Rome, depicting a woman at prayer.

THE NILE IN ROME
This marble statue from the second century A.D. represents the personification of the Nile. It was located in the temple of Isis in Rome.

# Myths, Legends, and Traditions

Roman mythology did not attain the complexity of its Greek counterpart, but it was far from negligible; and, while there was no Homer or Hesiod, it had an extensive, well-constructed, and in many ways surprising body of stories and beliefs.

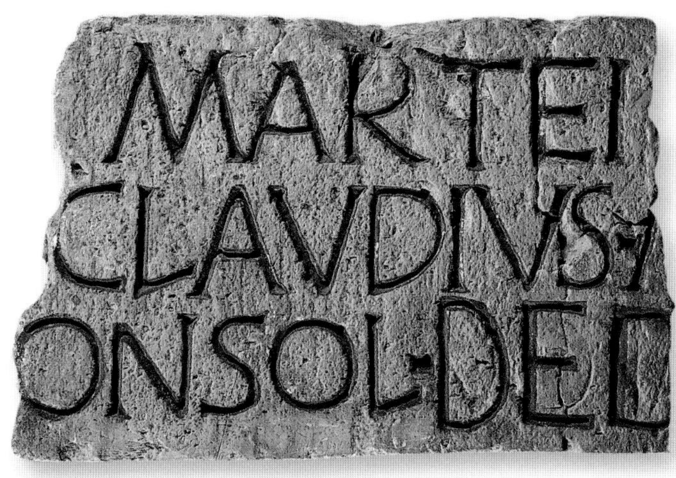


**Dedicated to Mars**
March, the first month of the archaic Roman calendar, was dedicated to the god of war, mentioned here in an inscription from the republican era.

The first Latin myths were probably tied to divinities that were thought to predate the birth of the cosmos. There also were myths that referred to gods who emerged later, however, and others tied to the civilizing actions of heroes, deified ancestors involved with a sort of creation that was linked, above all, to the birth of various settlements. Janus, Saturn, and Vulcan were primordial divinities. Perhaps more recent was the cult of Fortuna Primigenia, seen as the mother of Jupiter and Juno—a mythological theme absent from Rome (probably because it conflicted with the state religion) but clearly present at *Praeneste* (Palestrina). Picus and Faunus, daemon-kings of ambiguous appearance, are conspicuous among the civilizing heroes. They merge human and animal characteristics (Picus is the totemic figure of the woodpecker, a sacred and oracular bird, while Faunus combines the characteristics of the wolf, the goat, and the serpent, depending on the version and locale). Mars and Ops were a very ancient divine couple. The latter, dispenser of royal power and abundant harvests, appeared earlier in certain tombs that can be dated between the late Bronze Age and the early Iron Age. The myth of Ops is interwoven

**Personification of the Tiber**
This marble statue from the second century A.D., which comes from the temple of Isis and Serapis in Rome, depicts the personification of the Tiber, protecting the she-wolf and the mythical twins Romulus and Remus.

**Bearded Mars**
This gold coin, one of the first minted in Rome (c. 196 B.C.), shows the head of a bearded Mars on the front.

with that of Mars, the young sovereign with exceptional warlike abilities, who supposedly was her husband and rival: the destruction and fury of war both in opposition to and united with the satiety and warmth of abundance.

## *Birth Myths*

Many of these myths converge or were made to converge in the larger mythological construction of Rome related to the city's birth and destiny. Thus, according to one possible genealogy, Picus, the woodpecker, son of Mars, joined with a nymph, producing Faunus, the wolf-goat-serpent that in turn joined with Fauna, who gave birth to Latinus, the first king and eponym of the Latins, and the first divinity not to have any monstrous or animal aspect. At the time of the Tarquins, these sagas were superimposed upon the legend of Hercules, who had produced Latinus with a daughter of Faunus. Then there is the myth-legend of Romulus, the son of Mars and a Latin princess (she too a distant descendent of Mars) and founder of the Urbs, venerated in his divine aspect as Quirinus.

**Strong as a Bull**
Detail from the Sarcophagus of the Labors of Hercules (third century A.D.).

## *Glorifying Epic Poetry*

Under Augustus the myths of the city's founding were organized anew by Virgil. His *Aeneid*, taking up various legendary and mythological tales already widely disseminated, introduced Ascanius Iulus as the forefather of the Romans. Ascanius was the son of Aeneas and founder of the *gens Iulia* to which the emperor belonged. Thus it perhaps is incorrect to say that Rome did not have its Homer, but unlike Greece, its epic bard appeared in the culminating phase of the civilization's ascent, not at the beginning.

### ROME, SHE-WOLF, WOODPECKER

"On the banks of the river where the basket with the twins landed there grew a wild fig tree, which the Romans called *Ruminalis*, derived either from Romulus, or, better, from the suckling of the children there, and the ancients called the teat *ruma*. Beneath the fig tree, tradition continues, the infants stayed when the she-wolf came to suckle them; a woodpecker helped to nourish them and guard them. These two animals are considered sacred to Mars, and the Latins have particular veneration for the woodpecker. Thus one can understand how it was not difficult for their mother to have people believe that the father of the twins was Mars. According to others, the fable is rooted in the ambiguity of the nurse's name, for the Latins called not only she-wolves *lupa* but also loose women; and such was the wife of Faustulus, who nursed these children . . . ."

Plutarch, *Life of Romulus*, 4

**The Fortune in the Well**
The sanctuary of Fortuna Primigenia in *Praeneste*, present-day Palestrina (Rome), was home to one of the most important oracles and consultants in the archaic and republican eras. According to ancient sources, the divinity gave *sortes*, responses, which would be extracted from a well into which a child had fallen. *Above*, remains of the sanctuary.

**God of the Forests**
*Above,* a divinity related to the raising of sheep, Faunus generally represented wild, primordial forces. In the private world he was known as Sylvan (from *silva*, wood, forest). *Above*, a Punic terracotta mask, depicting a faun.

# Priestly Schools

Priestly duties were numerous and were distributed among a large number of people. The situation was made even more complex by the Roman religious world's tendency to incorporate foreign cults, each with its own priestly figures.

Religious activity took place on various levels. There were public cults that involved the entire Roman community; there were local cults, expressed by a city or a region; and there were private cults, centered in the priestly or professional schools and in individual families. On the whole, for the Romans a "priest" was anyone who carried out acts of worship at one of these levels: thus not only actual *sacerdotes*, or institutional administrators of a cult, but also magistrates and *pater familias*, those who managed, respectively, the civil and family aspects of religion.

## *Priests and Priestesses*

The priesthood, public or private, was for the most part a male prerogative. Women who had priestly functions were usually subordinate to a male figure. Even the vestals, the highest expression of the female priesthood in Rome, who had immense importance in the management of public matters, were placed under the guidance of the Pontefix Maximus, who fulfilled the role of *pater familias* for their particular organization.

The Fire of Vesta
The primary task of the vestals was to keep the fire perpetually illuminated in the temple of Vesta, the goddess-protector of the Roman state. *Right*, a relief from Rome that depicts a sacrifice to Vesta.

## *Priests and the Community*

Not all men were considered suitable for the priesthood; only Roman citizens fully qualified for public cults, and males of a family for domestic cults. What we would call vocation had no relevance at all. Men became priests by election or cooptation,

Invitation to the Banquet
*Below*, a relief with a scene of animal sacrifice. This type of ceremony was interpreted as a sharing of food with the divinity.

as in the "laic" magistratures. Priestly tasks were carried out not by spreading a faith but by scrupulously observing the rituals that it entailed—namely, the "contract" stipulated between the represented community and its gods. Consequently, magistratures and priestly roles overlapped in many areas of public life. Consuls celebrated numerous rites and sacrifices of the highest importance, they established the dates of religious festivals, they oversaw the auspices that were taken before every significant public act, and they even could decide about introducing a new cult to Rome. However, many important prerogatives were reserved for the specifically priestly schools, populated by those who were priests by profession (pontifices, augurs, decemviri, quindecemviri, septemviri, vestals). Such privileges included the celebration of specific cults, the inauguration of certain civil or sacred spaces (*templa*), the preservation of the Sibylline books for the purpose of drawing forth prophecies, and the organization of ritual banquets and processions. Then there were "specialized" schools (the *Feciali*, *Arvali*, *Salii*, *Luperci*, etc.), set aside for specific cults or rites of archaic origin. This vast complexity was gradually "normalized" in the imperial era, when the *princeps*, who oversaw all the priestly schools and directly or indirectly chose their members, substantially reduced each priestly structure to mere "executive" tasks, performed at the will of a single person—namely, the sovereign. This was not the least of the reasons that traditional religion had decreasing influence on the citizens of Rome.

**Chaste and Pure**
The priestesses of Vesta, chosen by lot among candidates ranging from six to ten years of age, remained at their post for thirty years. For this entire period, they had to keep themselves chastely pure under penalty of death. *Left*, The House of the Vestals in the Roman forum.

**The Priest's Chair**
*Right*, a priest's marble throne. This is an eighteenth-century reconstruction, executed on the basis of Roman models and using, in part, ancient materials.

## PRIESTS, GUARDIANS OF RITES

Traditional Roman religion did not deal with individuals but with society as a whole. It was a complex of cults and ceremonies that accompanied and involved every aspect of life. Completely without mystical or emotional features, it drew its power from the extremely strong integration between institutions and ritual aspects, which led Romans to consider it extremely risky to neglect the rites. What we would call faith had no place in this attitude.

Within this context, priests were not responsible for supervising the religious life of individual citizens. Their duties were to the Roman people as a whole, not the individuals who made up society. If a scandal arose tied to religious practices, this did not concern the priests but rather the magistrates, as guardians of public order. Thus during the Second Punic War, when the Roman people, terrorized by Hannibal's continuous victories, sought refuge in esoteric and foreign cults, it was not the priests who intervened, but the presiding praetor, who judged such practices to be an act of subversion against the state.

# Divination—Interpreting the Signs of the Gods

For Romans, the response of the divinities was of capital importance. Indeed, divination—that is, the art of interpreting the intentions of the gods—and the city of Rome came into being together.

**The Turn of the Screw**
The emperor Tiberius was forced to issue laws to limit the activity of the augurs and haruspices, whose influence over the lower classes was enormous.

When Romulus and Remus had to choose which of them would give his name to the city, the two twins trusted in the signs of the heavens, but they disagreed as to how these signs should be interpreted. A dispute arose in which Remus lost his life. This story conveys the entire relationship between Rome and this particular branch of the esoteric arts.

## *The Systems of Divination*

There were various systems through which signs sent by the gods could be interpreted. The most ancient was that chosen by the two twins, the founders of the city: observation of the flight and cries of birds. This practice was the prerogative of a specific professional group, the augurs, who had a prestigious and influential school in Rome. In the case of important decisions, an augur accompanied the consul in charge and provided an interpretation of the signs that the magistrate observed. Later a different practice developed, based on the examination of the entrails of sacrificed animals or on the evaluation of omens or natural portents: earthquakes, floods, comet paths, eclipses, and also less objective events, such as weeping statues or cows capable of speech. The results of the divination were referred to the Senate, which consulted experts in the matter—the haruspices—in order to understand which gods were angry and which rites had to be celebrated to placate them. Augurs and haruspices were jealous of their specific arts. However, citizens and authorities alike did not particularly admire the local professionals, and they acknowledged the greater skill of the Greeks and Etruscans in this field and turned to them in cases of particular danger or great importance.

**School of Haruspication**
The haruspices drew auspices, positive or negative, by observing the entrails of animals. This bronze model of a cow's liver with inscribed lines (second century B.C.) may have been used for educational purposes.

### THE DIVINE SEAL ON DECISIONS OF STATE

Roman divinatory practices can arouse our scorn, but they had undeniable value in the functioning of the Roman state. Magistrates, through scrupulous research and interpretation of auspices, seemed to ask—and then obtain—the endorsement of the gods for their own choices, which in this manner were rendered almost sacred and thus worthy of being shared and accepted by the people. For those in opposition, who had to criticize a decision approved and blessed by the gods, life became rather difficult, at times impossible. Julius Caesar himself saw many of his consular decisions weakened by "contestation" brought forth by his consular colleague, Lucius Calpurnius Bibulus, on the basis of observations of celestial phenomena.

## *The Importance of Auspices*

In ancient Rome no significant question, even of a private nature, was taken up without first consulting the auspices. This custom was preserved well into the imperial era and fell into disuse only after the full affirmation of Christianity. Military commanders carried with them cages of sacred chickens from which they drew indications about the right moment to initiate a battle or to ford a river. Public meetings could be postponed or interrupted if the presiding magistrates or the augurs who accompanied them noticed signs of ill omen, such as lightening in a calm sky or other similar occurrences (and the resulting political stakes are easy to imagine).

Naturally, notice was not always paid. One particularly decisive consul threw into the sea chickens that persisted in not eating before a naval battle—a sign considered particularly negative—sarcastically commenting, "If they don't want to eat, let them drink." But just as often one could find a mistakenly observed omen or a neglected negative auspice to explain something that went wrong. Among the middle and lower classes, especially, there was considerable respect for the judgments of the augurs and haruspices. Their influence was so great that the emperor Tiberius had to issue laws restricting their activity and decreeing that they could make divinations only before witnesses in order to protect those most at risk, often victims of fraud. It is true that in their works many Latin authors (Cicero in particular) mocked divination. But it is likewise true that the general behavior of Roman society with regard to this issue could be summarized in the classic saying, "It is not true, but believe it I do."

**Professional Etruscan**
The incomparable skill of the Etruscans in the field of haruspication was documented in a treatise that Cicero knew by the name of the Haruspicine Books, nothing of which, unfortunately, survives. *Left,* a small Etruscan bronze depicting a haruspex (third century B.C.).

**A Priest Holding a Liver for Divination**
This cover to a funerary urn (second century B.C.) depicts a priest who holds a cow's liver in his hand. It comes from Volterra and is the work of an Etruscan artist.

**Eternal Augurs**
These two figures in a ritual stance give the name to the Etruscan Tomb of the Augurs in Tarquinia.

# Religion in Private Life

Private religious life was the setting for the most ancient forms of worship, tied to the people's Latin origins and uncontaminated by the anthropomorphism of the Greek divinities.

The home represented the fulcrum of religious life for the Romans. Here the animistic forces typical of Italic religion were honored with little inclination toward the anthropomorphism that characterized the Greek divinities. The *penates* were the protectors of food supplies, the *manes* were venerated in order to honor the deceased, and the *lares* protected home and family, including servants. Along with these domestic entities, certain public divinities found a place within the context of private worship. For example, Vesta oversaw the domestic hearth as well as that of the state, and Janus protected the doorway of the house as well as those of the city. Each male individual then had his own tutelary numen (*genius*), which accompanied him in life and in death. Often depicted as a serpent, this deity embodied the generative force that guaranteed the continuity of the family line.

**The House of the *Lares***
Each Roman dwelling possessed a *lararium*, a chapel in miniature, dedicated to the *lares*. Generally, this had the form of a niche with little columns or pilasters, surmounted by a triangular tympanum and resting on a masonry base, such as this one, from the House of the Vettii in Pompeii.

**Divinity of Passage**
The Arch of Janus in Rome, shown here in a nineteenth-century painting by Ippolito Caffi, was erected in the fourth century A.D. in honor of the divinity of "transitions." In fact, house doors, streets, and certain obligatory passages that opened onto public thoroughfares were sacred to Janus.

**Family Portraits**
This statue, known as the "Barbarini Togatus," depicts a man holding images of his ancestors.

## *Continuity of Worship*

Unlike public cults, the Romans' domestic cults effectively underwent no modifications during the centuries. Generation after generation, the *lares* continued to receive the offering of fire, the *genius* that of pure wine, the *penates* that of perfume. The sacred function entrusted to the *pater familias*, assisted by his sons, was celebrated in the name and often in the presence of the entire family, and sometimes, as in the case of weddings and funerals, of the entire neighborhood or community. The head of the family, in fact, was the custodian and person in charge of ritual tradition, which he had received from his ancestors and had to, in turn, hand down to his descendents.

## *Ancestor Worship*

In family religion, the worship of ancestors was extremely important. Indeed, the continuity of the family represented survival beyond the time of the individuals, each of whom felt, not isolated, but rather part of a centuries-old organism for which he or she could ensure continuity. This is the context for the typically Roman-Italic custom of bringing back to life the family's famous ancestors during a funeral of a family member. The bier was followed by actors dressed in clothes appropriate to the rank of each ancestor and wearing wax death masks (*imagines maiorum*), molded from the face of each family member and jealously preserved in a well-protected cabinet in the house. At the end of the ceremony, after the virtues of the deceased had been illustrated, they began to speak about the ancestors whose masks were present; beginning with the most ancient, they expounded on the exploits and successes of each to the perennial pride of the family.

### THE "RIGHT OF PORTRAIT"

Aware of the strong emotional impact that the celebration of ancestors and their "resurrection" through *imagines maiorum* had on the people, the Roman ruling class instituted an actual "right of portrait" (*ius imaginum*) that limited the prerogative of such representations solely to members of the dominant oligarchy.

**_Religio_ and _Pietas_**
In the Roman world the term *religio* indicated respect by oath, while the scrupulous and faithful fulfillment of all obligations toward the gods, whether in a public or private context, was called *pietas*. *Left*, a mosaic with a scene of sacrifice.

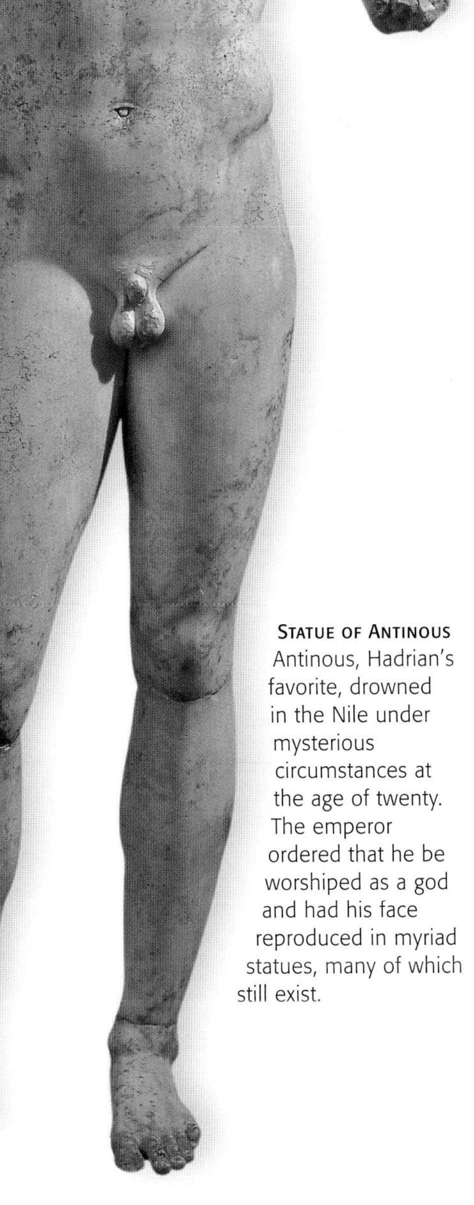

**Statue of Antinous**
Antinous, Hadrian's favorite, drowned in the Nile under mysterious circumstances at the age of twenty. The emperor ordered that he be worshiped as a god and had his face reproduced in myriad statues, many of which still exist.

# Funerary Rituals

In Rome death was a public event: the more sumptuous the funeral, the more illustrious the deceased and his *gens*—or so they appeared.

Funerary rituals were strongly influenced by Greek culture, with its celebration of individual qualities, and Etruscan culture, with its parallel exaltation of the clan (the *gens*) to which one belonged. These rituals tended, on the one hand, to honor and exalt the qualities (in the case of a man) or the virtue (in the case of a woman) of the deceased. On the other hand, they proudly represented the wealth, prestige, fame, and rank of the person's *gens*. In fact, if the death of a family member necessarily modified the balances within the family, it was not supposed to alter the external ones—namely, those relationships of power with other *gentes* and with the state.

## *The Rite of Passage*

Funerary rituals called for four fundamental moments: the public showing of the corpse, dressed in state; the funerary procession with the exhibition of masks (*imagines*) of ancestors; the funeral eulogy pronounced over the body of the deceased; the final pyre.

The management of the ceremony was entrusted to an undertaker's establishment, whose employees (*libitinarii*) took care of the numerous and complex tasks required by the ritual. They prepared the body, laid it out on the *lectus funebris* located in the atrium of the house, and organized the procession with flautists, mimes, dancers, and hired mourners who surrounded the grieving family and friends. If the deceased had been a powerful man who held high office,

**Public Exposition**
This relief from a funerary urn depicts a wake. The ceremony took place in the atrium of the house, where the corpse, after having been washed and sprinkled with unguents, was exhibited on the *lectus funebris*.

**Tears for Hire**
Hired mourners, shown here in a relief, were women paid to weep and create a scene of desperation at funeral ceremonies.

**Funeral Eulogy**
*Below*, a relief depicting the emperor Hadrian giving the funeral eulogy for his wife Sabina.

**Votive Offerings**
A funerary urn with votive offerings, originally from Gaul (first century A.D.).

the bier was surrounded by lictors, with their fasces edged in mourning, followed by bearers of placards that recalled the exploits of the departed.

The funeral eulogy (*laudatio*) assumed particular importance and was spoken from the rostra, the orators' dais in the forum. Some *laudationes*, such as Caesar's in honor of his first wife, Cinnilla, were remembered many years later. Antony's discourse over the body of Caesar inspired the immortal poetry of William Shakespeare.

### CREMATION OR BURIAL?

Both types of funeral rites coexisted in Rome. The choice depended on the era or, sometimes, family tradition (the deceased of the *gens Cornelia*, for example, traditionally were buried and not cremated). Ancient historians maintained that the oldest rite was burial, which was replaced by cremation, but archeological research shows that the two modes coexisted as early as the eighth to seventh century B.C. Cremation prevailed only from the fourth century onward, and the practice continued for the most part throughout the first century A.D. Cinerary urns ranged from simple terracotta vases for people of humble rank to true works of art (shaped like altars, houses, caskets), made from marble and even gold, for the most wealthy or illustrious figures. Beginning with the reign of Hadrian, burial became more widespread until the practice almost totally replaced cremation, a development that gave rise to the great period of Roman sarcophagi.

## *The Funeral Banquet*

The funeral ceremony concluded with a ritual banquet, the *silicernium*, which took place near the tomb and to which all participants in the procession were invited. A portion of the food was placed next to the tomb, signifying that the ceremony was, first of all, in honor of the deceased. The banquet also functioned as a purification rite and a return to normality for the family, which from that moment on resumed its journey in the world. However, such solemn tributes were not bestowed on all. The less wealthy, whose families could not allow themselves the cost of such ceremony, received more modest funeral rites from the association to which they belonged. The state paid for the funerals of the *capite censi*, those who did not own property, and the poet Martial has left a representative description of one such event: "Four public grave-diggers who carried one of those corpses that burn by the thousand on the poor wretches' pyres." Even in death, all were not equal.

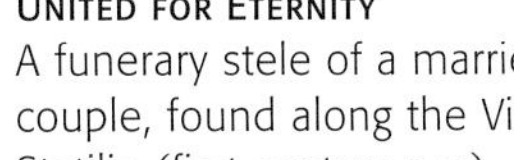

**United for Eternity**
A funerary stele of a married couple, found along the Via Statilia (first century B.C.).

**Miniature Sarcophagus**
A cinerary urn in alabaster (first to second century A.D.) in the form of a house.

# Superstitions and the Practice of Magic

Amid the vagabonds and idlers who thronged the streets of Rome, magicians and wizards of every type were particularly numerous, and they profited from people's credulity and superstitions.

During the Second Punic War at a moment of great uncertainty about Rome's fate, astrologers, palmists, interpreters of dreams, and sellers of amulets had become so numerous and pestiferous that the authorities had to take drastic measures to expel them from the city. This was an ineradicable phenomenon, however, that spread relentlessly, particularly under the empire, with magic often appearing in a "scientific" guise.

## *White Magic and Black Magic*

This cauldron contained everything: country quacks who carried out popular magic rituals meant to safeguard the harvests; ambiguous female figures who furtively gathered bones and herbs in the necropolises to prepare magical potions; necromancers who practiced sorcery and ritual murders of newborns; sorcerers who prepared "tablets of transfixion," extremely cruel curses written on lead tablets, to harm opponents in sports, rivals in love, or political enemies. During the Antonine era, the figure of the philosopher-magician gained popularity. This was a sort of initiate who brought together the practice of magic, religious meditation, philosophy, scientific investigation, and medicine, in a search for contact with celestial powers in order to improve understanding and modify reality. During this period, a distinction was made between black magic *(goetica)*,

**Giving Fortune a Hand**
A bronze votive hand with apotropaic symbols, capable of keeping evil influences at bay.

### WORDS OF MAGIC

The word *magus* (with its derivations *magia, ars magica, herba magica*) appears in the Latin language at the time of Cicero. Initially, it indicated simply someone who came from Mesopotamia, the land of origin of many practitioners of the esoteric arts. It soon took on a negative connotation, however, to indicate wizards, astrologers, healers, and mystificators of various types. In the time of Tiberius, the term was enriched with a specific legal connotation, indicating those who practiced criminal magic. The other words connected with the magical arts also took on more or less negative significance, from *maleficus* and *veneficus* (makers of spells and poisons)—often identified with sorcerers, shamans, and the like—to *striges* (literally "vampires") and *sagae*—which indicated the female practitioners of the profession, namely, witches.

**Pendant for an Amulet**
*Above*, an Etruscan *bulla* from Vulci (fourth century B.C.). The bulla was a metal pendant that contained an amulet. In the Roman world, children wore them hanging from their necks until adulthood.

**The Sorceress and the Wayfarer**
Painting from the House of the Dioscuri in Pompeii, in which a sorceress offers a magical potion to a wayfarer.

scorned as base witchcraft directed exclusively toward evil deeds, and white magic (*teurgia*), which allowed the realization of pure and beneficial goals—a view that must have had a strong influence on subsequent eras.

## *A Futile Struggle*

To stem the spread of superstition and the practice of magic, emperors often resorted to draconian measures. Augustus, in A.D. 13, ordered the burning of two thousand parchments with magic-related contents. Tiberius, Claudius, Vitellius, and Diocletian reiterated proscriptions and condemnations against those who practiced magic. But it was a futile struggle. Only the advent of Christianity—which equated all practice of magic with acts contrary to the one possible faith, that in God, and at the same time gave a strong mystical character to its own beliefs in an attempt to satisfy the population's strong need for the supernatural—eliminated, at least apparently, superstitious practices from the European panorama.

**The Massacre of the Innocents**
The epitaph of a young boy, Giocondo, who died at the age of four at the hands of a cruel witch, documents one of the most tragic aspects of the practice of magic: the ritual sacrifice of young innocents during the course of satanic ceremonies. The inscription concludes with an excruciating admonishment to parents: "Guard your children carefully, if you do not want to have your heart pierced by despair." *Right*, a Pompeian mosaic shows a scene from a comedy that may involve magic.

**On the Door of a House**
An *oscillum* in white marble with decoration in relief, from Pompeii (first century B.C.). Small sculptures like this, usually consecrated to Saturn or Bacchus, were hung on the doors of houses to ward off evil.

# The Infancy of a Language

For centuries, until relatively recent times, Latin was the universal language par excellence, used for scientific and literary works of greatest importance. Its beginnings were modest, however, and in many ways are still unknown.

Traces exist of the most ancient poetic texts in the Latin language. These were religious songs such as the *carmen* of the Arvali (an extremely ancient fellowship formed to celebrate rites related to the earth). What has survived is a late compilation from the third century A.D., but it seems faithfully to revive the original text. We also know of the existence of *carmina convivalia*, performed during banquets, and others celebrating the glorious feats of ancestors—the first compositions of epic Latin. However, the initial poetic forms that were more characteristic of Rome are the Fescennines and the *satura*. The former derived their name *(fescennina licentia)* from a city in southern Etruria; these were farcical and not infrequently licentious strophes that various interpreters improvised and exchanged in a context that is defined as pre-theater. In a certain manner these are the most ancient ancestors of commedia dell'arte. The *satura*, however, represented a more refined genre with accompaniment of music and dance.

## *Theater*

Roman theater emerged from contact with the Greek cities of southern Italy, and it was an imported genre for quite some time. It is no accident that the first author in this field was a Greek slave deported from Tarentum. The Latin word itself for comedy, *Palliata*, from *pallio*, a Greek garment worn by actors, indicated its provenance. Only in the second half of the third century B.C., with the coarse but lively work of Titus Maccius Plautus, did original dramatic compositions written in Latin by Latin authors appear on the stage.

**An Imported Genre**
A theatrical mask in terracotta from Magna Graecia.

**The Theater of Mérida**
One of the best-preserved Roman theaters is the one in Mérida, Spain, which could hold up to 5,000 spectators. Mérida was founded in 25 B.C. by Augustus under the name *Emerita Augusta*.

### A DANGEROUS PLACE

Rome received its first permanent theater, built by Pompey, only in 55 B.C., at a time when such structures had already existed for some time in many Italic cities of considerably less importance. Until then, the Romans had to be satisfied with temporary theaters built in conjunction with sanctuaries where festivals were dedicated to divinities and dismantled at the conclusion of the festivities. This did not reflect parsimoniousness on the part of the magistrates charged with such constructions, but rather the suspicion of the dominant oligarchy in Rome that theatrical sites, as gathering places, might facilitate potentially seditious assemblies.

**The Theater of Pompey**
What remains of the Theater of Pompey are, above all, the ruins of the central *cavea (left)*, used as foundations for new buildings, which still follow the original curvature.

**Tablet and Stylus**
Rome was acquainted with writing very early on. It was introduced into Italy in the late eighth century B.C. by Greek colonists and was put to broad use. Nonetheless, the level of literacy among the population always remained below twenty percent. All cities had scribes, who, in return for payment, wrote for those who were illiterate, by incising letters on wax-covered tablets.

## *Prose*

The hotbed of Roman prose was the political competition. The first texts were international treatises affixed to the walls of temples, *Fasti* (civil and religious calendars), and Annals, the record collected by the *pontefix maximus* of the principal events that occurred during the year, particularly the orations given by citizens in the Senate or on the rostra approving or opposing a political decision or law. This had considerable influence on the character and structure of the language, which assumed the same solemn and idea-packed tone with a love of lapidary concision and effective phrases, which became typical.

But historiography, a genre in which the Romans later excelled, contributed little to the initial development of the language, and it emerged from the Greek model rather than from an indigenous impulse. The first chronicles of Rome were written in Greek, such as one by Fabius Pictor. Cato the Censor was the first to write a historical work in Latin, but he wrote more as a statesman, a protagonist in the political and social struggles of his time, committed to spreading his ideas, than as an impartial historian. This was destined to become a model, and for a long time history was a literary genre controlled by the dominant oligarchy. For the members of this ruling class, it was almost an obligation, after having experienced firsthand the events of their time, to present their own personal historical reconstruction.

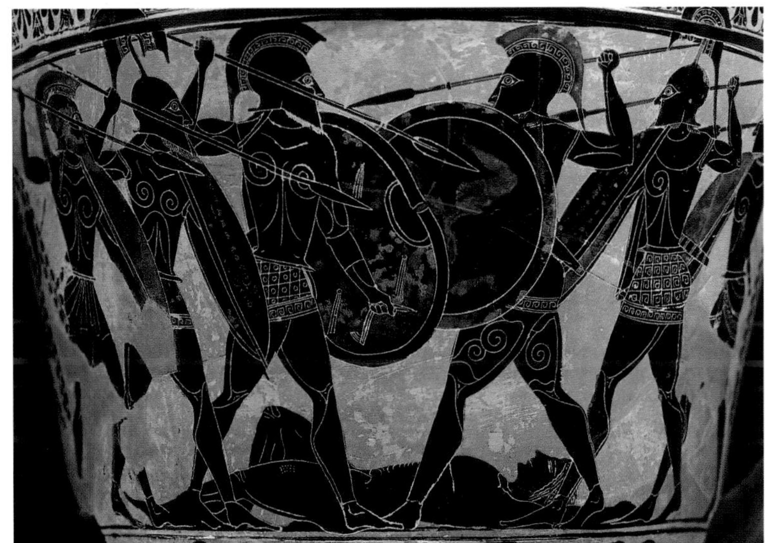

**Greek Epic**
In addition to introducing theater to Rome, Livius Andronicus translated Homer's *Odyssey* into Saturnian verse. The great Greek epic thus entered in complete fashion into the Roman cultural world, which already was familiar with its characters and episodes through decorations on ceramics. The decoration illustrated here, originally from Pharsalus, depicts the battle for the spoils of Patroclus.

# The Discovery of Sentiment

Until the first century B.C., the Latin poets were split between the writing of epics and theater, with tragedy clearly predominant. Only comedy remained to represent the pleasant and playful side of literature.

THE RAPE OF GANYMEDE
One of the most famous episodes of Ovid's *Metamorphoses* tells how Zeus transformed himself into an eagle to abduct the young Ganymede and make him the cupbearer of the gods.

In time, new generations appeared on the Roman scene, eager for innovation and worldly refinements, a refuge from the gloomy disorders of civil wars. This cultivated and demanding public found its bards and inspirers in poets such as Gaius Valerius Catullus, Ablius Tibullus, and Publius Ovidius Naso, who straddled the age of Caesar and that of Augustus. These three authors gave the Latin language—which until that time had been characterized by a rather serious and sedate gait, suited above all to public proclamations and legislative texts—the supple sweetness of a graceful idiom, shaped to praise the joys and sorrows of love.

## *Catullus*

Born in Verona about 84 B.C., Catullus is one of the greatest Latin poets. He abandoned the concept of literature as a celebration of the collective values of Roman life, and his lyric poetry gave voice to individual sentiment. The sentiment of friendship and, especially, the burning experience of his love for "Lesbia," a cultivated and refined woman identified by historians as Clodia, a well-known aristocratic Roman, were the central motifs of his inspiration. Catullus also was capable of ferocious enmity, such as he harbored for Julius Caesar, a frequent target of his literary barbs. Catullus died about 54 B.C.

THE GROTTOS OF CATULLUS
The so-called Grottos of Catullus are the vestiges of a large Roman building that overlooked Lake Garda near Sirmione. According to tradition, this was the villa described by Catullus in his poems.

## *Tibullus*

We know very little about Albius Tibullus, who perhaps was born to a wealthy family in Latium about the time that Catullus died, between 55 and 50 B.C. Conscripted into the legions of Octavian in the struggle against Marc Antony, Tibullus got to know

### THE POETRY OF CATULLUS

"Let us enjoy life, O Lesbia mine, and the pleasures of love . . . . Give me a thousand kisses, and then a hundred, then another thousand and then another hundred . . . . "

Beyond its apparent simplicity and spontaneity, the poetry of Catullus is extremely refined and is expressed in an original blending of elements of spoken language and deliberately affected terms. Here are two other splendid examples:

"I hate and I love. Perhaps you wonder how I do it. I don't know; but I feel that this is what happens to me: it is my chagrin."

"And now these offerings . . . that you enjoy. They are bathed in many fraternal tears; I honor you forever, O brother. Farewell."

Marcus Valerius Messalla Corvinus during his military service. Corvinus, himself an aristocrat and a poet, took the young writer under his wing and introduced him to the circle of intellectuals protected by the emperor. Tibullus was one of the major elegiac poets of the Roman world. Unhappy in love (but without the fury of Catullus), he wrote with melancholy abandon in limpid and elegant verses of the two women he loved and his nostalgia for the simplicity of rural life. He died about 19 B.C.

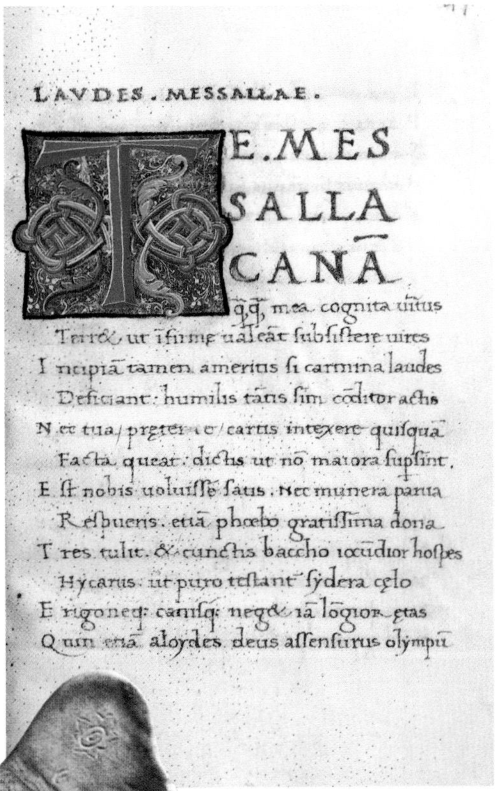

**The Poems of Tibullus** An illuminated codex from the fifteenth century with the poems of Tibullus.

## *Ovid*

*Carmen et error:* to have written verses and to have participated (or witnessed) something better left ignored. This, for years, was the complaint of Publius Ovidius Naso, who was born in 43 B.C. in Sulmo and died in A.D. 17 in Tomi (present-day Constantsa, in Romania), bemoaning the cold and the squalor of that place to which he had been exiled by the emperor Augustus, nine years before. His great works, including *Ars amatoria* and *Metamorphoses*, taught Romans not only to love but also to express love of self with polished sweetness. As for his "error," perhaps it was merely a question of having witnessed, at too close proximity, the amorous adventures of the imperial women (and perhaps even instigated them, according to infamous gossip). This was sufficient to earn him exile, where his muse, accustomed to exalted society, had to submit to singing the *Tristia*, the sad songs without hope of one who is far from home.

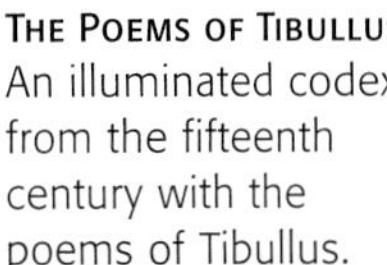

**Perfect Sentiment** A marble group depicting the couple Amor and Psyche.

**The Art of Love** Ovid's *Ars amatoria* is a didactic poem in three books, which instructs how a man can win a woman and keep love alive and how a woman can make herself loved. *Right*, Ares and Aphrodite in a fresco from Pompeii.

# ORATORY

To move, delight, convince: these, according to the great Cicero, were the goals that a good orator must set for himself.

Oratory, that is, the art of "speaking well," was the principal tool for politics. It was practiced in assembly confrontations and for the dispensation of law, an essential part of Roman political life with which it was inextricably bound.

## *The Apprenticeship of the Forum*

The political role of oratory was ever present for Romans. In his treatise *De oratore*, Cicero points out how the substantial difference between Romans and Greeks lay in the fact that the latter learned oratory from the lessons of paid teachers, while the Romans were trained in the art from infancy. They modeled themselves on the example of eminent figures in social and political fields, pursuing those careers and learning the art of eloquence firsthand. This was the so-called "apprenticeship of the forum," which aimed to create not only able speakers but also and above all the future holders of political office, capable of using their discourses to influence the positions of the Senate and the people's assemblies.

## *Greek Influence*

During the wars in the East, Roman aristocrats were fascinated by the elegance and effectiveness of Greek rhetoric, based on a vast philosophical and literary culture that

### TRICKS OF THE TRADE

Today, Lucius Crassus is much less known than Cicero, Caesar, or Hortensius. In his time, however, he was a greatly esteemed orator, skillful enough to be authorized to add the title of *Orator* to his name. He was a true virtuoso of the word, capable of inspiring the minds of his listeners with language that was broad and rich in quotations but at the same time immediate and direct. To obtain these results, he resorted to embellishing refinements of speech with enormously effective theatrical tricks: taking large strides toward the dais, gesturing emphatically, even, on one occasion, having his discourse accompanied by a flautist who, hidden behind a curtain, musically emphasized the most suggestive passages.

**Cicero's Letters**
Cicero's correspondence, made up of 774 letters, sent principally to his brother, Quintus, to other family members, and to his friends Atticus and Brutus, make it possible to reconstruct the personality and psychology of this great Roman orator and man of politics. *Right*, a marble bust of Cicero.

**The Training Ground of Orators**
The Roman forum, the appointed place for public and private business, was the commercial, administrative, and cultural center of the capital.

allowed them to capture and hold the attention of the public.

The great orators of the last century of the Republic—Cato, Lucius Crassus, Hortensius, Cicero, and Caesar—were all followers of the various Greek schools of oratory. (There were numerous schools, but the two principal ones were the "Asian," which was more figurative and grandiose, and the "Attic," which was more sober and refined.)

## *Cicero*

The greatest of the Roman orators was Marcus Tullius Cicero (106–43 B.C.), a lawyer, man of politics, and tremendously convincing writer. He was influenced by both schools of Greek rhetoric, which he sought to mediate by forming an intermediary style that was not as brisk and spare as the Attic and not as turgid and dense with ideas as the Asian. (This position reflected his political views, which were oriented toward balance, above all in the social field, where he supported the *concordia ordinum*, that is, harmony among social classes).

Cicero brought oratory to its highest level. After him, this noble republican activity began to decline not so much because of the difficulty in equaling models like Cicero and Caesar but because of the disappearance of political debate, now impeded by the dominant and increasingly autocratic position assumed by the emperor, who made all decisions.

**Cicero's Tomb**
Cicero was killed in Formia, where he had a villa, by assassins hired by Marc Antony, whom the great orator had attacked violently in the Senate, giving his 14 orations known as the "Philippics." *Inset*, Cicero's tomb in Formia.

**Togate Magistrate**
The art of oratory found an ideal stage in the halls of the tribunals, where lawyers battled each other before a judge and members of the public.

# A Sense of Destiny: The Historians

Sallust, Livy, Tacitus, Suetonius: few civilizations can equal the Roman world's array of historians, who were capable of analyzing with objectivity and relentless sincerity the events and motivations of their own society.

**Domitian the Terrible**
Tacitus's *Historiae* presents a final sentence of condemnation against this cruel and despotic emperor. Commenting on his death, the historian wrote, "Now finally breathing space returns."

The Greeks invented historiography and, with Herodotus and Thucydides, provided its models. From them, the Romans learned this art, this "possession for all time," as Thucydides called it. At first they entered the field somewhat clumsily, but soon their historians were producing works that were worthy of their Greek models. First Sallust and then Caesar skillfully and astutely recounted the wars of their time (against Jugurtha in the case of Sallustius, his own military campaigns in Gaul and the civil war with Pompey in the case of Caesar).

It was during the early imperial era (first and second centuries A.D.), however, that Roman historiography reached its high point with expressive and engagingly dramatic accounts of events from the past.

## *The Great Fresco of Roman History*

Titus Livius, born in Padua in 59 B.C., is the great narrator of Archaic Roman events. The work to which he devoted the majority of his life, known as *Ab Urbe condita (From the Foundation of Rome)*, appeared in various stages over a forty-year period.

**First Page**
*Above*, a page of a fifteenth-century codex with the beginning of the *Ab Urbe condita* by Titus Livius. The work was widely disseminated during the Renaissance and it inspired, for example, numerous theater pieces that were fashionable in the sixteenth century.

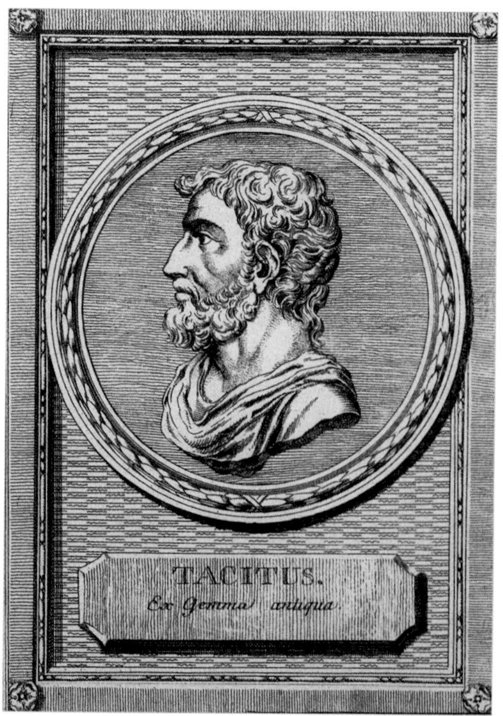


**The Works of Tacitus**
The *Historiae*, in 12 books, expounded the history of Rome from Galba to Domitian (A.D. 69–97), while the *Annales*, in 16 books, described the reigns of the earlier emperors from Tiberius to Nero (A.D. 14–68). The first four books of the *Historiae* and the first six and last six of the *Annales* have survived. *At right*, an eighteenth-century engraving of Tacitus in profile.

Unlike earlier historical works, such as those of Sallust, which were dedicated to the narration of individual historical periods, Livy's work embraced the entire arc of Roman history from the city's founding to contemporary times. His approach for sketching out the history of Rome was broadly echoed by subsequent historians. Livy's 142 books (only 35 of which have survived to the present day) enjoyed immense fame both in the Roman era and in the Renaissance, and they in turn inspired important political and historiographic works, such as the *Discourses on the First Decade of Titus Livius* by Niccolò Machiavelli).

THE GARDENS OF SALLUST
The places where Sallustius worked intently on his studies were principally the gardens of his Roman residence, which occupied the entire valley between the Quirinal and Pincian hills. These gardens contained various buildings and an extremely noteworthy collection of artworks. This striking piece, a richly decorated marble krater, is one of the sculptures found in the area over the course of time.

## *Imperial Tragedies and Greatness*

Livy, who wrote at the time of Augustus, sketched a coherent portrait of the birth and assertion of Roman dominion—the history of the Republic. But the great historians of the following era focused their attention on the deeds and misdeeds of the emperors, by then the principal if not sole moving forces behind events. This personalized narrative reached its heights in the work of two great writers, Cornelius Tacitus, who wrote during the period immediately following the Flavian dynasty, and Gaius Suetonius Tranquillus, who lived under Hadrian and was his librarian and secretary. The books of Tacitus—*De Agricola*, *Historiae*, *Annales*—are not only illuminating historiographic essays but also literary works of high stylistic value. Suetonius, less skillful on a literary plane, is nevertheless an inexhaustible source of information and anecdotes, which are abundant in his works *(De viris illustribus*, *De vita Caesarum)*, written according to the traditional biographical scheme of Greek and Latin literature.

The pages of these authors include curious bits of information, gossip, sometimes horrifying details, stories of conspiracies, abuses of power, crimes (perhaps invented, the result of disparaging propaganda that emperors tended to employ to diminish the status of their predecessors), but also enlightening opinions and memorable portraits of famous men. In any case, they are always unforgettable reading.

GALBA AND THE EAGLE
This engraving, from a seventeenth-century treatise on physiognomy, compares the face of Galba with an eagle's head.

### OPPOSITION TO THE REGIME

Suetonius has left us merciless portraits (not only morally but also physically) of the emperors of the first century A.D. For example, he writes that Augustus had a neck covered with itchy eczema, a limping gait, and was afraid of lightning. Galba is described as a short and corpulent man with pale eyes and a hooked nose and limbs distorted by gout. Claudius is like an unstable and inept simpleton, an object of scorn and a target for olive and date pits thrown by his courtiers. The contrast with the stately and majestic view given by propaganda and imperial portraiture could not be more strident: a veritable manual of "counter-information."

# Spiritual Guides for a World in Crisis

While the Roman world entered a period of long and inexorable decline, it increasingly began to question itself, its beliefs, and its destiny.

As the imperial era proceeded from the first to the third century, philosophers and masters of rhetoric gradually replaced poets and historians as society's spiritual guides. They revolutionized language, intellectual horizons, and the view that the entire Latin world had of itself.

## *The Prince's Counselor*

Lucius Anneus Seneca, born in Corduba (Córdoba), Spain, about 4 B.C., moved to Rome while he was still young to complete his studies, and there he devoted himself to a career of public debate. Under the reign of Claudius, he was expelled for having had a relationship with Julia Livilla, the sister of the deceased emperor Caligula, but he returned to Rome after the emperor's death and Nero's ascent to the throne. For a certain period, Seneca was an influential counselor to the emperor but fell into disgrace (accused of involvement in a plot against Nero) and committed suicide in A.D. 65. His philosophical work, of immense moral depth, is the highest expression of the stoic code that characterized the Roman ruling class of the time and provided it with a severe, demanding ethical conscience. While according to historians such as Cassius Dio, the conduct of the philosopher was not always on the same high level as his stated principles, his writings are among the most inspired and ethically committed in all classical literature.

## *I Believe Because It Is Absurd*

*Credo quia absurdum*, "I believe because it is absurd," is one of the most well-known maxims of Tertullian, a lawyer, rhetorician, and former military man born in Carthage about A.D. 150. As an adult, he converted to Christianity and became a passionate scholar, defender, and propagandist for the faith. He was famous for his paradoxical phrases and for the enthusiasm with which he fought for the cause and which pushed him to the brink of heresy. In him the Roman world had the prototype of a figure that would become common in later centuries: the intransigent and impassioned Christian thinker, capable of acting as a moral point of reference for a world decreasingly convinced of its values.

## *The Last Philosopher of Antiquity*

Born in Egypt in A.D. 205, a student of philosophy in Alexandria and a reverent

**Presumed Portrait of Plotinus**
We do not know if the portraits of Plotinus are authentic. In fact, the philosopher once refused to pose, stating, "Isn't it bad enough to drag around this image in which nature has imprisoned us? Must I agree to leave behind me an image of that image, as if it were a work worth seeing?"

**The Death of Seneca**
*The Death of Seneca* by the French painter Jacques-Louis David (1748–1825) depicts the dramatic moment of the suicide of the philosopher, who was suspected of having taken part in a plot against Nero. Seneca cut his veins and, while he awaited death, wanted also to drink hemlock. His wife, Pompeia Paulina, attempted to follow his example but was saved.

disciple of the philosopher Ammonius, Plotinus was the most influential philosopher of the late Roman world. His vast production (reorganized by his disciple Porphyry into six groups of nine treatises) revived the lessons of Plato, adapting them, however, to the very different cultural and moral climate of his time when Christianity and mystery-religions such as that of Mithras had great influence on society. Finally, he attempted without success to establish in Campania a city of philosophers based on his ideas.

Plotinus had immense influence on both his contemporaries and later periods, in part because of the strong connections between his mystical and religious views of the world.

**Paladin of the New Faith**
Tertullian's most important work is the *Apologeticus*, probably the very first text in Latin Christian literature. It consists of a legally based and logical defense of Christians against accusations of treason and contempt for the state religion. *Right*, a mosaic from the basilica of Aquileia, which depicts the Good Shepherd.

**Versatile Genius**
The literary work of Seneca embraces many different genres and subjects, from philosophy to geography and from poetry to tragedy. Seneca's reputation was so great that this bronze *(below)*, discovered in the Villa dei Pisoni in Herculaneum and now known as Psuedo-Seneca, was long thought to represent him.

### ADVICE TO WOMEN

"It is time that you showed yourselves embellished with the makeup and the ornaments of the prophets and the apostles, resorting to the white of simplicity, the red of chastity, painting your eyes with modesty, your mouth with silence, wearing as earrings the word of God, attaching to your neck the yoke of Christ. Bend your head before your husbands and you will be sufficiently adorned; occupy your hands with spinning and keep your feet at home: you will have more pleasure than if you were covered with gold.

Dress in the silk of honesty, the fine linen of sanctity, the purple of modesty: and thus adorned, you will have God for a lover."

Tertullian, *The Ornaments of Women*, II, 13

**Pagan Frivolity**
Tertullian would not have been pleased by the appearance of the wife of Tertius Neo, portrayed in this Pompeian fresco with her elaborate hairstyle, refined earrings, and elegant purple garment.

# The Senate and the People

*S.P.Q.R.*: these letters (an acronym for *Senatus PopulusQue Romanus*, "The Senate and the People of Rome"), which appeared wherever Roman civilization arrived, summarized the dyarchy that supported the fortunes of both city and empire for centuries.

**Senatorial Imprimatur**
Sestertius of the emperor Trajan with the letters *s.p.q.r.*

The Senate was not only the most prestigious but also one of the most ancient Roman institutions. According to tradition, it had been created by Romulus himself. It was a council of elders *(senes)*, made up of the heads *(patres)* of the most ancient and noble families. With the passage of time, those who had held the highest offices, such as the consulate and the quaestura, were also elected *(conscripti)*. This was the derivation of the traditional phrase used to indicate senators, *patres conscripti*. In order to meet, the Senate had to be convened by a magistrate in office: a consul, praetor, or tribune of the plebs. Once convened, its power was immense. It advised consuls and dictated political policy, dealt with state finances, took care of public safety, oversaw the state bureaucracy, designated ambassadors, and issued senatorial decrees *(senatus consulta)* that were binding for magistrates. In cases of danger, it could even issue a *senatus consultum de re publica defendenda* (senatorial decree in defense of

**A Senator's Garment**
*Left*, a marble statue of a togate man. Senators wore a broad purple stripe along the hem of their togas as a sign of recognition.

**Life as a Slave**
During the Republic, slaves did not enjoy political rights, and they were legally considered the private property of their owners, who could do with them what they wished. *Above*, a relief depicting slaves at work in a marble quarry.

the state) that established martial law or its Roman equivalent. Its members enjoyed privileges that underlined their rank. They wore a garment edged in a broad purple stripe, the *toga praetexta*, and shoes of a particular style; and they had available the best seats in theaters and at public ceremonies. They made up the true ruling class of the Roman state, a fact of which they were proudly aware.

## *The People, from Political Object to Subject*

In Rome, the term "people" did not indicate the entire population but only those who enjoyed political rights. Among these, there were profound divisions based on wealth and social rank. Citizens voted not by name but by tax brackets, and the votes of the two wealthiest classes exceeded those of all other classes combined, who therefore had much less political weight. Many magistratures were thus initially reserved for patricians and forbidden to plebeians—that is, to those who did not belong to the ancient senatorial families. However, through long and often bitter struggles, at times with recourse to extreme means such as secession from the city, the lower classes succeeded in having their voices heard and in organizing themselves so they could be counted in the political arena. One fundamental tool for this ascent was the tribunate of the plebs. This was a magistracy whose supporters, protected by complete personal inviolability *(tribunicia potestas)*, could irrevocably veto any decision, law, or act that might harm the interest of the plebs. The other essential tool was the *concilia plebis*, assemblies of all the plebeians, whose deliberations *(plebiscita)* assumed the status of law, after, however, senatorial ratification. This created a sort of "state within the state," but for a long time the result was the maintenance of a dynamic equilibrium with the other powers of the Republic, giving rise to one of the most successful and long-lived political experiments in history.

**Solemn Procession**
This fragment from the so-called Acilia sarcophagus (third century A.D.) shows a senatorial procession led by the young emperor Gordian III.

### SENATORIAL MEETINGS AND DECISIONS

The magistrate who convened the Senate always had to indicate the date, hour, and place (usually the *Curia Hostilia* or some temple), as well as the agenda. Meetings could last at most from sunrise until dusk. Participation followed a rigid hierarchy: consuls spoke first, then other magistrates in office in order of rank, then patricians, and finally plebeians (and, among the various social groups, the order ranged from eldest to youngest). Furthest down in the senatorial hierarchy were the neophytes of lower class, who by law could not speak. They were the *pedarii*, those who could make known their decision only "with their feet," that is, by moving from one area to another when there was voting (which generally occurred *per discessionem*, by people gathering to the left or to the right of the president of the assembly).

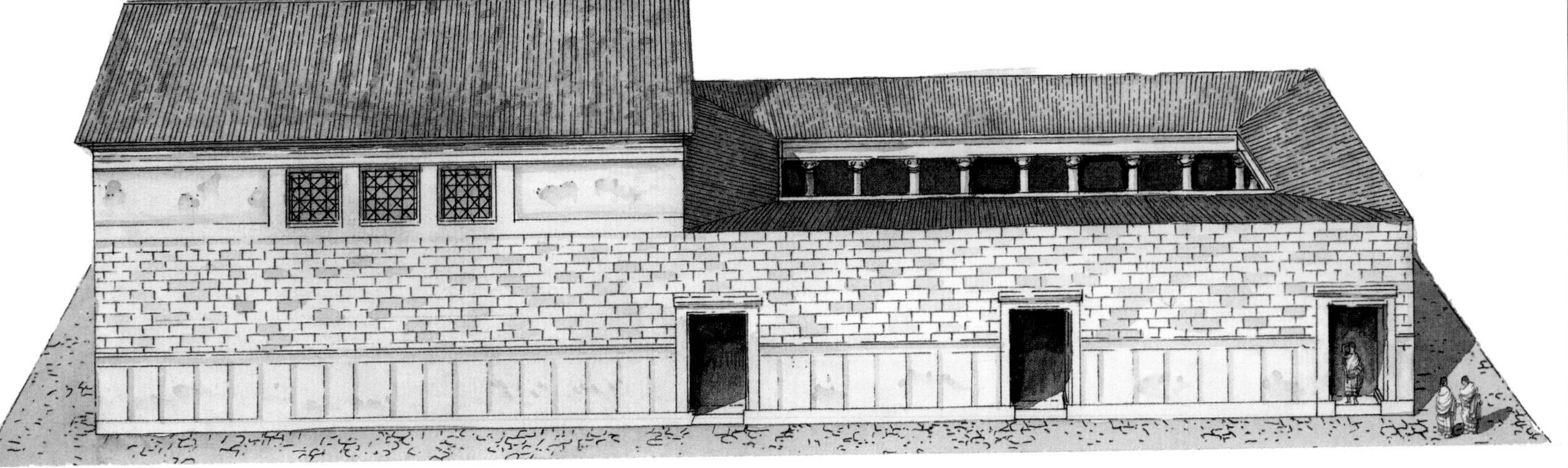

**The Senate Building**
Reconstruction of the *Curia Hostilia*, the building where the Senate met. In 29 B.C. the assembly moved into the *Curia Iulia*, the construction of which was begun by Julius Caesar and completed by Augustus.

# Civil Power and Military Power

Rome emerged as a democracy in which military service was one of the obligations linked to the enjoyment of citizenship. But continuous wars led first to the creation of a professional army and then to the use of armed forces as a personal power base for commanders.

**Portrait of Septimius Severus**
Septimius Severus, the founder of the Severan dynasty, was named emperor in A.D. 193 by the legions of Pannonia, which he commanded.

In early Rome, the army was based on citizen-soldier identity. Bearing arms was both a right and a duty for the citizen (almost always a farmer-landowner). In cases of necessity, a soldier was enlisted for the anticipated duration of a campaign, he paid for his own weapons and was incorporated into the ranks of a legion, and he returned to his lands after being discharged.

**Surprise Enlistment**
In archaic and republican times, all Roman citizens from the ages of 17 to 60 could be enlisted at any moment without warning. Recruitment was of two types: *dilectus*, regular conscription, and *tumultus*, extraordinary conscription in cases of unforeseen danger or sudden attack by the enemy. *Below*, a relief from the second to first century B.C. depicts a battle between Romans and Italians.

Officers were the magistrates who were elected for that year: consuls, praetors, quaestors. The succession of wars, which extended over increasingly widespread theaters of war, made it difficult to maintain this tradition. Continuous losses decimated the class of small landowners, and uninterrupted campaigns took farmers away from their fields for, not months, but years on end, and threatened their economic position. The annual rotation of commanders increased the risk that the army might be entrusted to an inept general.

## *The Birth of the Professional Army*

Between the third and first centuries B.C., a series of reforms—among which, those of Gaius Marius in the late second century were fundamental—opened the army to the nonproperty-owning proletarian classes. These people enlisted not out of civic duty but because they were attracted by the possibilities for adventure, booty, and lands to be assigned at the end of their service. This marked the beginning of a professional army. It entailed some positive innovations, such as the tactical reorganization of the legions into cohorts. This was made possible by the long training that conscripts finally could undergo, by the efficient standardization of weapons, insignia, and procedures typical of a professional army, and by the reintegration into the ranks of small landowners, thanks to settlement in colonies set aside for discharged veterans. The reform of the army also had negative effects, however, primarily the increasingly close tie between commanders and soldiers to the detriment of army loyalty to the state. This allowed leaders such as Marius, Sulla, Pompey, and Caesar, who had strong personal charisma, to utilize the troops for their own political purposes and in the end to turn the army into an arbiter of Roman politics.

## *The Power Base*

The birth of the *principate* was the consequence of the civil wars unleashed by political men who were at the same time able generals. There was a reason that the title wielded by the person who held power, *imperator*, was military in origin. However, the idea of the subordination of military order to civil structure was so strongly rooted that, from the time of Augustus until the late second century A.D., military commanders had to come from the ranks of the senatorial or equestrian orders, assimilating their values and ideals. Later, however, the permanent state of war at the frontiers and the consequent military effort supported by the empire led to a progressive militarization of the entire state structure, until, in the mid-third century A.D., there was a complete reversal of the situation. From that time on, not only did the *viri militares* live out their entire careers in the ranks of the legions, but also a military career became the key for entry to high office in the empire. This was the overthrow, dictated by the extreme danger of the situation, of the entire concept of the Roman state.

**Stele of a Praetorian**
To avoid sudden attacks, special laws prohibited the stationing of armed troops in Rome. The situation changed with the empire, when the sovereign's guard, the praetorians, were quartered in the city. *Left*, stele of the praetorian Pomponius Proculus.

### THE GENERALS' LANDS

The change in status of the military from the second century A.D. on, also entailed a shuffling of the importance of the various provinces of the empire. Thus the Balkan lands (Illyria and Pannonia in particular), where professional armies were traditional, acquired greater significance. Many of the emperors of the third and fourth centuries came from this area: Decius, Maximinus the Thracian, Trebonianus Gallus, Valerian, Diocletian, and Constantine. Indeed, some historians speak of a veritable Illyrian lobby (to use a modern term).

**The Soldier's Wife**
Stele of Sestus A. Macrinus, a tribune of Legion VI Victrix, and his wife.

**Trebonianus Gallus**
A general of Balkan origin, Trebonianus Gallus reigned for only two years, from 251 to 253. He was killed in the battle of Interamna (present-day Terni) by the usurper Aemilianus.

# The Magistracy

Reserved Seating

A relief from the republican era of the *sella curulis*, the distinctive seat reserved for magistrates and consuls.

The Roman magistracies, which came into being at the dawn of the Republic, continued to survive, at least in name, even during the imperial era, resulting in one of the most enduring periods of political continuity in history.

The succession of Roman magistracies (what the Latins called *cursus honorium*) was defined between the fifth and fourth centuries B.C. and lasted almost unaltered throughout the entire republican era. Two consuls were at the top of the hierarchy, holders of the *suprema potestas* (supreme civil power) and the *imperium maius* (military authority). As long as they were in agreement (in fact each could block the other's initiatives), the two consuls theoretically held unlimited power in times of peace and war. They convened and presided over the Senate, proposed laws, commanded the army, oversaw public order, and imposed taxes and tributes. Their extremely high rank was emphasized in various ways. In peacetime a consul wore a *toga praetexta* edged in purple, and during times of war a purple *paludamentum*. They were granted *ius imaginum* (the right to be represented in effigies and to be able to exhibit images of their ancestors). A consul sat on a *sella curulis* (a seat reserved for high magistrates) and was accompanied everywhere by twelve lictors, who were provided with fasces with axes inserted, a symbol of authority.

The Magistrate's Escort

All magistrates had the right to be escorted by lictors, whose number varied, depending on the importance of the position. *Below*, a relief depicting a lictor.

One step down was the praetor, a sort of "minor consul" (called, in fact, a *collega minor*), who availed himself, in narrower form, of all the prerogatives of the consuls. Initially established as a military magistrate, over time the praetor became the person in charge of the administration of justice between Romans and between Romans and foreigners in the provinces.

Consuls and praetors were the most important curule magistrates because they were endowed with *imperium*, or military power. The lesser magistrates followed in sequence: the tribunes of the plebs (ten each year), the aediles (entrusted with the archives, urban planning, food supplies, festivals, and public celebrations), and the quaestors, who were responsible for financial matters (taxes, tributes, booty of war, and war expenditures). At the lowest level, finally, stood "the twenty-six" *(vigintisexviri)*, who carried out official tasks as police, justices of peace, managers of the mint, and building engineers.

## *Extraordinary Offices*

Apart from ordinary political careers, there were two exceptional positions: dictatorship and censorship. The dictator, named at the suggestion of the consuls in situations of mortal danger for the Republic, assumed absolute power over all state apparatus for six months. The position of censor, instead, was held for five-year terms by two former consuls or former praetors. Censors were charged with taking a census

**Public Works**
Appius Claudius Ciecus, remembered here in a eulogistic stele, was the most illustrious representative of the *gens Claudia* in the republican era. Censor and consul, he was remembered over time above all for two public works projects that he undertook: the Appian Aqueduct, the first in Rome, and the Via Appia, which linked Rome and Capua.

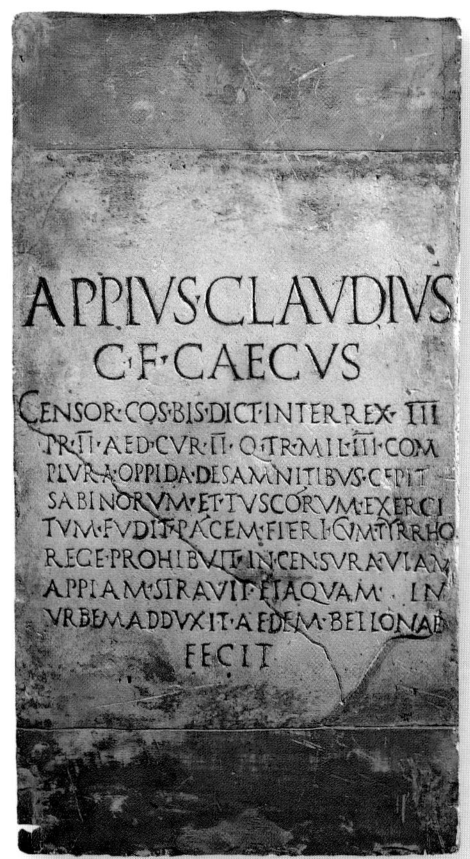


of citizens, deciding the taxes they had to pay, supervising their public and private behavior, and establishing the composition of the Senate—that is, determining who had the right to enter or remain there and who did not.

## *The Balancing of Powers*

All posts, except dictator and censor, were annual and carried out by a team; and each had a valid counterweight to their power in the other magistracies. All had to respond to the assemblies that elected them, the *comitia*. In Rome, governing was much more an exercise of parliamentary balancing than of force. Those who succeeded, step by step, in climbing the various stages of the *cursus honorum* to reach the consulate had to be endowed with great personal qualities and extensive wealth, which was consumed in large part by their ascent. This left the Senate (the only body in which members remained in office for life) the true arbiter of public life in Rome. Things changed only under the empire because the emperor relied not on the various traditional magistracies (which, however, continued to survive, although drained of significance) but on officials nominated directly by him.

### A JOURNEY IN STAGES

Custom, if not always law, rigidly established both the stages of the *cursus honorum* and the times of life when these could be attempted (the correct age for competing for the various magistratures). A Roman politician's highest aspiration was to attain each post in *suo anno*—that is, the first year it was considered valid. This was proof of exceptional political sway and personal charisma: what the Romans called *auctoritas*, a politician's most precious asset.

**Bust of Cato of Utica**
A follower of the stoic ethic, Cato of Utica (95–46 B.C.) covered the entire *cursus honorum* of Roman politics. It is said that he never missed a single session of the Senate, out of a sense of duty but also out of fear that unscrupulous colleagues might pass an unjust law.

**Daily Bread**
The aediles' tasks included the *cura annonae* ("management of foodstuffs"), which involved control of quality, prices, and correct weight of goods. *Left*, a relief with the presentation of bread to the magistrates.

# The Price of Fame

*Evergeteis*, "benefactors," were wealthy citizens who took on tasks that we today consider the role of the community: erecting temples, financing public festivals, offering opulent sacrifices in the name of the city. Without these people, the entire administrative system in the ancient world would not have been able to function.

In Rome public positions were not remunerated and, on the contrary, cost a great deal. A person who wanted to assume office had to ingratiate himself with the electors through acts of munificence, offering games, banquets, festivals, and gifts. Once in office, he was expected to pay out of pocket for the expenses required for holding the position: paving streets, erecting temples or buildings for public use, compensating officials employed to perform duties for him, even enlisting and arming legions. This concept, which went by the name *evergetism* (from the Greek *evergetès*, "benefactor"), was ingrained in the ancient concept according to which the ideal of life was *otium*, "leisure," a concern for non-remunerative matters. This was seen in opposition to *negotium* (from *nec otium*, "not leisure"), in other words, work or business, which was considered debasing. Thus politics was the "work" of the upper classes, whose members were available to make any sacrifice that might arise. And the sacrifices were considerable. Many political men literally were ruined in their quest for approval and fame (often paying back loans at interest, once an office was assumed; Caesar, for example, repaid tremendous debts contracted during his political career with revenues from his activity as administrator in the province of Hispania). In small cities, where the burden of being a benefactor was shared by a limited number of families, it was sometimes difficult to find candidates for public office. But the

**Domitian's Expenses**
Domitian gave extremely generously to public works projects, as well as to the construction and restoration of buildings and streets. He made frequent donations in money and in kind to citizens and was responsible for splendid spectacles in the Coliseum and in the stadium that he built. *Below*, quadriga (chariot) racing depicted in a splendid mosaic discovered in 1806 at the Roman circus in Lyons.

**Bread and Circuses**
This formula was coined by the poet Juvenal (first to second century A.D.): "Now that votes are no longer sold, the people have lost all interest in politics: they, who once bestowed commands, consulships, legions, and all else, now concern themselves with none of this, and long eagerly for two things only—bread and circuses." *Left*, mosaic from the amphitheater of Sisa (Tunisia), depicting "games."

**Catalogue of Public Works**
This fragment shows a series of public buildings in Rome, all dating from the emperors of the Flavian dynasty: *from the left*, a triumphal arch, the Coliseum, two more arches, the first of which as seen from the side, and a temple. The fragment was most likely part of the sepulchral monument of the builder who had carried out the public works depicted.

tradition was so deeply rooted that no one ever thought of modifying it, at least not until the advent of Christianity, which shifted the focus from acts of civil munificence to those of personal charity.

## *The Philosophy and Practice of Beneficence*

The concept of public beneficence developed in Greece in the fourth century B.C., and it was the Greeks who codified the rules. Donations had to be exclusively of a public nature and could not be made in order to obtain tangible benefits, but only for political recognition and admiration. In the Roman world, beneficence was the other face of oligarchy. Because public positions were the prerogative of the wealthy, it was considered natural for them also to shoulder the consequent burdens. The distinction between public and private was rather blurred, not to say absent. Moreover, acts of generosity were an excellent means of gaining consensus and, after all, of depoliticizing the lower classes. In the imperial era, this concept was codified in the formula *panem et circenses* (bread and circuses). The beneficence of the emperors, who regularly offered the plebs wheat and festivals, was a common political practice, useful for guaranteeing the favor of the people.

### THE SEARCH FOR CONSENSUS

Marcus Cornelius Fronto, a Latin writer originally from Numidia who was a teacher of Marcus Aurelius, provides an illuminating description of the practice of beneficence as a tool for organizing consensus. Speaking of Trajan, he writes: "He never neglected the actors and other protagonists of the circus and the amphitheater. He fully understood that the Romans are conquered by two things above all: distributions of wheat and public spectacles. The rule of an emperor is judged by the measure of amusements no less than by serious things. Neglecting important matters can lead to greater damage, but neglecting amusements provokes more discontent. And if donations gratify only the plebeians enrolled on the wheat-lists, and even these only once when their name is called, everyone is gratified by spectacles." In other words, imperial munificence was a way to gain the consensus of the masses and avoid governing solely on the basis of the "strong powers": army, bureaucracy, and senate.

**Baths of Centumcellae**
The emperor Trajan had the port and baths of *Centumcellae*, present-day Civitavecchia (Rome), built on lands that he owned.

# The Administration of the Provinces and the State

Roman bureaucracy was very different from that of our own time, and in many ways it was improvised under pressure as needs arose.

It was only in the imperial era that a professional body of officials was established to manage the various administrative branches of government. And yet the system worked, and for centuries it supported one of the largest political-military structures of the ancient world.

## *The Administration of the Provinces*

The word *province* originally indicated "sphere of activity of a magistrate," that is, the task that he was assigned or that he assumed upon entering office. The word maintained this significance as long as conquests were confined to the Italian peninsula, which, despite infinite ethnic and geographic divisions, was thought of by Rome as a unified whole. When subsequent wars led to Roman rule over territories outside the Italian peninsula, however, a need was felt to name certain officials (initially from the praetorial ranks) specifically to govern the new territories (Sicily, Sardinia, Corsica, then gradually Spain, Macedonia, Greece, Africa, Gaul, and Asia Minor).

Thus *province* began to signify "administrative district distinct from Italy." The administrative system of these provinces took shape slowly through many changes and modifications. It became customary to assign the government of each territory to a former curial magistrate (consul or praetor) upon the expiration of his elective position. The mandate (*imperium pro consule* or *pro praetore*)

THE ROMANS IN SPAIN
Roman columns of the ancient temple of *Augustobriga* in Spain. The Roman occupation of the Iberian Peninsula, which began during the second Punic War, ended with the last and definitive conquest under Augustus.

**The African Province**
The African province not only furnished Rome with wheat and olive oil but also provided many illustrious men: jurists, senators, knights, and writers. *Below*, view of the ruins of Djemila in Algeria, the ancient colony of *Cuicul*, founded under the emperor Nerva.

**Government Official**
*Above*, marble sarcophagus of the prefect Tiberius Flavius Miccalus.

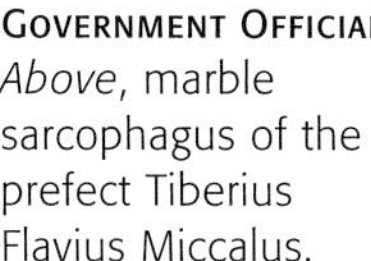

generally lasted one year but also could be extended numerous times. In the province, the governor had almost absolute powers; he minted money, established taxes, commanded troops stationed in the region, and administered justice. Such broad powers inevitably led to a high level of corruption and extortion. (Proof of this can be seen in the numerous and increasingly severe laws *de repetundis*—namely, laws against corruption, issued over the centuries.) Moreover, the system was complex and inconsistent, but it remained, until the end, the basis for Roman administration of the territories outside Italy.

## *Imperial Bureaucracy*

Among the principal reasons for the passage from Republic to empire were functional problems and a muddled administrative system. Therefore, the emperors, continually seeking to improve it, created a structure of professional officials who were entrusted with positions previously assigned through election or designation by assembly. The old magistratures, like the provincial system of government, remained formally unaltered, but the men who held the posts were no longer truly elected but appointed by the sovereign. Often these were not even people of senatorial rank or Roman citizens of ancient origins, but imperial freedmen. The new system clearly increased the efficiency and uniformity of government, at the price, however, of an increasingly oppressive centralized authority, which inevitably led to a substantial paralysis of the imperial administration. Moreover, as in any rigidly bureaucratic system, there was an increase in corruption, nepotism, and patronage. Finally the system's costs exceeded its advantages, and it ceased being the glue that held the empire together—but not before it had established a model that would long inspire later generations.

**City and Country**
The history of the Gallic provinces is characterized by geographic differences between the south, where many cities were built, such as *Massilia* (Marseilles), *Arelate* (Arles), and *Nemausus* (Nîmes), and the region to the north and west of the Massif Central, where the countryside played a decisive role. *Below*, the Pont du Gard, the famous aqueduct built at the time of Augustus, which brought water to Nîmes.

# Insignia of Power

Few peoples were as sensitive to insignia of rank and power as the Romans, who also meticulously codified their use. These were the highest expression of authority that the state delegated to its magistrates and, as such, were venerated.

From the beginning of their history, the Romans developed a strongly articulated idea of power. Even during the royal period, nothing could have been further from their way of thinking than the Eastern concept according to which each man was a subordinate of the sovereign to whom all power and honors were due. On the contrary, they thought of power as a well-balanced totality of separate authorities, each with its specific rank. When the monarchy gave way to the Republic, this vision could be expressed fully, permeating every aspect of public Roman life.

**Otacilius Oppianus, Magistrate**
This relief on the cippus (funerary stone) of Otacilius Oppianus, found in Graveson, France, depicts a chair reserved for magistrates.

**The Eagle of Rome**
Symbol of Rome's military power, the eagle sculpted in stone *(as shown at left)* appeared in all cities of the empire and, cast in bronze, was part of the insignia of the legions.

## *Fasces, Curule Chairs, Togas*

From the beginning, a complex symbology was developed to express an idea of such strong power. In some ways similar to the symbology of today's military, these accouterments and items of clothing immediately must have evoked for the viewer all the dignity of the *imperium*. The lictor's fasces, made up of tightly bound rods into which an axe was inserted, indicated the power of the principal magistrates. There were folding chairs of a particular shape for the magistrates themselves, and the *lituus*, a crook-shaped staff, for professional augurs. Clothing also expressed the rank of the wearer. The toga, a draped garment, complicated to wear but extremely effective, was the distinctive apparel of all Roman citizens. Senators, however, had the right to edge their togas with a broad purple hem (*latus clavus*); knights were granted the right to a similar but narrower hem (*angustus clavus*); a victorious general had

### THE SOOTHSAYER'S MANTLE

The garment we now call a mantle was known by different names in Rome, depending on the style. *Mantle* was the specific garment worn by the haruspices, the soothsayers who read omens from the examination of animal entrails. This hooded fur cape, very similar to those found earlier on small bronze nuraghic figures, may date back to prehistoric garments.

**Regulation Uniform**
Small bronze depicting a haruspex dressed in the traditional hooded cloak (fourth century B.C.).

**Etruscan Lituus**
The lituus, a liturgical instrument and insignia of the augurs, was Etruscan in origin, as seen in this discovery *(above)* from a tomb at Cerveteri (sixth century B.C.).

the exceptional privilege of wearing a completely purple toga, the *toga picta* (but only on the day of his triumph). Military commanders could flaunt the scarlet tunic (*paludamentum*) and, on their armor, sashes of various styles depending on rank, and so on. Even priests wore unmistakable and distinctive signs, such as the *apex*, a leather helmet surmounted by a lance-point shape, worn in public.

## *Continuity in Time*

Many insignia of power were Etruscan in origin, but the meticulousness with which these were codified and displayed—making them veritable archetypes of the power they represented—was utterly Roman. Their importance endured every bit as long as the entire history of Rome. In fact, the imperial period did not do away with Republican symbols and, particularly in its late stages, added other insignia. These too were destined to survive long into the future as indications of imperial rank, such as the radiated crown, the scepter, and the globe (symbol of power over the terraqueous orb).

**Togate Men**
A relief of men wearing togas, originally from Brescia. The colored border on a toga specified the role and function of the wearer.

# *Civis Romanus sum*

"I am a Roman citizen": throughout the entire Mediterranean region, for centuries, this proud declaration confirmed one's status as the dominant race, masters of the world. But the price for this privilege was high.

Rome emerged as a city-state within an area populated by other, often more powerful city-states, and it owed its survival and expansion to the continuous use of arms. For this reason, being a Roman citizen meant above all being a potential soldier. Any man between the ages of seventeen and sixty could be drafted at any moment; even when he was not called upon to defend the city with arms, he had to subordinate his existence to that of the *civitas*, the community of citizens of which he was a part. In exchange, he enjoyed political rights—namely, the possibility of influencing the direction of the state, either by standing as a candidate for public office or simply through his vote. Not all citizens, however, were equal. Those who had more, had to give more, but they also counted more. Each citizen, depending on his income, was registered in one of five tax categories. Each category, in turn, was divided into "centuries," groups of one hundred people. Votes were calculated by century, and if the number declined, the category changed. The first category counted more than the second, which counted more than the third, and so on.

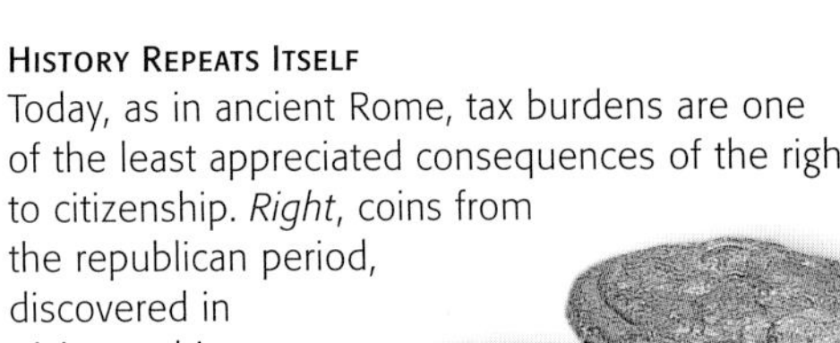

**History Repeats Itself**
Today, as in ancient Rome, tax burdens are one of the least appreciated consequences of the right to citizenship. *Right*, coins from the republican period, discovered in Civitavecchia.

**The Counting of Citizens**
Detail from a relief from the Campus Martius in Rome, which depicts census taking (second century B.C.).

### THE CENSUS

The census, or recording on civic lists, was obligatory: all Roman citizens had to register. In ancient times, the operation took place in the Campus Martius, outside the pomoerium boundary, in order to extend participation to citizens in the army, who were prohibited from entering the city. The head of each family had to make a declaration to the censor, giving specific information and providing an estimate of his property, as well as taking an oath that guaranteed the truth and good faith of his statement (what we would call a formal declaration or affirmation). Such statements specified "name of father, age and name of wife and children." At the end of the census, the censors compiled the civic lists in which the citizen found his designated place. A religious festival—the *lustrum*—marked the end of the census, a vital operation that recorded changes in Roman society every five years.

In practice, actual power was in the hands of the top categories, made up of the wealthiest citizens. In compensation, they paid the most to arm themselves (equipment was the responsibility of the citizen, not the state), theoretically served the longest in the army, and paid out of pocket for the high expenses connected with carrying out public duties.

## *The Problem of Citizenship*

As long as Rome was a small city-state, the system functioned quite well. Things became more complicated when, with the conquest of Italy, Rome's allies were burdened with duties even greater than those imposed on Roman citizens (the requirement to furnish men for the legions and auxiliary troops, to pay tributes and taxes, to adopt the foreign policy of the ruling city), without any benefit in exchange. The demands of the citizenry gave rise to a strong movement, which in the first century B.C. provoked an extremely harsh conflict (the Social War) between Romans and the Italic peoples. It was only with Caesar and Augustus that the problem began to be

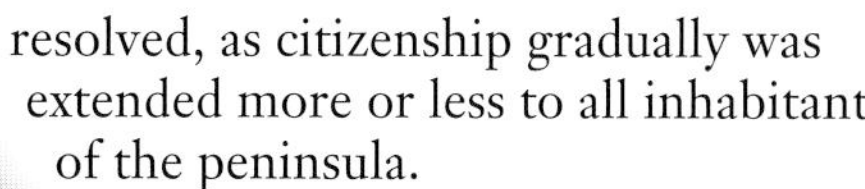

resolved, as citizenship gradually was extended more or less to all inhabitants of the peninsula.

## *The Edict of Caracalla*

The inhabitants of the empire had to wait another two centuries, and it was not until A.D. 212 (or 213) that Caracalla issued the *Constitutio Antoniniana*, which granted Roman citizenship, and thus political rights, to all free males who lived within the imperial borders. The historian Cassius Dio implied that this probably was done for financial reasons—namely, the goal of imposing new taxes on the new citizens. In any case, the *Constitutio Antoniniana* acknowledged that Rome now had completed its historic mission: civilizing all lands under its rule, which from that moment were to participate fully in the life of the empire, contributing to the determination of its policies and its choices of government.

**Etruscan God of War**
At the end of the Social War, the Etruscans were the first to obtain Roman citizenship. *Left*, a small Etruscan bronze, probably of Laran, the Etruscan god of war (fifth century B.C.).

**Called to Arms**
*Left*, relief on an alabaster urn, depicting a soldier taking leave of his wife.

**Imperial Edict**
*Right*, inscription bearing an edict of Caracalla, following the *Constitutio Antoniniana*, in which the emperor requested that taxpayers pay their taxes with greater zeal (A.D. 215).

# Administration of Justice

Legal culture is without doubt one of Rome's brightest legacies, and it is still the basis of law in all Western countries.

The most ancient source of Roman jurisprudence is a famous body of laws promulgated about the fifth century B.C., the so-called laws of the Twelve Tables. These nullified the priests' privilege of administering the law, which until then had been passed down orally. Century after century, Roman jurisprudence changed profoundly, although some elements remained constant over time.

**Legacy to Be Handed Down**
Page of an illuminated codex of Justinian's *Corpus Iuris Civilis*.

Each year the body of laws was revised through the promulgation of a sort of framework of laws or unique text, known as the praetor's edict. It was not until the imperial era that Hadrian took the initiative to give definitive form to the edict, entrusting its drafting to the jurist Salvius Iulianus; the new legislation then became known as the "perpetual edict." The role of judge was granted to elected magistrates; toward the end of the imperial era, however, the figure of the professional judge emerged. Official proceedings were unknown: for a trial to begin, it was necessary for a complaint to be lodged by one party. The accusation initially was asserted directly by the plaintiff; only the defense had the right to a lawyer. Trials of great importance were reserved for the Senate, just as under the empire the crimes of treason, extortion, and serious violence were reserved for the emperor. In the provinces, legal jurisdiction was given to the governors; in Rome, generally, it was granted to the praetors (this is the derivation of the

**Justinian's Legislation**
The emperor Justinian, depicted here in a mosaic from the basilica of San Vitale in Ravenna, organized the *Corpus Iuris Civilis*, a colossal legislative compendium that summarized the entire judicial experience of the Roman world.

TABLES I–V
According to the most reliable reconstructions, Tables I–III concerned trial law; Table IV, family law; and Table V, hereditary guardianship, trusteeship, and succession. *Above*, relief showing the opening of a will.

present-day Italian term *pretore*, a lower-court judge).

## *The Course of a Trial*

The presiding magistrate initially was limited to authorizing and organizing a trial, giving the parties a preliminary hearing, and determining the appropriate legal formula (called the *in iure* phase). If the accused admitted guilt, the magistrate issued the sentence; otherwise the trial phase (*in iudicio*) began, taking place in the forum or in the surrounding basilicas. After addresses by the parties, witnesses for the prosecution and the defense were heard, and then the jurors gave their verdict (*A* for *absolvo*, *C* for *condemno*). At this point the presiding magistrate issued the sentence and established the punishment. Its enforcement was entrusted to his lictors, who functioned as judicial police.

TABLES VI–XII
Tables VI–VII concerned legal transactions, property, and real estate restrictions; Tables VIII–IX, crimes and criminal trials; Table X, sacred law. Tables XI and XII contained appendices and additions to the previous tables. *Left*, a relief depicting the sale of fabrics.

The condemned could file an appeal against the rulings made by the magistrate during the preliminary or penalty stages but not against the trial, the verdict of which could not be appealed. In such cases, the appeal was entrusted to a magistrate of a higher rank or, during the imperial era, directly to the *princeps* (who sometimes arrogated the appeal to himself without waiting for the postponement of the proceedings). If the accused was absolved, he could sue the accuser for *calumnia*.

## *The* Corpus Iuris Civilis

The reorganization of all Roman legislation into a systematic entity was achieved by Justinian (A.D. 482–565), the emperor of the East who conceived the monumental *Corpus Iuris Civilis*, which still is considered one of the foundations for law and jurisprudence. The *Corpus Iuris* consists of four parts: the "Institutions," a fundamental and elementary legal treatise; the "Digest" or "Pandects," extracts of works of Roman jurists; the "Code," a collection of imperial constitutions; and the "Novels" (or "new laws"), laws issued by Justinian himself.

# Crime and Punishment

"A punishment for every crime" was a valid saying for the ancient Romans. However, many of these punishments were horrible to our modern way of thinking, and even the scale of misdemeanors and punishments was very different from what we use today.

**Capital Punishment**
A Roman mosaic from the second century A.D., illustrating the torture of a man condemned to be torn apart by wild beasts.

**Awaiting Judgment**
This sculpture depicts a Gallic prisoner in chains who awaits his fate.

However strange it may seem, the least widespread penalty in Rome was one that we consider normal—namely, detention. The very idea of locking someone in a cell for a period of time was foreign to the Latin mentality. In practice, a Roman citizen, especially one of high rank, was subject to two punishments considered "honorable," or not socially defamatory: exile, either temporary or permanent, and suicide. The latter was carried out by cutting one's veins, taking poison, starving oneself, falling on one's sword, or strangling oneself with a special noose, the *laqueum*, which many aristocrats always carried on their persons.

**The Suicide of Cato**
Cato the Censor, one of the most famous men of politics in the republican era, sided with Pompey in his dispute with Julius Caesar. When Caesar prevailed, Cato did not await the judgment of the victor, and on an April night in A.D. 46 he drew his sword from its sheath and plunged it into his chest. The episode is evoked in this seventeenth-century painting *(below)* by Gian Battista Langetti.

## *The Death Penalty*

The death penalty, however, was very common and was inflicted for a vast range of crimes and in an impressive variety of fashions. Decapitation was initially inflicted with the lictor's axe and then, in the imperial era, with the sword. Flogging, an extremely ancient punishment, was used above all in military circumstances. Sorcerers, those who burned the harvests, and passive homosexuals were condemned to the stake. Crucifixion was the specific punishment reserved for slaves and was even called *servile supplicium*. In the imperial era, punishments increased in frequency and cruelty. A sentence *ad bestias* was a condemnation to be torn apart in the circus; combustion entailed dressing the condemned in tunics soaked in sulfur or pitch and setting them afire. Then there was castration (another punishment for homosexuals) and the pouring of molten lead down the throat (a torture inflicted by the emperor Constantine on some female slaves who had persuaded or helped a young woman of good family to run away with a man).

## *Punishments Reserved for Women*

According to *mos maiorum*, traditional Roman custom, it was considered *nefas*, impious, to condemn women to public punishment or even to forms of physical violence. The death penalty that the law prescribed for adulterers and also for women caught drinking wine generally called for starvation. There are only rare references to women who were strangled or beaten to death. The penalty always took place in a family setting, because custom dictated that a woman's death be hidden from view. The case of *incestae* or defiled vestals, those who had broken the vow of chastity to which the members of the sacred body were bound, was typical. The punishment was carried out in the "field of iniquity" near the Porta Collina of the Servian walls; the victims were buried alive in an underground chamber containing a small bed, a ration of bread, water, oil, and a torch.

The most sensational exception in this respect was the public exhibition of suffering inflicted on Christian women. According to Roman beliefs, these martyrs formed a special group—women who had rejected the very structure of traditional society and thus could not invoke the rights granted to its adherents. Public exposition and degradation were part of the punishment.

PORTRAIT OF THE CHIEF VESTAL *(above)*
The vestals were distinguished by a vow of chastity; anyone who broke this vow was condemned to death.

### THEFT PUNISHED BY DEATH

According to the laws of Table XII, theft could be punished by death if it occurred at night, a circumstance considered particularly antisocial and worthy of contempt. If, instead, it occurred by day, the victim could kill the thief only if there were aggravating circumstances, such as the use of weapons by the wrongdoer. Even in this case, however, the injured party first had to call for help, alerting the neighbors (who could act as witnesses) before taking action.

AN EXCEPTION TO THE LAW
Roman women were prohibited from drinking wine. Devotees of Dionysus were granted this privilege in order to reach the states of inebriation and exaltation required for the rituals in which they participated.

# LAWYERS AND JURISTS

In ancient Rome, the legal profession was considered a noble mission, practiced free of charge in the service of the community. Later, it became a handsomely rewarded activity and in the end also accommodated somewhat untrustworthy "amateurs."

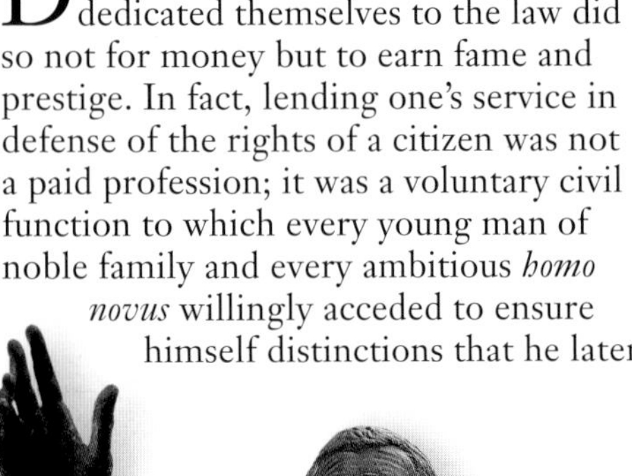

During the republican era, those who dedicated themselves to the law did so not for money but to earn fame and prestige. In fact, lending one's service in defense of the rights of a citizen was not a paid profession; it was a voluntary civil function to which every young man of noble family and every ambitious *homo novus* willingly acceded to ensure himself distinctions that he later

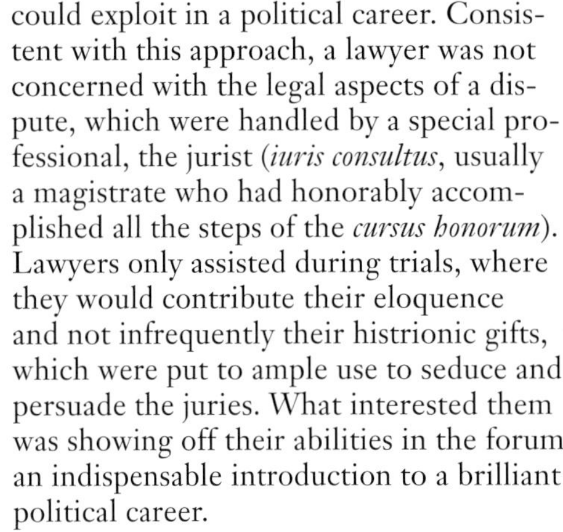

could exploit in a political career. Consistent with this approach, a lawyer was not concerned with the legal aspects of a dispute, which were handled by a special professional, the jurist (*iuris consultus*, usually a magistrate who had honorably accomplished all the steps of the *cursus honorum*). Lawyers only assisted during trials, where they would contribute their eloquence and not infrequently their histrionic gifts, which were put to ample use to seduce and persuade the juries. What interested them was showing off their abilities in the forum: an indispensable introduction to a brilliant political career.

## *A Noble Profession*

During the early imperial era, political struggle ceased and the law became a true profession. Although some continued to practice spontaneously and without remuneration, it became customary to pay lawyers regular fees; from the time of Claudius, their work became legitimized and regulated by a law that, among other things, established a legal limit of ten thousand sesterces for legal bills.

**LAWYERS' FEES**
In republican Rome, it was forbidden to request payment for services as a lawyer. But, as always, once a law was passed, a loophole was found. In this case, it was customary for the client to "donate" a considerable sum (or a work of art, a piece of land, a villa, etc.) to his lawyer. Because no law prohibited generous actions, everything was in order. *Right*, one of the first gold coins minted in Rome (circa 296 B.C.).

**THE HARANGUER**
This famous statue, dating from the first century B.C., depicts a lawyer making a display of his eloquence.

**THE BASILICA IULIA**
The ruins of this building, based on a rectangular plan with three naves, are still visible in the Roman forum.

**ARGUMENT IN COURT**
*Above,* a painting from Ostia Antica depicting an argument in court.

## *The Triumph of Swindlers*

In the late imperial era, the ancient bond between politics and law had broken down completely. The law, like so many other fields, had become populated by people of dubious ethics if not by outright swindlers; they turned this once noble activity into an almost fraudulent means of support. Any individual with a gift for glibness and a small fund of legal ideas could turn himself into an orator and prey upon humble people with little means. Such tricksters seduced their clients with the illusion of amazing profits to be gained through recourse to the courts and involved them in endless trials that were often disastrous, except for the pockets of the defense. These pettifoggers were the plague of the forum, and they gave the legal profession a bad reputation that would endure over the centuries.

### THE THEATER OF THE LAW

The Romans were not only incurably litigious, they were also great "consumers" of legal spectacles. Watching a trial was a bit like going to the theater. Pliny the Younger gives us an animated description of what went on in the central hall of the Basilica Iulia, built by Caesar and completed by Augustus (the basilica was the building that the Romans used for trials). The praetor who presided over the hearing sat on a platform, to the sides of which were the 180 *centumviri*, or judges, who made up the court. Opposite, on wood benches, were the litigants, accompanied by friends, relatives, clients, and defense lawyers. At the back of the hall and in the side naves, the spectators crowded together, watchful for any dramatic surprise or "discovery" by the lawyers. In the case of small or average trials, four cases were debated at the same time in four separate halls, created by dividing the basilica with curtained partitions. The din and confusion were considerable, but no one, it would seem, complained.

# The Creation of Consensus

The power of the emperor was based above all on the army, but in a society as complex as Rome's, this power could not rest exclusively on the use of force. It was indispensable to guarantee, as much as possible, the consensus of the emperor's subjects.

In this regard, one of the most skillful emperors was the first: Augustus had to legitimize his autocratic power in the eyes of the citizens, who still cherished memories of the recent Republic. Under the capable orchestration of Maecenas (a notable citizen of Arezzo and the sovereign's "minister of culture," as we might call him today), an efficient "propaganda machine" was created with the task of glorifying the emperor, his lineage, and his accomplishments. The numerous poets "discovered" by Maecenas—such as Virgil, Horace, and Ovid—were central to this operation, and they were handsomely funded to create poetic works consonant with the goals of the dynasty. It is to the great credit of this noble Etruscan (the term *Maecenas* has come to mean patron of the arts) that he was insightful about

**Commemorative and Triumphal Arches**
The function of arches was to glorify a person or an event, sometimes independent of a military triumph. All arches were surmounted by statues, generally in gilded bronze, which depicted knights, emperors, and their family members.

**The Baths of Caracalla**
The emperor Caracalla wanted to give Rome a truly grand bath complex. He had this built on the slopes of the Aventine, covering over 11,000 square meters, including the enclosure. The central space alone was as large as the present-day basilica of St. Peter's. The baths were surrounded by gardens *(below)* in which the Romans strolled and sunned themselves.

**Publius Vergilius Maro**
The most important of the so-called Augustan poets was Publius Vergilius Maro (Virgil), the author of the *Aeneid*, shown above in a third-century-A.D. mosaic.

choosing poets suited to the goal. Indeed, they had the tact, restraint, and balance to carry out the task, and they avoided the pitfalls of flattery and exaggeration that would become habitual in the future. Maecenas was responsible not only for the exaltation of Augustus and his lineage but also for the writing of some of the most beautiful pages of Latin literature.

THE GIFT OF MAECENAS
Outside Tivoli (Rome) the ruins of the villa that Maecenas gave to Horace are still visible. The poet lived here for much of his life.

### THE LURE OF POWER

Maecenas was both a skillful connoisseur of art and a wise judge of men, adept at using his seductive personality to best advantage. His relationship with Horace was typical. The poet, who had fought with Brutus at Philippi, was presented to Maecenas by Virgil. Horace wrote that the first time he was brought before Augustus's powerful adviser, he could only manage to stammer a few words, so intimidated was he. Some months later, Maecenas, who had been equally lacking in words, asked him to call and had him spend time with his closest friends. Horace always remembered with rapture the early days of their friendship and the walks they took together on the outskirts of Rome. Exchanging only a few mumbled phrases, they immediately understood each other in a friendship made up more of silences than of words.

## *The Discrediting of Adversaries*

There was negative as well as positive propaganda, and it was widespread. It assumed above all the form of the "critical revision" of the past (in particular the recent past), employed systematically to discredit previous emperors or dynasties. Thus by contrast, current sovereigns were legitimized and elevated. The major practitioners of this corrosive "art" were historians such as Tacitus, Suetonius, and Cassius Dio. It is in large part thanks to them that we know about the private vices and atrocities perpetrated by the Julio-Claudian dynasty, although these probably have been magnified or exaggerated.

## *Means of Mass Communication*

Architecture was another widely used tool of propaganda: temples, aqueducts, basilicas, baths, ports, roads, and forums constituted proof of magistrates' and emperors' largess, benevolence, and concern for the public good. The list is vast and includes the *Ara Pacis Augustae*, Hadrian's tomb (now Castel Sant'Angelo), the Pantheon, the imperial forums, the baths of Caracalla, and the basilica of Maxentius, to mention only projects in the capital (gigantic works were erected throughout the empire). All these monuments were meant to celebrate the builders but also to recall the glory of Rome for eternity.

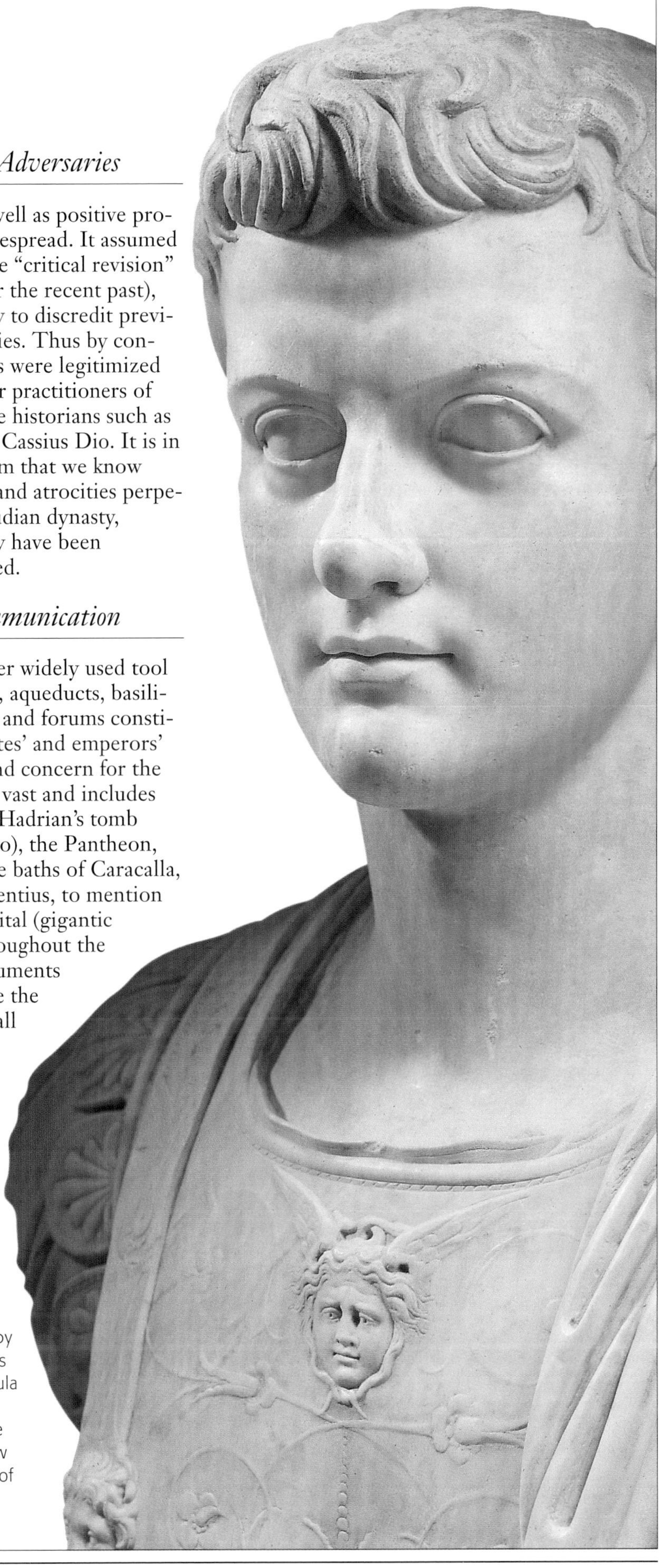

BUST OF CALIGULA
Tiberius's successor was one of the victims of the "critical revision" practiced by Roman historians. Suetonius divided his writing on Caligula into two parts separated by this phrase: "Thus far I have spoken of the emperor, now I shall describe the actions of the monster."

# Rome's Fighting Men

**At a Gallop**
A small bronze statue, originally from France, which depicts a Roman knight.

During the monarchy and the Republic, Rome did not have an army; it was an army. Every citizen was considered a soldier and had the right/duty to bear arms in defense of his country.

Military service was obligatory. Only the poorest citizens were exempt, based on the principle, firmly rooted in ancient society, that those who had property had the most interest in defending it. Moreover, it was considered the soldier's responsibility to procure his own equipment, so that only those who were able to afford it could go to war. At the age of seventeen, a young Roman man put on the *toga virilis*, a sign of coming of age. He was enrolled in the lists of *iuniores*, and from then on could be called to arms at any moment. It was impossible to avoid this duty, and reluctant recruits risked having their property confiscated and being reduced to slavery. A recruit procured his own equipment and was sworn in and subjected to the draconian discipline of the legions, aimed at turning him into a combatant capable of facing any wartime situation. For this reason, farmers were considered to be the best soldiers: a harsh life, patient subordination to the unpredictability of climate, and a familiarity with physical exertion made them ideal candidates for the Roman army, where discipline, tenacity, and obedience were the most appreciated qualifications. The birth of the professional army, between the end of the republican era and the beginning of the principate, radically changed the structure and concept of the army. Soldiers, now recruited for the most part from members of the proletariat who saw a chance to escape a precarious life and enrich themselves with booty or an allotment of lands upon discharge, gave their loyalty not to the state (a remote and scarcely significant entity for them) but to their commander. Confined for years and decades in military

**Planned Campaigns**
Before the great expansion of Rome, wars consisted essentially of annual campaigns within Italy. These allowed soldiers to return home for winter and then leave again in the springtime. *Left*, a calendar found in the Campus Martius in Rome.

**Shield of War**
A Roman shield of war; detail from a mosaic in the basilica of San Vitale in Ravenna.

encampments, they identified less and less with everyday citizens of the empire, who were settled in the cities and countryside. The army was in many ways an extraneous body that defended a society that was, in turn, extraneous to it. Finally and not insignificantly, the growing cost of a permanent army increasingly burdened the state banks to the point of causing their collapse.

## *Punishments*

Discipline in the Roman army was severe and maintained by extremely harsh means. A broad series of punishments were established for a soldier who broke the military code; these ranged from a fine (*pecuniaria multa*), to a lashing (*castigatio*), to demotion (*gradus deiectio*), to dishonorable discharge (*ignominiosa missio*, as opposed to *honesta missio*, the honorable discharge that awaited those who had served "with loyalty and honor"). In the most serious cases, the death penalty (*supplicium*) was applied. If the offense was committed by an entire unit, the punishment might be decimation, the removal at random of ten percent of the guilty, who paid for all.

## *Pay and Discharge*

The pay of the legionnaire (*stipendium*) was low, even when military service became a profession. It could be supplemented, however, with the spoils of war, a portion of which generally was granted by the general to the troops. And there was, like a mirage around which a soldier's entire life gravitated, the promise of the "settlement" upon completion of his service—that is, the allotment of lands in one of the colonies established in the provinces or on properties confiscated by the state from rebels or traitors. This payment, along with the granting of Roman citizenship to those who did not already enjoy this privilege, permitted both a comfortable old age and the veteran's access to citizen magistracies in the colonies or their native municipalities.

**Early Warfare**
The battle between the Romans and Sabines in a famous canvas by the French painter Jacques-Louis David.

# Weapons and Equipment

The Roman army owed its victories more to discipline, consistency, and unshakable faith in itself and its commanders than to superiority of arms. But weaponry and tactics were not overlooked, and the army became the most formidable war machine in history.

The Romans often lost the early battles in a conflict, but they regularly won the final ones, a demonstration of their great capacity to learn and to develop tactical flexibility. It was an army of infantry, the tactical unit of which was the legion, made up initially of three thousand foot soldiers with heavy arms—1200 *hastati* in the vanguard, 1200 *principes* in the second line, and 600 *triarii* as reinforcements—to which 1200 *velites* of light infantry and 300 knights (*equites*) were added for scouting and pursuit. The defensive arms of the heavy infantry (the same for the three formations) consisted of a tunic of bronze mail (*pectorale*), which covered the torso, a rectangular shield (*scutum*) with a convex surface, and a helmet with a plume at the top. Offensive arms consisted of a double-edged sword (*gladius*) and two heavy javelins (*pila*) for the *hastati* and the *principes*, two long lances (*hastae*) for the *triarii*. A *velite* had, as his only protection, a sword and javelins and a light shield (*parma*), as well as a helmet, sometimes covered with wolf skin.

Marius, the first general who permanently enlisted citizens who were not landowners, began the transformation toward a professional army; he reorganized the legion into 10 tactically self-sufficient divisions (*cohortes*) of 600 foot soldiers each, abolished the light infantry, and replaced it with divisions of auxiliary troops (*auxilia*) provided by Rome's allies. Each division had its own insignia (as the legion had its eagle), which was given great symbolic value, like present-day flags, in stimulating esprit de corps. After the battle between Crassus and the Parthians, other improvements were introduced: armor clad in metal plate (*lorica segmentata*) gave the legionnaires greater protection against arrows than the metal-mesh tunic, and modifications were made to the *pilum* (which bent as soon as it hit its target so that it could not be reused by the enemy and now had the addition of a counterweight to improve its balance and give it a greater range). This tactical

**The Infantry Weapon**
A Roman sword in its sheath, made from bronze, wood, and bone.

**A Bivouac for Soldiers**
A group of Roman soldiers depicted in a mosaic from the sanctuary at Praeneste (Palestrina).

**The Organization of the Legions**
This drawing illustrates the alignment, discussed in the text, of the Roman legions in the time of the monarchy (1) and after the reforms instituted by Marius (2).

STELE OF GAIUS AND QUINTUS VETIUS
*Above*, decorations worn by the brothers Gaius and Quintus Vetius: nine *phalerae*, two *torques*, and two *armillae*.

## DECORATIONS

The Roman army made large use of decorations for valor. There were two orders: the *dona minora*, conferred on ordinary soldiers and noncommissioned officers, and the *dona maiora*, reserved for officers ( tribunes, prefects, and legates). The soldiers' decorations consisted primarily of bracelets (*armillae*), neck rings (*torques*), and medallions (*phalerae*) and generally were made of silver. The most prestigious decorations were the crowns, of which there were different types, depending on the act of valor carried out. The civic crown was awarded to a soldier who had escaped the enemy and saved a Roman citizen, when witnessed by a general. A soldier who was the first to scale the walls of an enemy city was granted the *corona muralis*. The most rare and coveted prize was the *corona obsidionalis* or *graminea*, a simple crown of grass, awarded to a soldier who had saved a city under siege or the entire army from extreme danger.

structure and equipment remained substantially stable until nearly the end of the empire. There were marginal changes, such as the increase in effectiveness and functions of the cavalry, the frequent adoption of the long sword instead of the *gladius*, and the increase of the *auxilia*.

## *War Machinery*

The true difference between the Romans and most of their enemies was the constant presence, along with the legions, of war machinery (catapults, battering rams, *vinee*—portable platforms for scaling walls—and assault towers) utilized effectively for sieges. From the second century A.D. on, hurling machines, mounted on wheels, also were used on the battlefield as veritable field artillery, providing useful support for the troops. Here, too, it was not a question of devices that were unknown to the adversaries but rather the systematic and rational use to which the Romans put them.

THE EQUIPMENT OF TITUS CALIDIUS SEVERUS
His metal-mesh tunic, crested helmet, and greaves are sculpted on the funeral stele of the centurion Titus Calidius Severus *(below)*.

# Enemies

Over the course of its very long history, Rome had to confront many different enemies, each with its own strong and weak points. Latin commanders and troops were skilled at knowing how to adapt successfully to different situations and tasks.

In the beginning, Rome found itself confronting people who were similar in origins, culture, language, and social and military organization, such as the various Italic peoples (Latins, Samnites, Picenes). Or they faced civilizations with which they had frequent dealings, such as the Etruscans, often adapting their techniques, traditions, and beliefs. With these populations, conflict was between equals on a tactical and logistical level. The contrast lay in the discipline, spirit of sacrifice, and perseverance demonstrated by Rome: similar weapons and organization but a different spirit.

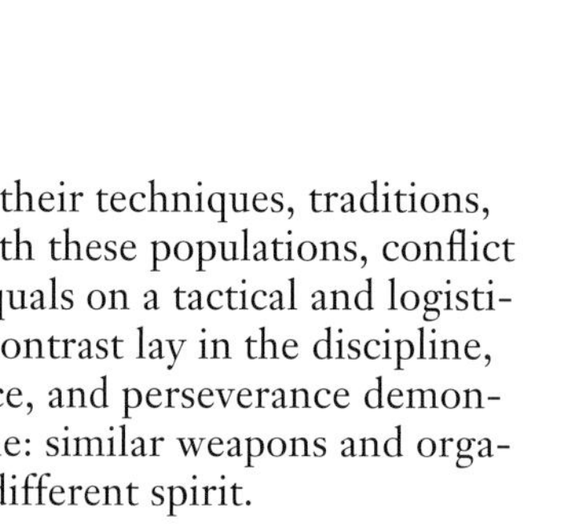

**Bust of Pyrrhus**
Hannibal considered Pyrrhus the greatest commander in history. To his contemporaries, the king of Epirus was second only to Alexander the Great.

**Dacian Helmet**
The wars against the Dacians, fought by Trajan along the Danube frontier in the second century A.D., were among the most glorious of the entire imperial era. *Above*, a silver Dacian helmet.

## THE GREATEST ENEMY

For Rome, in all its history, there may not have been an enemy more dangerous than Hannibal Barca, the Carthaginian general who was able to bring war all the way to the Italian peninsula and the only one who succeeded in defeating the Romans in four large consecutive conflicts. The Roman historian Cornelius Nepos wrote of him: "With his genius he went beyond all other commanders, just as the Roman people had gone beyond all others in courage." But Hannibal was beaten by the tactical ability of the legions more than by the genius of his Roman adversary, Scipio. Scipio had armed his men with the *gladius hispaniensis*, longer and more effective in battle than the Italic sword. Moreover, he divided his legions into mobile divisions, which were able to open up to allow the charge of Carthaginian elephants to pass through, then go back and regroup to face the enemy infantry.

**Hannibal at the Gates!**
Hannibal Barca, depicted here in a sixteenth-century fresco, brought the risk that Rome might be erased from history's stage. His name remains proverbial as a synonym for imminent danger: "Hannibal is at the gates!"

## *Confrontation with the East*

An entirely different kind of confrontation presented itself when, having proven its hegemony over the central Italic peninsula, Rome found itself opposing first the Greek cities of the south (and their overseas defenders, such as Pyrrhus), then Carthage, and finally the Macedonian, Greek, and Hellenistic troops. The initial contact with these forces almost always was disastrous—a long tradition of war that dated back to the Persian Wars and to Alexander the Great. The elephants of Pyrrhus terrified the Roman troops in Lucania and threw them into disarray, just as the brilliant maneuvers of Hannibal destroyed not only the armies of the Republic but also the morale of its soldiers. With the Eastern potentates, the Romans had to contend with their strength of numbers: hundreds of thousands of combatants brought to the battlefield. Here, the victorious weapons proved to be the tactical flexibility of the Roman legions and the capacity—shown by generals such as Quintus Fabius Maximus, Scipio, Marius, Sulla, and Lucullus—to learn from defeats and to turn the enemy's own tactics against it. The Romans were so aware of their superiority in command and tactics that they believed four armed and equipped Roman legions could vanquish any Eastern army, whatever the size.

COMBAT AT CLOSE RANGE
Detail of the relief on Trajan's Column that depicts a barbarian brandishing a sword against a Roman soldier.

THE FACE OF THE ENEMY
Marble portrait of a barbarian prince (third century A.D.).

## *The Furor of the Teutons*

The most difficult enemy to confront, one that in the end would break Rome's millennial civilization, was the barbarian horde that poured from the north in increasingly frequent waves. The Gauls under Brennus already had threatened the very life of the city. Caesar took ten years to subjugate Gaul, more than a century was required to pacify Spain, and northern Britain never could be conquered. The Germanic tribes destroyed the legions of Varus between the Rhine and the Elbe; and in the end the Vandals, Goths, Franks, Burgundians, and Alemanni overwhelmed the Roman *limes*. For centuries, the Romans held their northern adversaries at bay through the organization of their legions, their skillful use of fortifications, their astonishing campaigns of devastation (Tacitus tells of a Scottish chief who said, "They create a desert and call it peace"), and in the end their enlistment of barbarians to combat other barbarians. But the *furor teutonicus* led the Cimbri and Teutons to hurl themselves naked, drunk with violence, against Roman armor; and for the Romans, the price—economic, human, and moral—became ever greater and, in the end, too high to pay.

# Defensive Systems

Fortifications were crucial to the maneuvers of the legions. Cornerstones of territorial defense, barriers to hold the barbarians outside the empire, they were one of the most significant elements of the Roman military system.

The Romans were masters of the art of fortification, whether permanent or temporary field structures. The concept of *oppidum*, a fortified settlement in defense of a territory, was taken from the primitive Italic world. The Romans applied it systematically in their colonies, which were not only outposts of Roman civilization in surrounding territory but also essential fortified centers for that territory's control. Rome's most typical and significant invention, however, consisted of the fortified encampments *(castra)* that every Roman army erected at the end of a day's march.

**Defense of the frontiers**
*Right*, a relief from the Trajan Column, depicting a group of Roman legionnaires building a fortified encampment.

These were constructed according to a regular rectangular plan with the tent of the commander at the center and those of the various divisions set up in organized fashion, always in the same position. The perimeter was defended by a ditch, a rampart made with the earth excavated from the ditch, and a palisade created with stakes that the legionnaires carried with them. The *castra* guaranteed security during layovers and during the night and protection for foodstuffs, equipment, and mule trains. They also were a secure refuge if a battle was lost, and they represented a fundamental and irreplaceable fulcrum for field maneuvers—one that Roman generals and troops knew how to exploit with insuperable mastery.

## Control of the Border Territories

The "border," for the Romans, was not considered a continuous line behind which their defenses could be positioned. Rather, it was thought of as an area to be watched over, where particular attention was given to roads and rivers, following a principle that also was applied in areas distant from the frontier but strategic for communications and supplies. This type of defense was called *praetentura*, a term that indicated a chain of observation points along a road or a river valley. The presence of lookout towers, fortified settlements, and forts scattered over the territory was also due to the nature of the invasions by foreign peoples. Such invasions generally were not large shifts of masses of people but infiltrations and forays of small groups. For this reason, what really mattered was control of indispensable passes.

**Porta Palatina**
The Porta Palatina in Turin is one of the largest examples of a Roman urban gateway. It stood at the end of the *cardo maximus* on the north side of the walls.

**Lookout Tower**
*Right*, detail from a relief depicting a lookout tower along the Danube *limes*.

**VINDOLANDA**
The fort of *Vindolanda* (present-day Chesterholm in England) was built by Roman legions before 9 B.C. and later encompassed within the defensive system of Hadrian's Wall.

## *The Limes*

The expansionist thrust had propelled the Roman legions as far as the boundaries of Britain, beyond the Rhine and the Danube, into Mesopotamia, and down to the African deserts. When it ended, the Romans were faced with the need to defend the immense conquered territory from enemy incursions. At this point the tremendous experience that the Romans developed with fortifications found its highest expression. It was then that the concept of *limes*, a fortified boundary separating imperial from barbarian territory, emerged. Between the end of the first century A.D. and the middle of the fourth century, the frontiers of the empire were reinforced with a dense network of fortifications. These had the double task of accommodating Roman garrisons and blocking or at least draining barbarian infiltrations and incursions.

These fortifications were of various types. There were linear ramparts like those of Hadrian and Antoninus Pius in Britain, border fortresses like those erected on the Rhine and along the African *limes*, and encampments protected by trenches and supplemented with field towers and fortifications as in the wedge between the Rhine and the Danube in Germany. They all shared one goal: to use fortification technology to counter the inevitable attacks by larger forces and to facilitate the movement of Roman garrisons against barbarian penetrations.

**RECONSTRUCTION OF A *CASTRUM***
In the early imperial era, military encampments also functioned as logistical bases for offensives beyond the borders. Beginning in the third century, however, in order to deal with consistent and long-lasting incursions by barbarians, these assumed a prevalently defensive nature.

## *The Cities*

In addition to those of field and border, the Romans developed urban fortifications. Almost all their cities were constructed as masonry encampments with the same defensive scheme (ditch, walls, and towers) but on a greater scale. The city gates were a characteristic and distinctive feature. They were protected by two side towers and articulated as small autonomous castles, capable of effectively resisting even if the walls themselves fell. The Aurelian Walls in Rome are an excellent example of the Roman art of fortification; these were the first fortification built in the Urbs, during the time of the kings.

# The Pomp of Victory

The secret dream of every Roman general, the definitive consecration of his fame, was to parade as victorious commander and be carried in triumph through a rejoicing city.

If a Roman general, as the supreme commander of an army, had won a decisive victory over a foreign population, personally fighting in a battle in which at least five thousand enemies fell, he could then aspire to the honors of the triumph, the greatest recognition the Urbs reserved for its military leaders. The triumph came into being as a relatively simple religious ceremony of thanksgiving during which a victorious general entered the city with his troops, progressed to the temple of Jupiter Optimus Maximus, and gave thanks for his victory. Over time, however, the triumph became a magnificent holiday and a veritable ascension of the victor into the empyrean of heroes.

## *Preparation and Development*

The victorious general had to stop with his troops at the gates of Rome (going beyond the city boundary meant irrevocably losing the military *imperium*) and send the Senate his report. Based on his account, the assembly would decide whether a triumph was merited (often making the impatient commander wait for months or years). If the Senate's verdict was favorable, the date was set for the celebration, when all the people would turn out to see the triumphal procession pass by. Streets, squares, and monuments were festooned with garlands, temple doors were thrown open, and incense was burned on all the altars. The procession slowly departed from

**The Spoils of War**
*Above*, a marble representation of a Roman trophy constructed of captured armor mounted on a stake.

**The Moment of Triumph**
*Left*, a 1919 engraving by J. Hoffbauer, depicting a triumphal procession passing through the Roman forum.

**Panoply**
A decorative panel depicting a military trophy (panoply) with axe and shield.

the Campus Martius, passed beneath the Porta Triumphalis, crossed the Velabrum and the forum Boarium, skirted the Circus Maximus, passed into the forum and ended beneath the Capitolium. The victor, statuesque and imposing, wrapped in the *toga picta*, his face reddened with cinnabar, made the journey in a triumphal chariot. He was acclaimed by the entire city, amidst his soldiers and evidence of his victory (principal enemy prisoners, chariots loaded with the spoils of war, and paintings and models that illustrated the salient episodes of the campaign). Arriving at the Capitolium, he ascended to the temple of Jupiter, gave back to the god the crown and scepter that he had proudly worn for the ceremony, executed the ritual sacrifice, and presided over a celebratory banquet offered to the soldiers, the authorities, and all citizens.

## *From imperium to imperator*

The triumph had its greatest pageantry during the Republic, when it represented a reward for the citizen who had honored the *imperium* (power) granted to him by his equals. In the imperial era, the head of the army, the sole holder of *imperium* was the princeps, who by no coincidence was called the *imperator*. Generals were considered a mere extension of the sovereign, and they rarely (if ever) were awarded a triumph. On the contrary, the emperor appropriated the right to wear the *ornamenta triumphalia* as "full-dress uniform" in state ceremonies, and these trappings thus went from being exceptional to being habitual. Little by little, the very custom of the triumph declined even for emperors; the last was celebrated in 302 for Diocletian. Yet it is precisely the imperial era that has left us the greatest memorial of triumphs: the majestic arches erected in the forum to celebrate victorious emperors.

**Triumphal Arch of Orange**
Between the Augustan and Tiberian eras, an impressive number of triumphal arches were erected in Narbonese Gaul. The one in Orange is particularly noteworthy, with three barrel vaults and decorated with themes of the military triumph, including arms, trophies, and prisoners.

### SOME REPUBLICAN GENERALS HONORED WITH TRIUMPHS

| | |
|---|---|
| 209 B.C. | Fabius Maximus for the victory over the people of Tarentum. |
| 201 B.C. | Scipio Africanus for the victory over Carthage. |
| 168 B.C. | Lucius Aemilius Paullus for the victory over the Macedonians. |
| 105 B.C. | Gaius Marius for the victory over Jugurtha. |
| 61 B.C. | Pompey for the victory over Mithridates. |
| 46 B.C. | Caesar for the victory over the Gauls. |
| 29 B.C. | Octavian celebrated three triumphs: for the victory over the Dalmatians, the victory at Actium, and the conquest of Alexandria. |

# The Troops of the Princeps: The Praetorian Guard

The praetorians, an army unto themselves, were the armed guard of the *princeps*, and on more than one occasion they controlled the fates of emperors and empire.

The praetorian guard of Rome was created by Augustus in 22 to 21 B.C., following a conspiracy that had endangered the stability of the empire and the very life of the *princeps*. The guard was made up of a variable number of *cohortes* (from nine to sixteen) stationed from the time of Tiberius directly in Rome. This was a substantial, if not formal, deviation from the law that prohibited the presence of an armed corps within the city. The head of the guard was a *praefectus* *praetorio* of equestrian rank, who, given his extremely delicate function, enjoyed the total faith of the emperor and played a significant role in the life of the court. The corps, made up of professional warriors who had been carefully trained and hardened to meet any demand, constituted the elite of the Roman army. It was often a key element in struggles of succession, as, for example, on the occasion of the assassination of Caligula in A.D. 41, when it was the praetorians who acclaimed Claudius as his successor. Their influence diminished during the second century, when a stable imperial power maintained tight control over the state. Then they gradually became more important during the upheavals of the subsequent century to the point where Septimius Severus decided to disperse the guard and reconstitute it with soldiers taken from the legions of the field army. The praetorian guard was perceived as a threat once again during the reign of Constantine, who decided to disband it completely.

**Officer with Helmet**
Head of an officer wearing a helmet with the characteristic crest of feathers or horsehair.

**The Emperor's Guard**
A relief depicting officers and praetorians. The latter could be distinguished by the armor fitted to the torso and decorated with bas-reliefs.

## *The Organization, Recruitment, and Life of the Praetorians*

Each cohort, commanded by a tribune, included six centuries for a total of approximately one thousand infantrymen, supported by a cavalry division. Soldiers initially had to be all volunteers and holders of Roman citizenship. Over time the percentage of non-Italic soldiers kept increasing until Septimius Severus simply authorized their total exclusion from the ranks of the praetorian cohorts. Service lasted sixteen years (compared to the twenty to twenty-five years for "ordinary" legionnaires), and the pay was excellent: 500 denari a year under Augustus, raised to 2,500 during the time of Caracalla. This wage was augmented by significant gifts on the occasion of celebrations or in recognition for particular services rendered. The everyday life of the praetorian, as long as he was not engaged in military campaigns or special missions, was a great deal better than that of an ordinary legionnaire. The daily routine called for morning training on the drillfield, followed by body treatments at the baths, a meal in the dining hall, and time-off. Rations were much more lavish than those of the army and included daily servings of meat. During their free time, the praetorians had all the attractions of the capital at their disposal: theaters, spectacles, gladiators, taverns, and *thermopolia* (the bars of the time). They were quartered at the *castra praetoria*, built by Tiberius on the Viminal hill, just outside the Servian walls. This was a vast, fortified quadrangular area that accommodated dormitories for the troops, lodgings for officers, the commander's headquarters, warehouses, an armory, stables, and even a field hospital—all completely self-sufficient.

**COMMAND OF THE *CASTRUM***
In every Roman *castrum*, the *preatorium* was the commander's residence. *Left*, ruins of the *praetorium* of the Roman army in *Lambaesis*, Algeria.

### INSIGNIA OF THE PRAETORIAN

Every citizen immediately recognized the troops of the praetorian guard, because of the image of the emperor on their standards and their unmistakable clothing: armor fitted to the torso instead of the *lorica segmentata* typical of the legionnaires; short skirt with *pteryges* (leather strips to protect against blows); crested helmet with high visor; and oval shield with lightning bolt insignia. They were the armed wing of power, a fact of which they were well aware.

**BALDRIC**
A bronze baldric with a scene of a struggle between barbarians and Romans. Worn slung over the shoulder, from right shoulder to left hip, the baldric supported the sword.

**MEDALS FOR VALOR**
Relief depicting military insignia with numerous awards.

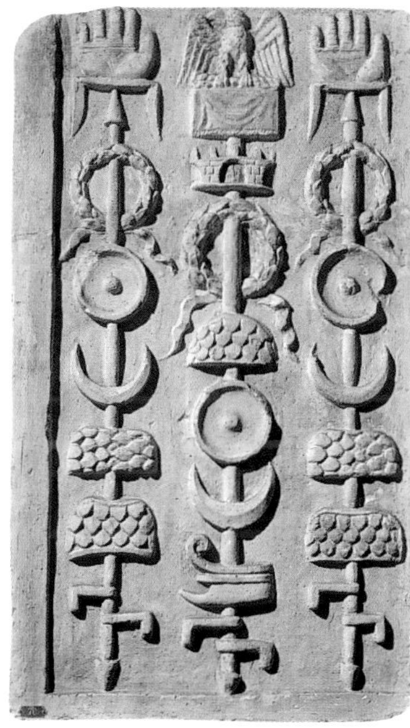

# Agrarian System

A complex and efficient agrarian system was the basis for the entire structure of the Roman state. This included the systematic organization of territory, the division of lands for production purposes, and the large-scale trade of farm products.

**Grinder for Grain**
A grinder made from lava stone, found in Pompeii, used for grinding grain (first century A.D.).

For a very long period, Roman civilization was based on agriculture, indeed on the identification of farmers with citizens. According to tradition, Romulus created a small landholding of two jugers (approximately five thousand square meters)—the *heredium*—that long constituted the functional unit of Italic agriculture. It was said that Romulus distributed one juger to each male inhabitant of the new city to give him the minimum amount of property required for full citizenship. This is very likely a simplification or a convoluted interpretation, but it demonstrates the importance that Rome attributed to small farms. Over the centuries, the Romans created tens of thousands of *heredia* and set up a complex system for the organization of land—"centuriation"—one of the distinctive features of Latin civilization. Put very simply, this consisted of the measuring and regular division of land into large

**The Mosaics of Tabarka**
The fifth-century-A.D. mosaics from the Roman villa of Tabarka in Tunisia provide excellent documentation about farms and farm life. *Below*, a farm with granaries, typical houses, and stables.

**Plowing**
*Above*, a small votive bronze depicting a man plowing. The Romans learned agricultural techniques from the Etruscans, who were already using plows drawn by pairs of oxen in the seventh century B.C.

square plots of two hundred jugers (approximately fifty hectares), called *centuriae*. These in turn were subdivided into small lots of two jugers each (*heredia*), distributed to farmers. Thus there were one hundred landowners for each *centuria*. Entire territories (the Po Valley in particular) were divided up methodically in this manner, creating an imprint on the land that still exists and can easily be seen in aerial photos or on maps. The cities founded by the Romans were also systematically divided into regular plots (*insulae*), which continued the organization of the territory. Indeed, roads often were laid out precisely as boundaries of fields in perfect correspondence to the organization of the city and the surrounding territory.

**The Land Surveyor**
This stele, belonging to L. Ebutius Faustus, depicts the implements of the land surveyor, the expert entrusted with the task of measuring and "centuriating" arable land.

## *Small Farms and Large Estates*

Small farms soon entered a period of crisis. The small farmer was finding it increasingly difficult to pay for his weapons, to spend long periods away from home in military service, and to deal with periods of bad weather. But above all, it was difficult to compete with a new agricultural system that began spreading through Roman society at the time of the Punic Wars: the large estate based on slave labor. Low labor costs, extensive single-crop farming, and the possibility for large landowners to cope more easily with a bad year, all combined to sideline the small farmers; many of them sold their farms to the large landowners and moved to the city, where they created a plebian citizen class with neither trade nor profession. The Roman rulers, from the Gracchi to Julius Caesar and Augustus, repeatedly attempted to breathe new life into the small farm, which they saw as an essential reservoir of men for the legions and a fundamental element of the social structure. But they achieved scant results. At the end of the imperial era, many territories ruled by Rome had estates as extensive as provinces with owners who often behaved like sovereigns ruling their own domains—presage of the feudal system.

### FREEDMEN AND SLAVES

The Roman writer Varro (first century B.C.) provides this illuminating portrait of the relationship between labor by freedmen and by slaves. "Now I will deal with the means necessary for cultivating the land. Some divide this subject into two parts: men and tools indispensable for agriculture; others into three parts: speaking tools (namely slaves), inarticulate tools (beasts of burden) and mutes (carts). Agricultural tasks can be entrusted to slaves, to freedmen, or to both. Freedmen can farm on their own, as many poor farmers do, with only the help of their families, or they can be recruited as farmhands when agricultural operations require it, for example, on the occasion of the grape harvest or hay making . . . . I have the following opinion about the use of freedmen and farmhands: it makes sense to have barren lands tended by freedmen and to resort to farmhands for heavier operations such as the harvest, the grape harvest, and the preservation of fruit, even on healthy lands."

Varro, *De re rustica*, I, XVII. 1–3.

# Cattle Raising and Sheep Farming

Cattle raising and sheep farming were closely connected to agriculture and constituted one of the principal food and economic resources of ancient civilization.

According to a widespread belief in the ancient world, reported by Varro in his writings, men had passed through three stages of civilization: the primitive gathering stage, in which they lived off what the land had to offer; the shepherding phase, when they began to capture and raise animals; and the agricultural phase, source of civilized life. In reality, sheep farming and cattle raising appear closely connected and complementary to agriculture. They can offer valid assistance, as in the case of animals used for plowing and transportation. What is certain is that these were fundamental activities and constituted one of the economic bases for Roman society. The most prized animals were cows, an inexhaustible source of meat, milk, butter, cheese, manure, horn, bone, hides, and

**Gallic Bull**
This small bronze statue of a bull comes from Gaul, an area that in ancient Roman times was a vast expanse of land studded with small farming villages, particularly in the northern region.

**Rustic Scene**
Detail of a sarcophagus with scenes of a farmer gathering vegetables and shepherds milking their sheep.

essential help for pulling carts and plows. These were services that amply compensated for the assiduous care the animals required and the need to harvest and store large quantities of fodder to feed them during the winter. Horses were extremely valuable not only for their utility as means of transport but also and above all for military and sporting use. They were costly to raise, maintain, and use, however, and only gentlemen could afford them. Farmers much

**Galloping Horse**
Bronze of a galloping horse, from Spain. This is perhaps an example of the breed that Julius Caesar in his *De bello gallico* called *caballus ibericus*.

preferred more rustic animals, such as donkeys and mules. Sheep, finally, were viewed with ambivalence. On the one hand, they were basic to animal raising in the Roman world (the Latin word for wealth, *pecunia*, comes from *pecus*, sheep), and they were well suited to the arid Mediterranean climate and required little care. Moreover, they supplied an abundance of wool, sheepskins, meat, milk, and cheese. On the other hand, they were "poor" livestock—nomadic and not well liked because they destroyed pasture and farmland. Although cows, horses, and sheep made up most of the livestock, there were other species that should not be overlooked. Pigs provided a meat that was greatly appreciated by all social classes, and farmyard animals—chickens, hens, geese—guaranteed eggs and meat. Dung was a precious byproduct, used to fertilize vineyards and barren fields. Beekeeping was an area apart and was a popular activity because of the exquisite end product, honey, which the Romans used widely in cooking.

## *The Care of Animals*

Given the high value that could be placed on animals and their products, raising livestock became a highly specialized activity for the Romans. This was true not only for horses, which were given almost "human" attention, but also for cows, other equines, and swine. Ancient agronomists distributed advice and recommendations about the best age to purchase, sell, and mate animals and how to feed them and cure illnesses that might strike them. The figure of the veterinarian, in the modern sense, was unknown to the ancients, but farm stewards had to have profound knowledge about medical compresses, diets, and above all blood-letting, considered a true panacea for every malady.

### ANIMAL SACRIFICES

In the Roman world, sacrifices were divided into two major categories: those that were bloodless, the offering of various products, such as the first yield of the harvest; and those that were bloody, the ritual killing of one or more animals. Oxen, sheep, pigs, or goats could be sacrificed, as well as other animals, depending on the nature of the divinity and the importance of the sacrifice. The animals, which had to be free of physical defects, underwent a rigorous ritual. Once chosen, they were held apart from any others, carefully prepared, washed, adorned with garlands, and readied for immolation—namely, sprinkled with *mola salsa*, a mixture of spelt and salt prepared by the vestals. Finally, they were led to the place of sacrifice, where the person performing the sacrifice (generally a magistrate or, in cases of private sacrifice, the *paterfamilias*) and the attendants responsible for killing the victim met. *Haruspices* who examined the entrails of sacrificed animals for omens, a long series of acolytes, and the public also were present. After ritual prayers, the animal was slaughtered and the flowing blood was collected and sprayed on the sacrificial altar, the entrails were extracted to be examined and then, after being cut into pieces and sprinkled with oil and salt, were offered to the divinity. The appropriately deconsecrated remains were then consumed by the bystanders.

**Nomadic Life**
Relief from the republican era, depicting a shepherd.

***Rhyton* in the Form of a Rooster**
A rhyton is a drinking vessel in the shape of an animal. The one depicted to the right, which comes from a dwelling in Pompeii, resembles a rooster. Such vessels were widespread in cultures in the ancient world.

# Quarries and Mines

Quarries were sources of marble for building; mines yielded metals for tools, weapons, jewelry, and coins. These materials extracted from the depths of the earth were vital for Rome, but the systems for working them were not particularly humane.

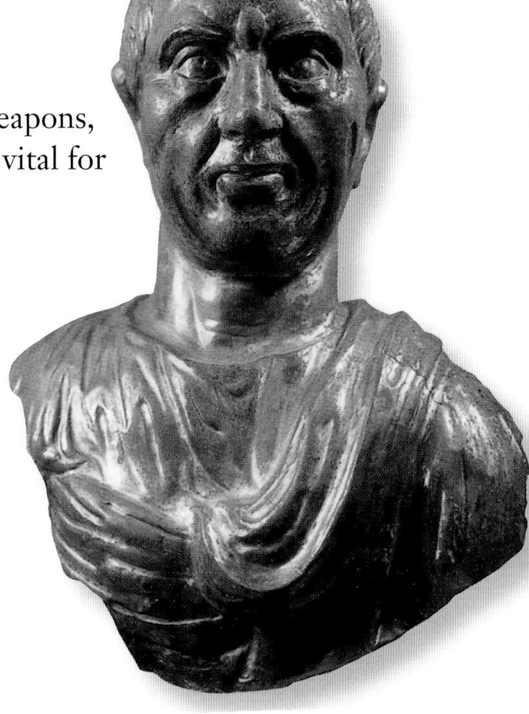

**Silver Processing**
A silver bust depicting a patrician, from *Vasio Vocontiorum* in Narbonese Gaul (present-day Vaison-la-Romaine, France).

To be condemned *ad metalla*, to forced labor in a mine, was one of the greatest punishments in the Roman world, for mines and sometimes quarries were among the harshest and most dangerous places. The problem mostly concerned mines because quarries were almost always open spaces. When the Romans began mining, the deposits of metals known to them, those that were close to the surface, were being depleted, so it was necessary to excavate underground mines, a difficult undertaking given the scanty knowledge of mineralogy and the rudimentary technical means available. In general, a mine was begun by digging a well—rectangular or circular—in which miners climbed down a rough grade or used ladders. Upon reaching the level of the vein of metal ore, work proceeded with horizontal excavations. Ventilation was guaranteed by the wells themselves (open at regular intervals in the land). Gas leaks were detected by lowering a lamp into the tunnel; if it stayed lit, the miners could safely descend. Small oil lamps inserted into hollows in the walls illuminated the excavations. Machinery such as Archimedes' screw (a device with a helix turning inside a tube) or a waterwheel was used to drain the water that often invaded the tunnels. Dikes, aqueducts, channels, and catch basins were constructed to convey the water necessary for breaking up the rock, removing layers with low metal content, and washing away detritus. Traces of this activity are visible on the land today.

## *The Products*

In addition to marble for building (which the Romans used a great deal and for which they developed a technique for facing walls with slabs), gold, silver, tin, copper, iron,

**Raw Material**
The unloading of iron materials from a boat, shown in a mosaic from Tunisia.

**Bronze Casting**
Small bronze statue from Pompeii, which depicts a lar wearing a short tunic and executing a dance step.

and lead were brought forth from the earth. With the exception of gold, these materials were not found in their pure state but rather as composites that had to be worked to extract the minerals.

### WHERE GOLD WAS MINED

During the imperial era, many of the gold-bearing rivers and gold mines that had been exploited by the Greek cities and by the Hellenistic kingdoms were depleted. The Egyptian mines were an exception, and these remained one of the most significant sources for the Romans, as well. New and extremely rich deposits were discovered in the Iberian Peninsula and, with the expansion of the empire's boundaries, in Dalmatia, Noricum, Britain, and Dacia.

In Italy there are remains of gold mines in present-day Piedmont and the Friuli-Venetia Julia region. However, production within the boundaries of the Roman empire was not sufficient to satisfy the enormous demand. Consequently, the precious metal was imported from distant regions, such as Arabia, India, and Siberia.

The Romans customarily used the word *bronze* to describe almost any alloy: true bronze (made from copper and tin), "Corinthian bronze" (copper, gold, and silver), "Campanian bronze" (copper, tin, and lead).

It does not seem that the Romans knew a direct method for producing steel, uniting iron and carbon, although they made successive fusions of ferrous materials in crucibles, in which coal and leaves of particular plants were mixed to produce a steel of rather variable quality. In any case, Roman metallurgy was able to provide society with implements that, all things considered, were suitable to the technology of the time—at the price, unfortunately, of frightful working conditions.

**The Most Exhausting Labor**
Relief depicting slaves at work in a marble quarry.

# The Organization of Labor

Professional associations, teeming artisans' workshops, and the harsh life of slaves: the Roman organization of labor was infinitely varied and complex, as much if not more so than today.

In the Roman world, there were a great many professional associations (*collegia* or *corpora*), which generally brought together entrepreneurs, wholesalers, merchants, or craftsmen. Rigidly controlled by the state, they enjoyed immense prestige that not infrequently spilled over into public life, where they became "collectors" of votes for agreeable candidates. One of the principal functions was to act as what today we might call a lobby—namely, to establish useful relationships with officials of the state administration. All associations had their own statutes, *lex collegii*, which laid out the regulations for community life and the criteria for selecting members. Provided they had money, the number of members could be quite large; women could join if they were wealthy and generous. Heading everything was the *patronus*, or patron of the association, the person responsible not only for administration but also for good relationships between members and outside officials. This explains why the patron often was chosen from among men of politics in the public eye or from influential members of the senatorial or equestrian classes.

**Slave Labor**
Seneca advised his contemporaries to treat slaves with humanity. "Be merciful and also cordial with the slave; include him in your conversation, consult him in your decisions, call him to your table." *Right*, black marble statue of a young slave.

## Tabernae *and Workshops*

In Rome *taberna* did not have the meaning it later took on in Italian. Instead, it

**Daily Bread**
The distribution of bread, shown in a Pompeian fresco (first century A.D.).

### WORK SCHEDULES

For Romans, the workday began early in the morning. In fact, the precariousness of artificial light made it indispensable to take advantage of daylight as much as possible. Even before dawn the streets were enlivened by the striking of blacksmiths' hammers and the calls of strolling vendors who arrived from the countryside with loads of vegetables and greens. Merchants of luxury items opened up in late morning, however, when wealthy clients, having recovered from their nocturnal exertions, finally went out. All things considered, the work schedule was not very different from that of our own time: many corporations imposed fixed hours on their employees, which generally did not exceed eight hours. As a result, those who began working at dawn could usually cease work around 2 P.M. Only certain categories, such as tavern keepers, barbers, and perfume makers, preferred to work longer hours in order to take advantage of the evening traffic of potential customers.

**Via *Biberatica***
*Above*, the Via Biberatica in Trajan's Market in Rome. The name of this street is derived from *bibere* ("to drink"), making it easy to guess the type of workshops that lined the street.

RECONSTRUCTION OF A WORKSHOP
The workshop of the House of Neptune and Amphitrite in Herculaneum.

indicated something similar to a medieval workshop, an atelier that exhibited and sold artisans' products. Roman cities (and Rome in particular) were filled with workshops of this type. In effect their presence constituted a raison d'être for the urban centers, where objects were produced (weapons, tools, works of art, jewelry) to be exchanged for agricultural products from the countryside. These workshops covered all the needs of daily life; there were bakeries, confectioneries, and perfumeries along with blacksmiths, jewelers, potters, glassmakers, and an infinite array of artisans who made up the urban manufacturing class. These often were organized into "chains" that produced a place's typical product (vases in Cumae, alabaster objects in Volterra, perfumes in Rome, weapons in northern Italy, and so on).

## *Slave Labor*

The presence of slave labor was fundamental to the ancient economy, particularly in Rome. Considered as "goods," the complete property of their owners, slaves provided a low-cost and high-yield labor force that was essential to many activities. There were rural slaves (*familia rustica*) who worked the fields—often vast landed estates—under the surveillance of a steward (*vilicus*), also a slave. There were city slaves (*familia urbana*) destined for personal service to their owner (barbers, porters, and dishwashers but also pedagogues, secretaries, and business managers).

In the final years of the Republic, great workshops also took root (pottery works, brickworks, factories, etc.) based on the intensive use of slave labor. Here, the slave became a "machine" of considerable efficiency and productivity, destined to repeat infinitely a few identical operations with a high degree of mechanical gestures and efficiency. This intensive exploitation not only displaced the artisan workshops based on free labor but also constituted one of the cruelest fates of the Roman slave.

SHIPBUILDER
The *fabri navales*, shipbuilders, had one of the most important professional associations in Ostia, the port of Rome. *Below*, the grave stele of the *faber navalis* P. Longidienus.

LUXURY ARTICLE
Relief depicting the interior of a shop selling cushions.

# Banks and Money

From moneychangers to workers specializing in financial transactions, over the course of centuries Roman bankers created the first "global" financial and commercial system.

**The Roman Coin Par Excellence**
*Above*, two sesterces from the imperial era. On the basis of a complex series of calculations, it has been established within a certain degree of accuracy that one sesterce was equal to 60 to 70 hundredths of a euro.

The moneychangers who, beginning in the fourth century B.C., began to open their stalls in the city were called *argentarii*, silver traders, by the Romans. Initially, they were limited to changing money, verifying its authenticity, and carrying out depository and cashier services. As early as the second century B.C., however, they were involved in auction sales, guarantees, loans at interest, and, of course, banking services. Unlike banking as we know it, a deposit did not yield anything for bankers or customers. In fact, according to Roman law, money given in deposit had to be simply guarded and returned upon the expiration of the term of deposit without gaining any profit. This apparently led savers to keep their money under the mattress (attested to by the frequent discovery of small treasures in excavations of Roman houses). Alternatively, people feigned that money given in deposit was really entrusted as a loan, and thus they could demand interest from the banker. However, loans were in turn subject to a maximum interest rate established by law, which for some time remained fixed at twelve percent. Then, in the later imperial era, in order to stimulate the economy, the government kept lowering what we now would call the discount rate, bringing it down to six percent. Naturally, the market reality was quite different. Usury was not uncommon, and despite the severity of the laws, there was always a loophole (and a good lawyer) to bend the rules.

## *Which coin?*

The Romans began to issue their own money (a bronze coin, the *as*, weighing approximately 327 grams, or one pound) in the second half of the fourth century B.C., later than the Greeks or the Carthaginians but in time to experience devaluation, the sad fate of all currencies.

Indeed, a century later it became necessary to mint a new coin, the *sesterce*, which, as its name indicates (*sestertius* means "two

### Money and Propaganda

Recent selections, research, and discussions about what images to place on "national" euro coins demonstrate the strong and deeply rooted cultural and political value that money continues to have, even today. In fact, the image placed on a coin expresses a message transmitted by the authority that has placed the money in circulation. In the Roman world, the depiction on a coin had particular importance because of its extremely broad circulation. It passed from hand to hand throughout the territory of the empire over a long period of time. In the late republican era, senators entrusted with minting coins already were taking advantage of this means to create propaganda about the glories, true or presumed, of their own families. From Augustus on, the coin was the principal support of imperial politics, depicting first of all the numerous virtues of the *princeps*; communicating, in a simple image, his military victories and conquests; or presenting dynastic policy through the effigies of his presumed successor.

**The Mint?**
Fresco from the House of the Vettii in Pompeii may depict a mint (or a jeweler's) with putti as silversmiths.

**Solid and Golden**
A *solidus* and an *aureus* minted by order of Theodosius I, both with the effigy of the emperor on the front.

**The Moneychanger's *taberna***
This relief shows a *taberna argentaria*, the workshop of a moneychanger.

## THE FILES OF CECILIUS IUCUNDUS

The excavations at Pompeii have brought to light the files of an *argentarius* of the time, Cecilius Iucundus: a series of tablets on which financial transactions of various sizes are recorded. These range from 520 sesterces paid for a mule to a complex transaction for a total of 38,079 sesterces. Most of Cecilius Iucundus's business (48% to be precise) involved sums between 1,000 and 5,000 sesterces, and a significant percentage (24%) involved transactions from 5,000 to 10,000 sesterces.

and a half times as great"), was worth two and one-half *asses*. The *sesterce* was to become the most famous Roman coin. Inevitably, it also suffered devaluation because of inflation (mainly to pay the costs of continuous wars), and so the various governing officials repeatedly had to create other coins, such as the *aureus nummus* of Julius Caesar (which over time kept its name but not its gold content, which slid from 1/42 to 1/60 pound). The emperor Constantine issued the *solidus* (which, despite its reassuring name, was worth less than the *aureus*: 1/72 pound). Then there was a confusing array of coins of lesser value—the *denarius*, the *dupondius*, the *binio*, the *follis*, the *tremissis*—made from different metals (silver, bronze) and tied by various fractional relationships to gold coins. All in all, this worked to the benefit of the *argentarii* scattered throughout the empire.

**Banker's Father**
This herm of the father of the banker Lucius Cecilius was discovered in the atrium of the House of Cecilius Iucundus in Pompeii.

# Trade

Thanks to their victories, the Romans c
that embraced all the lands around the M
was a source of wealth and well-being o

We can identify the moment—in the middle-republican era, approximately between the Punic Wars—when the Roman economy went beyond the limits of production and trade carried out almost exclusively for the satisfaction of needs. It was at this point that the economy became geared toward the production and acquisition of costly goods (marbles, works of art, precious textiles, exotic foods, well-educated slaves, and domestic comforts). Much of the population remained untouched by this phenomenon, which only had an impact on the upper classes; but the resulting expansion in trade was immense. Upkeep of the army constituted another stimulus to production and trade. To give an example, four legions required seventy thousand hectoliters of wine per year, which had to be moved from places of production to locations where the troops were garrisoned. And there often were fifteen or twenty legions in service at the same time. The availability of money tempted senatorial families to undertake lucrative financial activities, even though this was severely prohibited by law. They engaged in transport, loans, and trade (the slave trade, in particular, flourished with the principal center on the Greek island of Delos). Trade in oil, wine, culinary specialties, jewels, and works of art fostered commercial traffic along the Mediterranean routes and sustained a

**The Slave Trade**
Slave traders *(mangones)* worked in the forum or in workshops, exhibiting their "wares" in full view. Around the neck of each slave was a sign that gave personal information, from nationality to any physical defects. *Above*, a sculpture depicting a young slave asleep (first century B.C.).

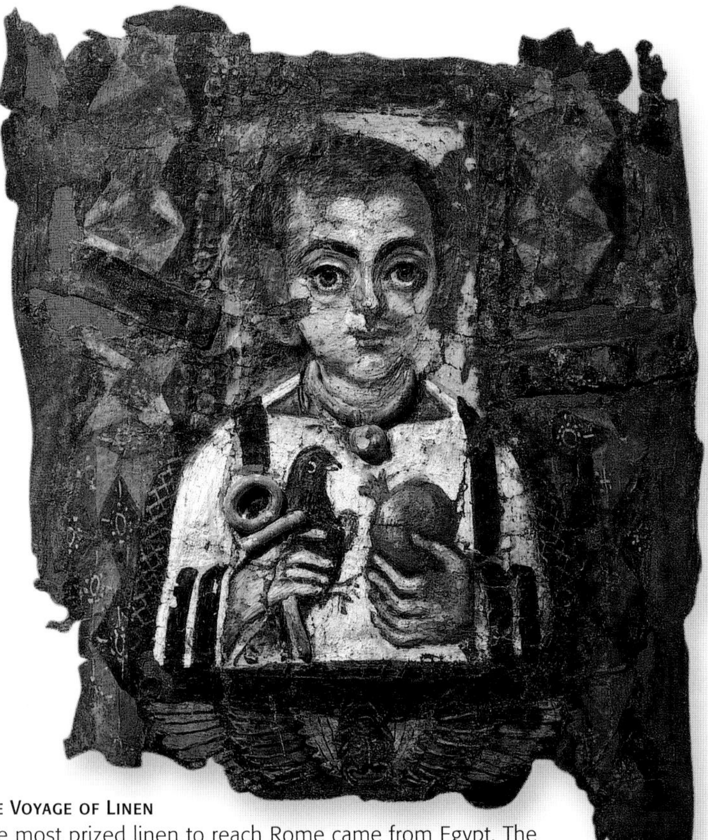

**The Voyage of Linen**
The most prized linen to reach Rome came from Egypt. The rough variety, used for making sails, was imported from Spain. *Above*, a baby's *sudarium* in painted linen (third century A.D.).

**The Arrival in Port**
*Below*, relief depicting two ships laden with amphorae, passing by the lighthouse at the entrance to the port of Ostia.

trade that would remain unequaled for many centuries to come.

## *"Industrial" Products and Agricultural Products*

During the imperial era, the presence of an enormous center of consumption like the capital strongly supported the production and trade of luxury objects. These ranged from jewels to textiles, tools of all types, weapons, kitchen ceramics, and foodstuffs (entire fleets were employed full time to transport grain from the provinces to Rome). However, the situation had its negative aspects. Italy, which could not sustain the competition of low-cost products from the provinces, became increasingly agrarian with the expansion of large estates at the expense of small farms. The various monetary crises of the empire had a strong impact on trade. Above all, the contraction of the population and its impoverishment as a result of high taxation led to the progressive self-sufficiency of the provinces between the third and fourth centuries. Thus, there was less of the "industrial" production (oil, wine, luxury items) that had been typical of the early imperial period, and more economic circuits of an increasingly restricted nature.

**AFRICAN CERAMICS**
Beginning in the second century A.D., the African provinces became known for the production of ceramic tableware, which soon began to be exported and appreciated throughout the empire. *Left*, a large decorated ceramic vessel.

### CARGO SHIPS

Much trade in the ancient world consisted of shipments of wine and oil, to the point where special ships were created for this activity, so-called cargo ships. Their holds were filled to the brim with amphorae arranged in *quicunx*—that is, various superimposed layers where the tips of the upper amphorae slipped into the spaces left by the necks of the amphorae below. This optimized the use of space and gave stability to the load. Straw or some other material capable of alleviating bumps and jolts was inserted between the amphora. To keep down costs, an effort was made to avoid having ships travel empty. Thus, for the return trip, building materials (finished marble, columns, lumber) often took the place of the amphorae of oil or wine that had filled the hold on the journey out.

**IMPORT-EXPORT OF HOUSEWARES**
A bronze pitcher, a ceramic vessel, and a glass pitcher made in Italy and discovered in Gaul. Most commercial traffic took place by sea.

The partition of the empire was economic even more than political and military, with East and West increasingly divided on this level, as well. During the fourth century, the epoch of the astute Italic *mercatores* who, invading the provinces, had created a great Mediterranean market was all but over. Wealth no longer came from trade but from the earth.

# The Treasury in Rome

It was not easy to finance continuous wars. The burden weighed heavily on citizens, even if it was in part alleviated by booty from the campaigns and by the tributes paid by subjugated peoples. For centuries, the fiscal policy of the Roman state revolved around this problem.

**Protector of Merchants**
Detail of a bronze scale with the head of Mercury, the god venerated as protector of merchants.

The taxation system in ancient Rome was organized in a way that would arouse the enthusiasm of certain neo-laissez-faire economists today. In fact, there was no provision for taxes on income from work, profits from capital, or property. Nor were there goals for redistribution, as in many present-day tax systems. (Far from deeming the accumulation of wealth to be negative, the ancient Romans considered it a highly desirable result.) Almost all the taxes imposed on citizens were indirect.

**Spoils of War**
*Below*, detail of a relief from Trajan's Column, which shows treasures taken from defeated peoples being carried triumphantly to Rome.

The principal one was the *portorium*, collected at varying rates (it was rather high for luxury items, lower for necessities) on the value of goods entering or exiting the city. In all periods, the only true tax that the state imposed on its citizens on the basis of personal income was the tax to support war expenditures. This was worked out in five strongly progressive tax brackets, which, however, also corresponded to considerable differences in political weight. Those who paid the most (and the citizens of the upper classes paid a great deal) counted more in city politics. It is important to remember that war not only called for spending but often yielded much in terms of booty, tributes from subject peoples, and slaves and lands to be divided up (here, too, with preference given to the wealthiest classes). Indeed, even Roman historians noted that the only ones to gain were the *mercatores*, the wealthy merchants who, after every campaign, hastened to take possession of the new markets opened up by the legions.

## *From Treasury to Taxation*

In times past, the state treasury had been kept in the temple of Saturn (the *aerarium Saturni*). During the reign of Augustus, the treasury was supplemented by an imperial fund, the *fiscus* (literally, "basket"). This contained revenues from taxes collected in Egypt and later expropriated from many other sources, from assets of people who died intestate to those who were fined, to half the value of assets recovered by chance and not claimed. It was also Augustus who created the *aerarium militare*, set up to liquidate sums paid to veterans. Two new taxes were imposed specifically to increase this special treasury fund: the *centesima venalium* (equal to a 1% sales tax) and the *vicesima* (5% tax on donations and inheritances). It seems incredible by today's standards, but the application of the 1% tax on transactions was the cause of broad and profound unrest, which in the end forced Caligula to decree its abolition. These were different times indeed.

THE GREAT OUTLAY OF TAXPAYERS
Payment of tribute, shown in a relief from Gaul.

## *Taxation in the Late Empire*

Increasing threats on the frontiers and the drastic reduction in population due to plagues, which cut in half the number of inhabitants in the empire, led to a progressive tax increase. Caracalla's historic decision to grant Roman citizenship to all male inhabitants of the empire has often been seen, even by ancient historians, as a means to increase revenues by increasing the taxable base. Under Septimius Severus, a new tax appeared, the *annona*, which could be paid in kind, with considerable advantage to the bureaucracy and, even more, to the army, which immediately could set aside provisions and assets without passing through complex systems of allotment. This was strongly disliked by the citizens, who preferred the *adaeratio*, payment in money. Things changed with the monetary reform under Constantine, when it became extremely burdensome to pay taxes because the value was expressed in the new gold *solidus* minted by the emperor, which was strongly revalued compared to coins in baser metals. From this time on, payment in kind tended to prevail—a precursor of the Middle Ages.

### *PUBLICANI*

In ancient times, the Roman state saw directly to the collecting of taxes. But in 123 B.C. with a law backed by Gaius Gracchus, a contracting system was introduced (or spread) for collecting tribute from the provinces. *Publicani*, or contractors, were granted the right to collect a tax in a territory; they paid a lump sum to the state and then recouped the money from the taxpayers. This freed the state bureaucracy from a heavy burden, but it encouraged abuses and corruption of every type. This system turned the *publicani* into one of the wealthiest but most hated classes in all Roman society.

PUBLICANI AT WORK
Relief of a grave stele depicting *publicani* collecting taxes.

# Building Materials and Techniques

Architecture was the Romans' art par excellence, the field in which this civilization left its greatest mark. Although the forms derived for the most part from the Greek experience, the use of materials and, above all, the building techniques were absolutely original.

**A Mason's Tools**
The equipment of masons in ancient Rome included trowels, compasses, and squares—tools that have remained more or less unchanged today.

The typical materials of ancient architecture were stone, brick, and wood for the structure of roofs. This was the basis for the elaboration of building forms (which under the Greeks had reached the apex of perfection) and the improvement of related building techniques. At the beginning, Rome also followed this path—for example, using mostly tufa, the soft volcanic stone that is plentiful in Latium. Soon (third century B.C.), however, a new, low-cost material was introduced, *opus caementicium*, which would completely revolutionize architecture. This was a mixture (we would call it concrete today), made from stone aggregate (*caementa*) bound together by a resistant mortar with a base of quicklime and sand, then poured into special molds. Compared to stone, it required considerably less labor and much less time for working and installation. Moreover, it guaranteed a high level of resistance, particularly if the mortar used was sand from Pozzuoli, the greatly renowned "pozzolana," which had superior static properties. Thus, it became customary to create the core of structures in *opus caementicium*, which would then be faced with valuable materials in imitation of traditional forms of Greek origin. And so, the latter lost their structural value to become simply ornaments for structures created using totally innovative methods.

**Building Machine**
In this funerary relief, a construction crane is depicted next to a building.

## THE FACING OF MASONRY BUILDINGS

The Romans worked out various ways to cover the concrete core of their structures. *Opus incertum* was very common, made from a facing of small irregular stones imbedded in concrete. Beginning in the first century B.C., the use of *opus reticulatum* became widespread. With this method, a series of "small bricks," pyramidal in form, were inserted with the top end facing into the cement core, creating a relatively regular grid of squares oriented at 45 degrees. In the imperial era, *opus latericium* was developed, whereby the facing was secured by courses of bricks inserted on edge, with the narrowest face into the concrete core. Brick facing could then be covered with marble slabs (*opus sectile*), which were plastered over or left exposed. In all cases, the application of uniform finishing elements made the work extremely rapid and productive in addition to guaranteeing walls of great cohesiveness.

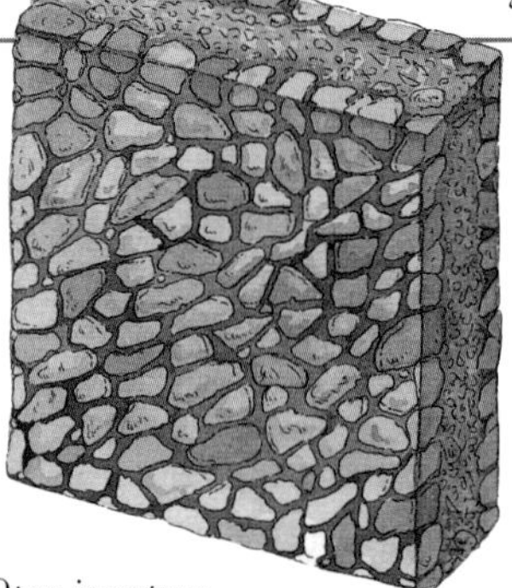

*Opus incertum*

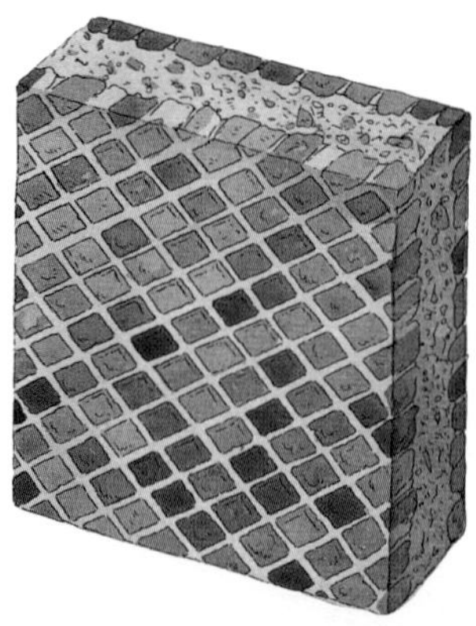

*Opus reticulatum*

## *Arches and Vaults*

The use of concrete was fundamental to another technical revolution, destined to have immense repercussions for the entire subsequent history of architecture: the adoption of the arch and the vault. The technique of the arch—a structure created from stone or brick elements arranged along a curved line so that each element pushes against the ones on either side, thus transmitting the weight—was not invented by the Romans. The Greeks and the Etruscans already knew about it, although they put it to very limited use. The Romans, however, adopted the arch on a large scale and made it the basis for their architecture. Above all, they applied it to the construction of vaults—namely, three-dimensional roof elements, quite different and much more complex than the wood trusses used by the Greeks.

These structures, which would have been difficult to create in stone or brick, became much simpler to build with concrete. In this way, an enormous and completely new field of experimentation opened up for Roman architects. It made possible temples like the Pantheon, grand halls like those of the baths, and vaulted spaces like those of Hadrian's Villa. The systematic use of arches and vaults became typical of Roman buildings and influenced the entire history of architecture to come.

**The First Arches**
The first Roman arches, almost certainly Hellenistic in derivation, were used in bridges or in utilitarian structures, particularly warehouses, from the early third century B.C. on. The monumental arched gateways, amply documented in central Italy, such as the Porta Marzia in Perugia *(left)* belong more or less to the same period.

**The Vault and the Dome**
Beginning with the arch, the Romans developed the barrel vault. The use of the cross vault, obtained from the intersection at right angles of two barrel vaults, dates back to the late republican era. A little later, the dome, or bowl vault, was introduced. It was obtained by rotating an arch around its axis of symmetry. *Above*, the interior of the dome of the Pantheon.

# Houses of the Romans—*Domus* and *Insula*

The *domus*, the typical house of the wealthy classes, was a variation of the traditional single-family dwelling found throughout the Mediterranean basin. The *insula*, however, a large block of residences, was an invention of Roman civilization.

The typical Roman house, the *domus*, evolved between the seventh and sixth centuries B.C. with a format that remained unchanged for centuries. This was a single-family dwelling (in the sense that this term had in Rome, where the *familia* included the various generations of a family and a large number of slaves). At the center was an atrium onto which the various rooms faced and from which they were illuminated. In fact, the exterior walls of the building were blank, with the exception of the entrance door and possibly some workshops (*tabernae*) inserted into the façade but without any communication with the rest of the house. The wing of the house opposite the entrance usually contained the public spaces: the *tablinum*, the owner's study, also utilized as a reception hall for visitors, and the *triclinium*, the dining room (sometimes divided into winter and summer triclinia). Behind these rooms was an open space, the *hortus*, which became a colonnaded courtyard, or *peristilium*, in the wealthiest and most important houses. The wings of the house to the sides of the atrium were generally reserved for the private rooms (*cubicula*) of the various family members. The entrance wing contained the kitchen and rooms for slaves. This scheme then had infinite variations, depending on the available space, the number of people

**The House of the Faun**
*Below*, view of the *peristilium* of the House of the Faun, an elegant Pompeian *domus* that gets its name from the statue of a dancing faun *(right)* found in its interior.

**Open-air Banquet**
*Above,* the summer *triclinium* of the House of the Cervi in Herculaneum.

in the family, the wealth and taste of the owner, and the height. Particularly in cities in the provinces, where land cost less and spaces were larger, it was not unusual for houses to be rather complex, with various peristyles and an intricate arrangement of spaces. But the classical layout with the atrium at the center and the house closed toward the outside was for the most part universally respected, from Britain to Africa, and was one of the constants of the Roman world.

## *The* Insula, *or Group Dwelling*

In many neighborhoods of Rome, but also in nearby Ostia, where housing needs were great and space was scarce, a completely new and specifically Roman type of dwelling came into being. This was the *insula*, or, as the name implies, a large building complex that occupied an entire block. Often the layout was the same as that of the *domus*: four wings built around a central courtyard. But these wings spread over many floors and were not occupied as single-family dwellings. Instead, they were divided into small or extremely small apartments (one, two, or three rooms), each rented to a different family unit. Crammed into these spaces were tradesmen, artisans, freedmen, professionals (doctors, midwifes, and scribes), and not infrequently young scions of the aristocracy who wanted to live away from the oppressive embrace of their families. Even if living conditions were infernal compared to today's standards—a constant uproar, discomfort, rather primitive hygienic conditions, and a serious and permanent risk of fire—the *insulae* were still a notable invention in terms of architecture and urban planning.

**ETRUSCAN ANTEFIX**
The antefix was a terracotta or marble ornament arranged along the cornice of the roof in Greek, Etruscan, and Roman buildings.

**WORKING-CLASS APARTMENT BLOCKS**
Reconstruction of an *insula*, the typical apartment block designed to be rented to working-class and lower-middle-class families.

### BARE WALLS, DECORATED ROOF

The exterior of even the most aristocratic Roman house was absolutely anonymous: when not masked by workshops, it consisted of a series of bare plaster walls with significant architectural form. Everything was "projected" inward. There was one place, however, where decoration could be glimpsed, or in certain cases might even be profuse—the roof. The surface covering was almost always in the Laconian-Corinthian style that originated in the Greek colonies of Sicily. It was characterized by flat tiles with raised edges alternating with semicylindrical bent tiles. Larger bent tiles protected the peaks and the hip line of the roofs; a series of decorative elements (slabs, cornices, antefixes) screened the ends of the wood beams and protected them from the weather. With the introduction of molded terracotta, the roof became the site of sumptuous painted openwork and relief decorations. Monumental openwork elements, acroteria, appeared on the bent tiles at the peak of the roof. The bent tiles at the ends were closed off by antefixes shaped like human masks. Sometimes these assumed the shape of fantastic animal heads. All elements visible from below were painted or ornamented with reliefs. Thus, they had a strong and evocative visual impact.

# Building Types

The Roman city boasted a variety and complexity of building types comparable only to modern cities. These constituted the greatest proof of the high degree of efficiency and specialization achieved by Latin civilization.

**The Triumph of Constantine**
Relief from the north face of the Arch of Constantine, depicting a wild boar hunt. The monument was erected in A.D. 315 near the Coliseum to celebrate the emperor's victory over Maxentius.

Single-family dwellings and *insulae*, temples, baths, theaters, amphitheaters, basilicas, streets and colonnaded squares, triumphal arches, celebratory columns, markets, libraries, mausoleums, circuses, aqueducts, massive structures and ports, bridges, granaries: these are only some of the building types that could be found in every Roman city—proof of the truly "urban" character of Latin civilization. No other ancient people came even close to this sort of diversification. Some of these—baths, amphitheaters, triumphal arches, aqueducts—are exclusively Roman and did not exist in other ancient civilizations. Others—theaters, celebratory columns, basilicas—while derived from other cultures, were profoundly rethought and modified. All these came together to make a Roman city a formidable complex that "framed" the life of the empire and contributed more than any other factor to the romanization of its territories.

## *Baths*

The widespread diffusion of building structures that had the function of satisfying certain primary needs of the population was typically Roman. But they fulfilled other functions, as well. The most striking of these perhaps were the amphitheaters, theaters, and circuses, where the immense Roman passion for spectacles and games found an outlet. The most useful structures were those that we would now call "infrastructures": wide paved streets, bridges, and markets like those erected by Trajan next to the imperial forums, aqueducts, and sewers. The most significant (and most typically Roman), however, were those destined for physical and mental well-being, such as the baths. These were places for the treatment of the body, where people could bathe in hot or cold water, receive massages, exercise their muscles in gymnastic activities, or relax at poolside. The baths also were social centers where readings of poetry and historic works took place, where well-stocked libraries could be consulted, and where friends and acquaintances could meet for philosophical and political discussions: one of Roman civilization's greatest creations.

**The Aqueduct of Segovia**
The aqueduct of Segovia (first century A.D.) is one of the boldest and most harmonious Roman architectural constructions, and it still traverses the Spanish city for approximately 800 meters. Built from square stone blocks, it has two tiers of superimposed arches that reach a height of 29 meters.

**The Baths of Trier**
Built in the fourth century A.D. and transformed into a fortress in the Middle Ages, the baths of Trier were among the largest in the empire. Impressive ruins *(above)* remain, as well as an extensive network of underground corridors.

## *Monuments of Power*

Almost all ancient peoples erected monuments to celebrate their rulers, gods, and triumphs, and the Romans were no exception. But some of the monuments they built, such as the triumphal arches and the celebratory columns, were extremely significant because they reflected certain peculiarities of the Roman world. The triumphal arch in particular is an entirely Roman "invention" that has no apparent analogy in other cultures of the classical era. It responds to the characteristic Roman need to exalt and commemorate generals who returned victorious from military campaigns and whose activities were the basis for the entire wealth of the state.

### THE FORMS OF BUILDINGS

The Romans were much more pragmatic than the Greeks, who attempted to reduce every type of building to a single archetype—that is, to a potentially immutable model. However, the Romans also established certain canonic forms for every type of construction, to be applied to every project. Thus for temples, a traditional rectangular layout on a high podium was preferred (except for certain major exceptions derived from features of worship, such as the Pantheon or the temple of Vesta). For theaters, the reinforced Greek semicircular form was repeated (with the important difference that the steps were supported by massive masonry structures and not resting against the slope of a hill, as in the Greek model; this allowed theaters to be built wherever needed, independent of the shape of the terrain). For amphitheaters, the elliptical or oval layout was standardized. Baths, particularly the most important ones, such as those of Caracalla and Diocletian in Rome, had a large central area surrounded by gardens. Aqueducts were built with various tiers of arches that decreased in height and width as they moved upward. Bridges were among the most varied structures in terms of layout. The shape and dimension of a bridge was strictly tied to the characteristics of the body of water that had to be traversed.

**In the Depths of the Amphitheater**
The word amphitheater is derived from the Greek *amphitheatron*, "theater in which spectators watch from all around," referring to the elliptical form of the building. *Above*, the underground areas of the amphitheater in Pozzuoli (Naples).

**The Pons Fabricius**
Built in 62 B.C., the Pons Fabricius in Rome *(below)* joins the Tiber Island to the left bank of the Tiber. Sixty-two meters long and 5.5 meters wide, it was constructed from blocks of tufa and peperino (volcanic rock). The central pylon, which supports two slightly depressed spans, has a small arch, designed to lessen the water pressure when the river waters swell.

# City and Regional Planning

The capacity to produce efficient systems of rationalization, colonization, and control of territory and to populate the territory with cities that functioned as tools for the export of Latin culture and for the political and cultural fusion between Romans and subject peoples was essential to the creation, consolidation, and maintenance of the empire.

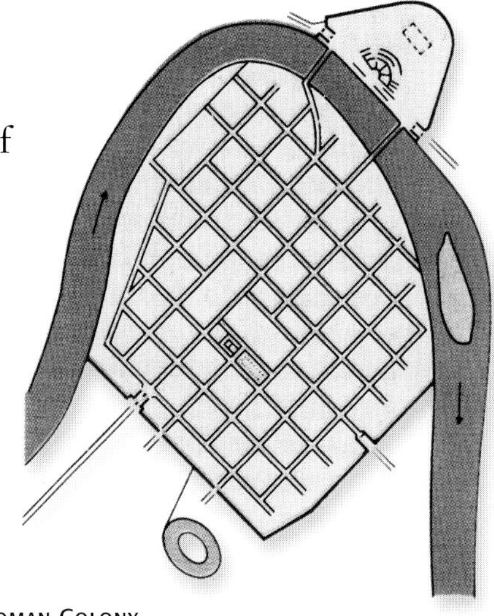

**Verona, Roman Colony**
The center of Verona is characterized by the *cardines* and *decumani* grid, typical of the Roman colonies, as seen in this map *(above)* from the *Corpus of the Gromatici*, a collection of Roman treatises on land-surveying and centuriation. Outside the enclosing wall was the Arena *(below)*, built in the first century A.D. and still perfectly suitable for use. Indeed every summer it is the venue for an opera season that draws tremendous crowds.

*Civilitas a civitate*, "civilization comes from the city," the Romans proclaimed. Surely they were thinking of their own civilization, which was essentially urban. Cities constituted an irreplaceable tool for the romanization of conquered territories. Throughout the empire, the Urbs exported an unambiguous model of the city, both as concept and as urban system. Conceptually, the city was seen as an administrative unit of the state—a cultural, military, and social center to which lesser settlements (*oppida, castella, fora, conciliabula, vici, pagi*) were subordinate and dependent. In terms of planning, the city was almost always organized around the intersection at right angles of two series of roads: the *cardines*, arranged from north to south, and the *decumani*, which ran east to west. The forum was built at the point where the principal *cardo* intersected the major *decumanus*, and the surrounding square was crowded with temples and public and commercial buildings. Typical Roman buildings were distributed throughout the main area of the city: a theater, baths, and so forth. Just outside the walls, there was usually an amphitheater, conveniently located so that inhabitants of

**The Via Aemilia**
The layout of roads had a strong and enduring influence on a territory. Evidence of this is provided by the Via Aemilia, built in 187 B.C. by Consul Marcus Aemilius Lepidus to link Rimini and Piacenza, which still gives its name to a region of Italy. *Above*, milestones from the Via Aemilia.

**The Western Portion of the Empire**
In the Augustan era, many cities of Gaul and Spain were given monumental centers (Arles, Nîmes, Tarragona) or enclosed within walls (Autum, Zaragoza, Barcelona). *Left*, a detail from a sarcophagus from Arles.

surrounding areas could also attend the spectacles.

The scheme for dividing a city into rectangular lots (called *hippodamic* by experts, from the name of the Greek planner Hippodamus of Miletus, who invented the system) was continued in the centuriation of territory. This was the division of farmland into regular lots of two hundred jugers, which was the basis for Roman agricultural colonization. In this manner, city and country were bound into a single, coherent plan of territorial organization, which left the typical imprint of the Roman mentality throughout the empire.

## *A Comprehensive Model*

The Roman urban planning model was also frequently imposed on lesser centers that had existed prior to the Latin conquest. Early on, the Celtic settlement of *Coninbriga* (present-day Coimbra) became the residential quarter for local notables and thus merged with the Roman city in the early imperial era. *Cularo* (today's Grenoble) was given a wall in the third century and, in the fourth century, was promoted to the rank of city with the name *Gratianopolis*. Even the *canabae*, the encampments that arose in the northern part of the empire next to legionary outposts, sometimes had buildings with monumental pretensions. Some, such as *Aquincum* (Budapest) and *Argentoratum* (Strasbourg), assumed the rank of city.

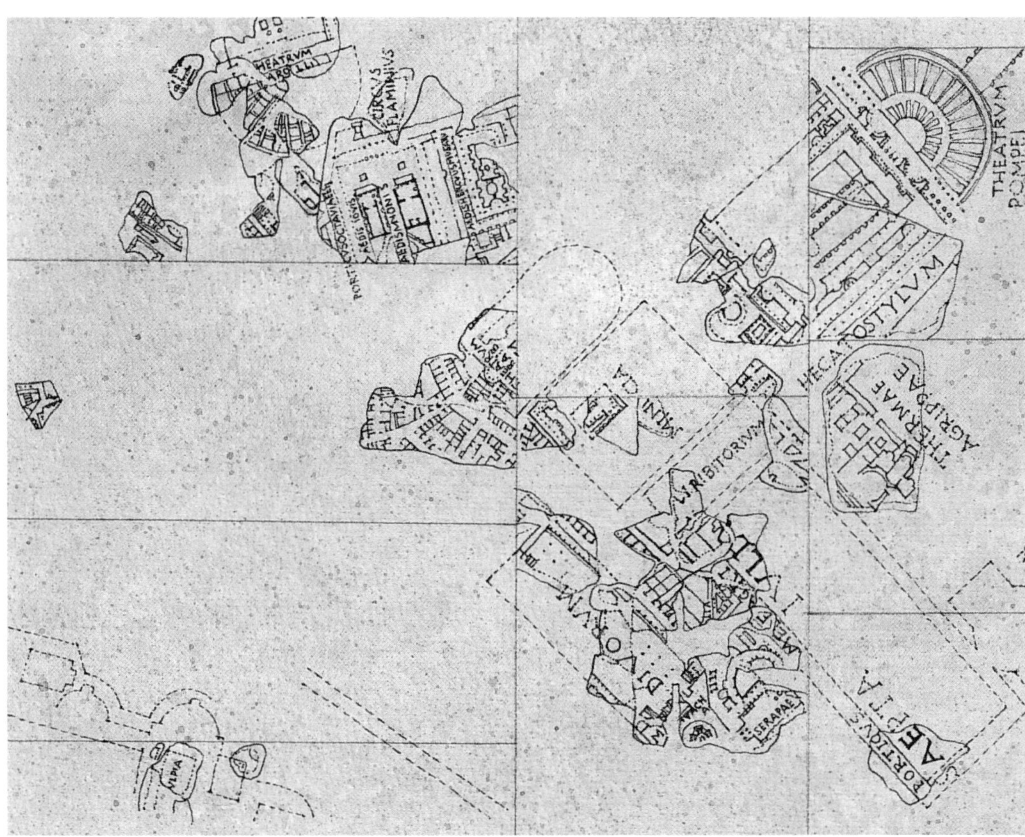


**A Partial Puzzle**
This drawing shows the reconstruction of the area of the Campus Martius, based on fragments of the *Forma Urbis* that have been recovered to date.

### THE *FORMA URBIS*

At the beginning of the third century A.D., a gigantic marble map of the city of Rome was made. For archeologists the surviving fragments represent a colossal puzzle to be reconstructed. This *Forma Urbis*, as it is called, originally measured 13 by 18 meters and was located in the Forum of Peace, built at the time of Vespasian. Created in sheets of marble that were meticulously connected to form a single surface, it represented, on a notably detailed scale (1:240) and in vertical projection, the entire fabric of the city. This included public and private buildings, temples, baths, streets, theaters, markets, and bridges. The names of many buildings are given. This leads people to believe that the project was created for a didactic, or what we would now call touristic, purpose. The map's tremendously precise rendering, however, not only of monuments but also of anonymous buildings demonstrates that it was compiled on the basis of a systematic and accurate relief of the type used for land surveys. And this is not an isolated creation, for we know from texts that similar *formae urbis* existed for provincial cities, as well.

# The Representation of Reality

Roman sculpture drew inspiration from many sources; and, in its more than one thousand years of history, it underwent an almost infinite series of stylistic variations. However, it steadily maintained one feature that makes it specific and distinctive: a passionate, irrepressible adherence to reality.

Ancient civilization did not love the portrait. Realistic representation was burdened with magical-religious ancestral ties, often forgotten but still alive on an unconscious level. It was not until the fourth century B.C. that Greek artists began to sculpt true portraits that, while not focusing precisely on physiognomic features, at least captured the moral characteristics of the subject portrayed. The Etruscans rarely departed from the depiction of various human types (the old man, the noblewoman, the obese person, and so on).

With the Romans, things were different. The worship of ancestors and their *imagines*, deeply rooted in the aristocracy, pushed sculptors to reproduce faithfully, as far as their technical abilities allowed, the

**Provincial Notable**
Numerous portraits from the republican era, from various Italian regions, survive to the present day, such as the bust to the right, from Fiesole (Florence). They provide significant testimony about the cultural climate of the Italic cities that, having overcome their differences with Rome, began participating actively in the political and economic life of the *res publica*.

**From Wax to Marble**
The origins of the portrait in ancient Rome may date to the custom of making wax death masks of family members. These images were then reproduced in the form of busts, first in wax, then in more durable materials, such as marble and bronze. *Below*, a relief depicting a sacrifice in honor of a deceased man. The presenter holds an image of his ancestor.

**Portrait of a Woman**
Roman portraiture has given us an immense gallery of personalities that, even today, bring to life the population of Latin society. *Above*, a bronze portrait of a noblewoman (first century A.D.).

DAUGHTER OF AUGUSTUS
During the era of Augustus and the Julio-Claudian dynasty, public portraiture underwent a change from a realistic to a more classicizing and idealized style. *Above*, a marble bust of Julia, the daughter of Augustus.

PORTRAIT OF VESPASIAN
Realism made a reappearance under the Flavians, as seen in this marble portrait bust of the emperor Vespasian. Later, under Diocletian and his successors, the features of the emperors were depicted in very stylized fashion to express the rulers' divine nature.

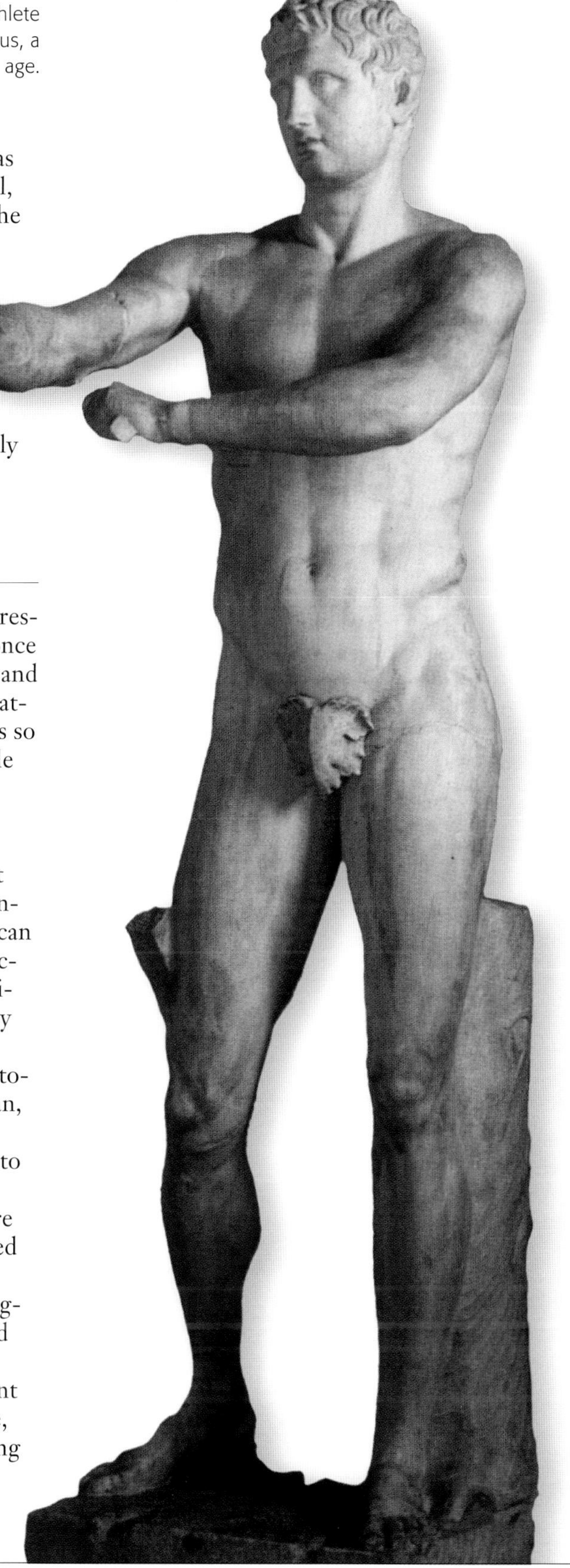

ROMAN REPLICA
A Roman copy of the *Apoxyómenos* ("Athlete scraping himself with a strigil") by Lysippus, a renowned Greek sculptor of the classical age.

specific physiognomy of their subjects. From the beginning, Roman statuary was involved with the portrait, in the faithful, sometimes merciless representation of the subject—an interest that never waned. Later Roman artists sought to capture not only the physical features but also the character of the person represented. This effort resulted in a splendid flowering of such work in the late republican and early imperial era, the golden age of Roman portraiture.

## *An Immense Production*

The works that have survived to the present day are but a fraction of those that once ornamented the houses, temples, roads, and squares of Roman cities. Most bronze statuary was melted down over the centuries so that the material could be reused. Marble sculptures often were thrown into kilns and burned up in order to extract lime. Nonetheless, the production of statues, reliefs, and decorations was so great that even the smallest surviving remnants constitute an immense legacy. In effect, we can speak of a full-fledged "industrial production" of sculptural products. Greek originals from the classical era were copied by the thousands to ornament villas, peristyles, palaces, and tombs. Not only aristocrats but every small provincial nobleman, newly-rich shopkeeper, and official with social-climbing pretensions felt obliged to fill his house with replicas of works by Scopas, Lysippus, or Praxiteles. An entire network of workshops and studios thrived on this activity. The great public works promoted by rulers to exalt their own dignity and that of their families constituted another source of work orders. All this activity has left us an incredible testament of extraordinary vigor, variety, and value, which place the Roman plastic arts among one of the great artistic creations of humankind.

# Painting and Mosaics

From celebratory paintings, created to be exhibited in triumphs, to refined mosaic compositions that embellished and enhanced floors and walls, Roman figurative art was without doubt one of the most versatile and original in the ancient world.

It is curious but also quite significant that Roman painting began with the celebration of the successes of war. In fact, as early as the third century B.C., a specific "triumphal" genre of pictorial representation was practiced along the banks of the Tiber. The goal of this art was to offer the people an illustrated account of victorious battles. The paintings were carried in triumphal processions and then brought to the Capitolium or wherever they might be admired by the greatest possible number of people. At more or less the same time, the first decorative paintings began to appear in sacred buildings, such as those in the temple of Salus, created about 304 B.C. by Fabius Pictor, the first Roman figurative artist that we know by name. We know little or nothing, however, about this work. The great archive of Roman painting and its trends appears later, for the most part in the Vesuvian centers buried by the large eruption of A.D. 79. Other works of the same type, discovered in Rome, particularly on the Palatine, can be added to this pictorial corpus. On the basis of these creations, in the nineteenth century the German scholar August Mau identified four styles of Roman painting spanning its evolution from the second century B.C. to the end of the first century A.D., a categorization that, with numerous adjustments, is still valid today. We know of another major line of Roman painting of an utterly different genre and source of inspiration. This work, connected with the Christian faith, began in the catacombs in the mid-first century and developed into the decorations of the Paleo-Christian basilicas built after the Edict of Constantine in 313. Nonetheless, painting always took second place to the great mosaic representations typical of Paleo-Christian art.

**Pebble Mosaic**
The oldest mosaic technique (but one used for centuries with results that were sometimes extremely refined) employed small colored pebbles and was in widespread use in the region of Greece. One of the most refined examples, depicting a hunting scene with Alexander the Great, comes from Pella in Macedonia.

**Tessera Mosaic**
The most common type of mosaic was made from tesserae, often glazed, with stupendous luminous effects. One of the most well-known motifs, replicated frequently in the late Hellenistic era, is of doves drinking water.

## *Mosaic*

If painting and sculpture are artistic expressions rooted in the stone age, mosaic is an original creation of Greco-Roman culture. Developed in Greece toward the end of the fifth century B.C., it was enthusiastically embraced in the Roman world. Originally, mosaics were composed of small colored pebbles; from the third century B.C. on, *opus tessellatum*, classic tessera mosaic, became popular. The Romans used it a great deal as a functional as well as a decorative element—for creating floors, for example, although today we consider this a medium primarily for wall decoration. The themes and techniques employed in the Roman world were nearly infinite and ranged from geometric compositions to floral and plant motifs, to scenes of hunting, war, and country life, to erotic, genre, and mythological subjects, and so on.

With the consolidation of the Christian religion, Biblical subjects, including depictions of saints, bishops, apostles, and doctors of the Church, became increasingly common. Indeed, mosaics (now almost exclusively for wall use) became one of most typical and widespread figurative expressions of Christian art, at least until the end of the Middle Ages.

Two Different Styles of Mosaic
Marble-inlay mosaic *(above)*, little used because of its great cost, was obtained from small sheets of precisely cut marble. The Paleo-Christian era was known for mosaics against a gold ground *(above right)*, where the figures stood out against a surface of gold tesserae.

Fourth Style in Pompeii
The frescoes of the House of Meleager in Pompeii *(below)* are a beautiful example of the so-called Fourth Style of Roman wall painting.

### THE FOUR STYLES OF ROMAN PAINTING

In 1872 August Mau theorized four styles of Roman painting, based substantially on the wall paintings of Herculaneum and Pompeii.

- **First Style** (widespread beginning in the second century B.C.): reproduction in polychrome stucco of structures and architectural elements.
- **Second Style** (first century B.C.): based on illusionistic paintings depicting complex architectural views with faux architecture that lead to other spaces and into distant natural settings.
- **Third Style** (age of Augustus and Tiberius): characterized by Egyptian-influenced and exotic decorative elements.
- **Fourth Style** (between 40 and 79 A.D.): walls painted with large mythological figures against strong architectural forms.

# Art and Craft

Ceramic, bronze, silver, gold, glass: Roman craftsmen worked skillfully in many different materials and created an extremely rich world of forms that still bring to life ancient Mediterranean culture.

**Ornamental Bronze**
A chariot ornament in bronze from Pannonia (third century A.D.), with Pan, Dionysus, and a satyr.

Contact with the Etruscans and then with the Greek cities of Campania acquainted the Romans with beautiful Attic ceramics and Etruscan black ware *(bucchero)*, with their elegant forms and ornate decoration. Later a veritable industry developed, based in the Greek islands, in the Peloponnesus, and in Campania, which furnished innumerable objects of everyday use—from amphorae to goblets and oil lamps to dishes—which were traded in every corner of the empire. This was an impressive production ranging from the roughest creations to items of supreme refinement and great value. Both techniques and forms often remained unaltered, sometimes for centuries; the result was one of the largest unitary markets in history.

## *Precious Metals*

Bronze was without a doubt the metal most widely used by the Romans. It was present in almost all aspects of daily life: furnishings, statues, innumerable useful objects (oil lamps, scalpels, objects for the toilette, dishes, pans, goblets, chalices, basins, ladles, and so forth). The Romans called it *aes*, the same word they used for copper, which was its principal component (from 70 to 90%, plus 10 to 30% tin and a small quantity of silver, lead, and zinc), and they were masters at working this material. Much more than iron (utilized in practice only for weapons and for specific tools that required considerable resistance), it was the basic metal for almost every creation in part because casting technology (in molds or by the lost-wax method) allowed it to be shaped with the greatest freedom and sense of fantasy so that effects of extreme refinement could be achieved. Silver and gold were considerably rarer, although war booty

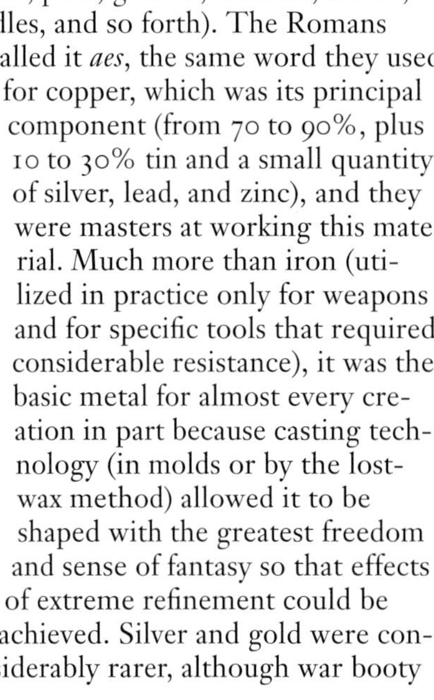

**A Masterpiece of Roman Cameo Glass**
The so-called Portland vase, one of the most refined works from the early imperial period, is decorated with complex scenes that may relate to the birth of Augustus and the Augustan age.

**Venus and Her Handmaidens**
The toilette of Venus, depicted on a silver vessel from Pompeii (first century A.D.).

CAMEO GLASS
This panel in blue glass and white vitreous paste depicts the initiation of Ariadne into the Dionysian mysteries. It dates from a period between the late first century B.C. and the early first century A.D.

brought them into the city in enormous quantity. More than for objects of ordinary use—limited to cups, basins, and drinking vessels—these rare metals were used to manufacture jewelry: necklaces, earrings, buckles, pendants, and bracelets. The forms were extremely varied, and yet the fact that similar objects were found even at opposite ends of the empire demonstrates the close ties between the various parts of the Roman world, particularly from the second century A.D. on. Thus a common taste developed wherever Latin civilization extended.

## *Fragile Glass*

The Roman world was the first to consistently appreciate and use glass objects. They were made by glassblowing, a technique that excluded the creation of large-scale objects but allowed Roman artisans to create objects of exquisite beauty and great artistic value. Skilled glass workers, generally from the East, were greatly appreciated in every corner of the empire. Their creations, which have emerged from excavations in ever-greater numbers, are among the most fascinating finds from the ancient world.

### A SECRET REVEALED

Roman glassmakers created objects of great artistic charm and superb workmanship, such as the famous "cameo glass" pieces, in which the basic form, created from various layers of different colors, was incised and polished, as in real cameos. These were often glass pieces with a blue ground and figures in white relief—highly prized in the ancient world as in modern times. Most Roman glass was simple, however, and without aesthetic pretenses; but a few pieces compensate for this formal simplicity with an extraordinary characteristic. If they are held against the light, they take on an iridescent coloration or change color (for example, changing from opaque green to translucent red). For a long time, it was thought that this extraordinary effect was due to a "secret" technique, lost over the course of time. Recent analyses, however, have shown that this was, much more prosaically, a simple deterioration of the material, often due to contact with the earth. In other words, it was a symptom of incipient decay, easily perceived to the touch. In fact, upon contact, small multi-colored flakes come off on the hands, a nightmare for restorers.

STAMPED CERAMIC
A typical Roman product was "stamped ceramic," recognizable by its brilliant coral red color. One such example, shown here, was found in Morocco (first century B.C.).

GLASS OF CHANGEABLE COLOR
A cup in green opaque glass that, placed against the light, becomes translucent red (fourth century A.D.).

# The Via Appia, "The Queen of Roads"

Created in 312 B.C. by the censor Appius Claudius to link Rome to Capua, the Via Appia was the first of the great Roman roads and the first to bear the name of its builder.

**Exceptional Transport**
*Above*, a relief from the Via Appia that depicts an elephant.

"Renowned, most excellent, queen of roads" was how the Via Appia was described in ancient times. Laid out in 312 B.C. by the censor Appius Claudius, it began initially at the Porta Capena and, after the building of the Aurelian Walls in the late third century A.D., at the Porta Appia, the present-day Porta San Sebastiano. The Via Appia linked Rome to Capua, the wealthy city that was the gateway to the south. In 268 B.C. it was extended to Beneventum, then later as far as Brundisium, thereby arriving at the large port that was the point of departure for Greece and the East. The Via Appia was the principal artery for trade and Roman military communications and was the most famous, significant, and well-traveled route in the entire empire. It was the first great Roman road to bear the name of the magistrate responsible for its planning—an honor never before granted to a Roman. Until that time, roads had taken the name of their city of destination (Nomentana, Tiburtina, Ardeatina, Praenestina) or of the peoples whose territories they traversed (Via Latina). A sole exception was the Via Salaria, which linked Rome to the Adriatic, source of salt *(sal)*, the precious commodity used for the preparation and preservation of food.

**The Roman Campagna**
The first stretch of the Via Appia outside the city preserves a bit of the charm of the Roman Campagna, which strongly influenced nineteenth-century literary figures and painters.

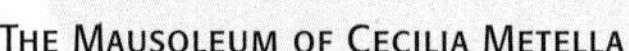

**The Mausoleum of Cecilia Metella**
At the third mile of the Via Appia is one of the most famous Roman sepulchral monuments, the mausoleum of Cecilia Metella. She was a member of a great noble *gens* of the republican era. The circular building still has some of its original marble-slab facing.

## *From Military Route To Commercial Highway*

Rome's principal reason for creating the Via Appia was strategic: to link the Urbs with the garrisons that were stationed to control Campania, where the Samnites had one of their strongholds. The original military function soon became secondary, however, and the Via Appia became the fundamental axis for the ever-growing trade between the capital and the territories of Campania, where the ports received goods from every part of the Mediterranean and where much of the mercantile and economic interests of the senatorial aristocracy was concentrated. The road also became the obligatory route for everyone—merchants, military, officials—who left for the East, and it soon became a crucial axis for the entire roadway system of southern Italy.

**The Column of Brundisium**
One of the two columns erected at the port of Brundisium to mark the end point of the Via Appia still stands, well preserved. The other, which collapsed in the sixteenth century, was later given to the city of Lecce, where it now serves as the impressive base for a statue of Sant'Oronzo.

## *Continuous Improvement*

Originally, the Via Appia was simply an unpaved road made by joining and straightening a series of earlier routes. Soon the urban section was paved, and then the rest. Its management became one of most onerous but coveted administrative positions in Rome, one that Caesar himself was happy to assume. Even during times of crisis, the maintenance and feasibility of the long road were of primary importance for the Roman state. The emperor Trajan focused great attention on the Via Appia, and, near the narrowing in the road at Terracina, he had excavated a bold "cut" in the rock, where the road was embanked to protect it from stormy seas. The emperor also improved the final stretch of road, which was renamed the Via Traiana.

### A ROAD OF MONUMENTS

The first stretch of the Via Appia outside the city is one of the most famous "postcard views" of Rome for archeologists and tourists. It is characterized by the silhouettes of monuments, including tombs and mausoleums of both great Roman families and humble citizens and freedmen, as well as a rolling landscape punctuated by clusters of pines. In fact, the entire route was studded with monuments, many of which were quite notable (such as the celebrated "Spindle" near Capua [*below*]), evidence of the road's immense importance.

# The *Domus Aurea*, Nero's Utopia

Immediately after the great fire of Rome in A.D. 64, Nero brought to completion a plan he had been considering for some time: a house worthy of an emperor in its size, sumptuousness, and symbolism.

**Entrance to the Palace**
*Above*, one of the entrances to the *Domus Aurea*. The complex occupied the entire southeast section of the Urbs.

The great fire of Rome was an enormous tragedy, but it also had a positive side: it provided Nero with a way to start work on his own urban planning projects, which called for the rebuilding of the city according to more modern and rational criteria, with broad roads and buildings distanced from one another to diminish the risks of another devastating fire. The emperor took advantage of the occasion to undertake, along with these projects "of public utility," a venture to which he attached particular importance: a palace that could be called truly imperial, which he named the *Domus Aurea*, "The Golden House."

**The Oppian hill**
View of the Oppian hill, beneath which lie the ruins of the *Domus Aurea*. The residence was built in an extremely short time, from A.D. 64 to 66.

## *Building Programs and Architects*

The grandiose design incorporated not only the Palatine and Esquiline into the complex but also the entire Caelian hill and the small valley below it, where the Coliseum later was erected. This was a veritable city within the city and even included a large lake, dominated by a gigantic statue of the emperor. Two architects, Severus and Celer, and one inspired decorator, Fabullus (or Famulus), were called upon to accomplish this project, and the emperor enjoined them to create "a dwelling worthy of a man." Although the people continued to love the emperor, the takeover of such a significant part of the center of the city aroused protests and grumbling, and construction costs skyrocketed. And so Vespasian, who ascended the throne after Nero's death, hastened to give back to the city the areas that had been expropriated by his predecessor, and much of the *Domus Aurea* was dismantled. Only a relatively small section was saved, on the Mons Oppius (Oppian hill), incorporated into the foundation of the large baths built by Trajan in A.D. 109.

## *Source of Inspiration for Architects and Decorators*

What remains is a complex of rooms articulated in two sections, which occupy a space of about three hundred by two hundred meters. To the west is a large rectangular courtyard, surrounded by porticoes, onto which an ample nymphaeum opens. At the center, the building narrows around one room, called the room "of the golden vault," characterized by a sumptuous decorative scheme. The eastern part revolves around a vast octagonal hall. Differences in concept are apparent, due to many possible causes, ranging from the presence of two different building yards with different designers to a chronological difference in the two wings. Nonetheless, the entire complex is unified to some extent by the superb decorative scheme that ornamented the palace and that, although partially destroyed, had a strong impact on Renaissance and Baroque artists that gave rise to an entire, prolific artistic school.

**Renaissance Tapestry**
The grotesques on this 16th-century tapestry were inspired by the paintings in Nero's *Domus Aurea*.

### THE ORIGINS OF GROTESQUES

Toward the end of the fifteenth century, people began to descend into the grottos of the Oppian hill and bring to light the wonders of the *Domus Aurea*. Many Renaissance artists, lowering themselves into the underground spaces, were struck by the style of the paintings preserved there. Thus they began to appropriate subjects and forms: fanciful plants and animals, human figures, and geometric motifs arranged in airy and bizarre compositions. Because these paintings had been discovered in the grottos, they became known as *grotesques*.

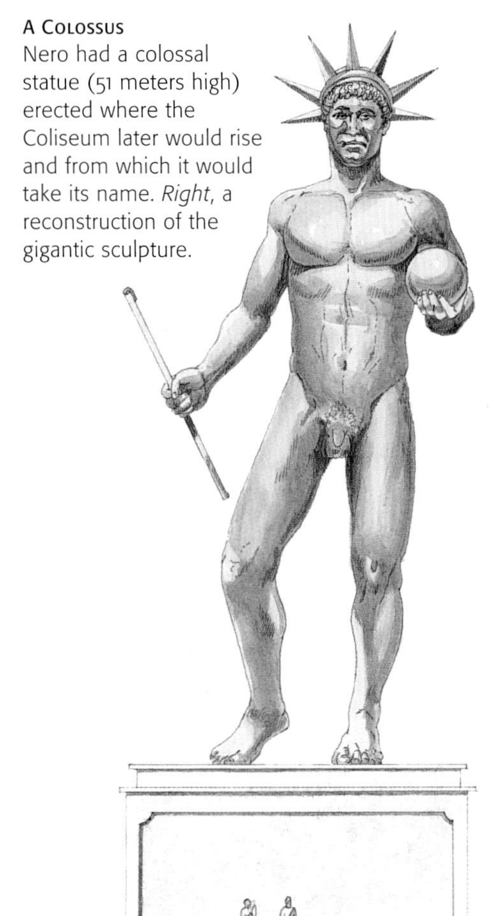

**A Colossus**
Nero had a colossal statue (51 meters high) erected where the Coliseum later would rise and from which it would take its name. *Right*, a reconstruction of the gigantic sculpture.

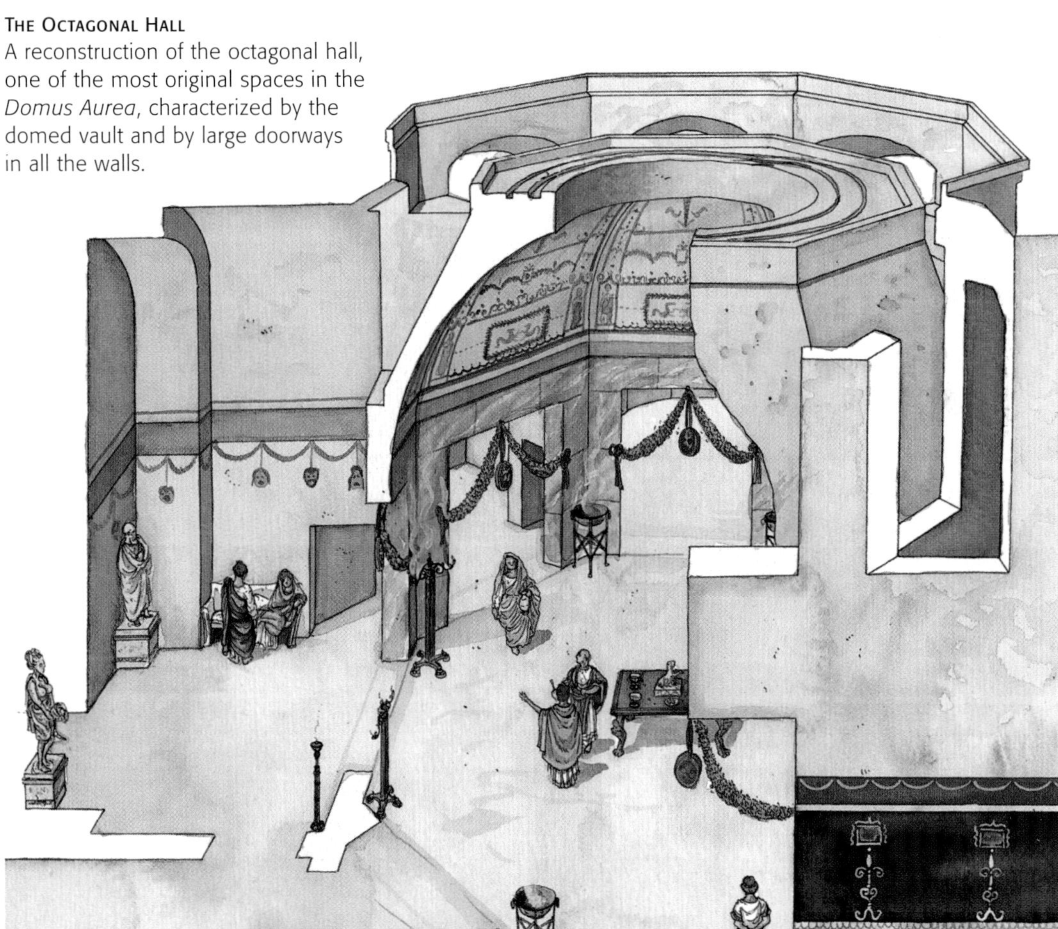

**The Octagonal Hall**
A reconstruction of the octagonal hall, one of the most original spaces in the *Domus Aurea*, characterized by the domed vault and by large doorways in all the walls.

# The Coliseum, Symbol of the Empire

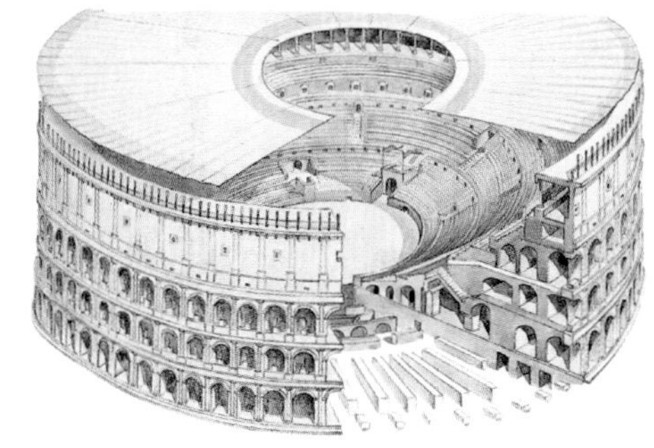

Begun under Vespasian, inaugurated by his son Titus, and completed by Domitian, the *Amphitheatrum Novum*, known today as the Coliseum, is the most famous monument in Rome, the symbol of Urbs and empire.

In the mid-first century A.D., Rome still lacked something other cities had had for more than a century: a large-scale masonry amphitheater capable of accommodating the spectacles people loved most: gladiatorial combats and *venationes*, hunting shows with ferocious exotic beasts. Taking an action with strong political consequences, Vespasian ordered the building of such a structure near the forum on the site of the artificial lake attached to Nero's *Domus Aurea*. Thus a building constructed for the people took the place of an emperor's arrogant private luxury. The great travertine ring, with four architectural orders reaching a height of fifty meters, enclosed massive theater-style seating that was reached through eighty arcades, each marked by a

### THE AWNING

The "marvelous technology" of the amphitheater was the *velarium* (*above*, in a reconstruction), the ingenious awning system that protected spectators from the sun. At the top of the attic, one still can see some of the corbels that supported a series of poles that projected over the building. Screens were attached to these, and, using a complex system of ropes, they were unfurled or rewound, according to need. The principle was similar to the one utilized for maneuvering boat sails. In fact, special teams of sailors were employed to work the awning, and barracks were built for them nearby.

**Bloody Spectacles**
A detail from a mosaic depicting combat between gladiators. This comes from Terranova near the ancient Latium city of Tusculum.

number to facilitate the flow of spectators. There were four principal entrances, corresponding to the axes of the oval. The largest was the *Triumphalis* gateway, by which entered the processions that initiated the spectacles. On the opposite side was the *Libitinaria* gateway, dedicated to the goddess Libitina, connected to the cult of the dead. In fact, this was the door through which the arena's victims were taken out. The stone seating area was divided into three concentric sections (*maeniana*). A fourth section, at the top, had steps made from wood (*maeianum summum in ligneis*). At the south end of the short axis, toward the Caelian hill, was the imperial box.

## *"When the Coliseum Falls, Rome Shall Fall"*

The immense structure in its present form has suffered much damage, particularly the interior, which was pilfered systematically over the centuries. The disappearance of the steps (*gradus*) and the arena have left exposed the interior and underground passageways that made up the "belly" of the complex—the distribution system that allowed it to function. The stage machinery (inclined planes, mobile and rotating platforms, elevators moved by counterweights), which made it possible to introduce scores of animals into the arena at the same time and to rapidly change the sets, has also disappeared. Despite the plundering, the amphitheater remains an impressive creation, worthy of the name Coliseum that it was given early on. Its bulk astonished everyone who visited Rome, to the point that it was considered the "spectacle" par excellence in the Urbs, indeed the city's symbol. In the Middle Ages, many believed in the prophecy made by the monk Bede in the eighth century: "While the Coliseum stands, Rome shall stand; when the Coliseum falls, Rome shall fall; when Rome falls, the world shall fall."

**Interior of the Coliseum**
As in today's theaters, the Coliseum had different categories of seats, which depended not on the price of the ticket (normally spectacles were free) but on the spectator's social class. The places closest to the arena were assigned to members of senatorial rank, the next tiers to members of the equestrian order, and so on, with a gradual rise upward in the tiers as the social order descended.

**The Missing Pieces**
Beginning in the fourteenth century, the Coliseum, already damaged by earthquakes, became a veritable travertine quarry from which material was taken to build many monuments in Rome. The removal ended in the eighteenth century, when Pope Benedict xv declared the Coliseum sacred because of the blood shed there by Christian martyrs.

# THE *PALATIUM*, HOME TO THE EMPERORS

On the Palatine hill, the sacred site where, according to tradition, Romulus founded the Urbs, rose the majestic residences of the Roman emperors.

Palace, *palazzo, palais, palast, palacio*: in many modern languages the terms that designate the city residence of kings and nobles are very similar, and this is no accident. The words derive from the *Palatium* of the Roman emperors, which in turn is connected to the name of the hill on which it stands, the Palatine. In the republican and early imperial eras, this area was still a residential zone, lined with the homes of the wealthy senatorial families most in the public eye. However, it also included some of the most sacred places of worship and sites related to the most ancient memories of Rome. Therefore, Augustus's decision to establish his own residence on the hill was not a casual one. The imperial residence was linked directly to the beginning of Rome's history. Despite this, the *Palatium* still maintained the appearance of a normal dwelling, if more luxurious. It was Augustus's successors who transformed it into a true palace, which gradually expanded until it occupied the entire hill. Indeed under Nero, the imperial palaces "overflowed" the Palatine to invade the surrounding areas, toward the Esquiline and the Caelian hills. After the period of Nero's megalomania, the imperial complex withdrew once again to the Palatine, occupying the hill with a series of new structures that, from the time of Vespasian, continued to be built in layers, more or less until the time of Constantine.

### IMAGE OF THE PALACE

Although the ruins of the imperial palace are very suggestive, in ancient times the *Palatium* must have looked quite different, with its colonnaded facades, walls painted or covered with multicolored marble slabs, paintings, statues, and sumptuous furnishings. The collections of the Palatine Museum give an idea of how it might have looked. Most of what remains are sculptures of the highest quality, but they are a pale reflection of the masterpieces that the palace must have held during its golden age.

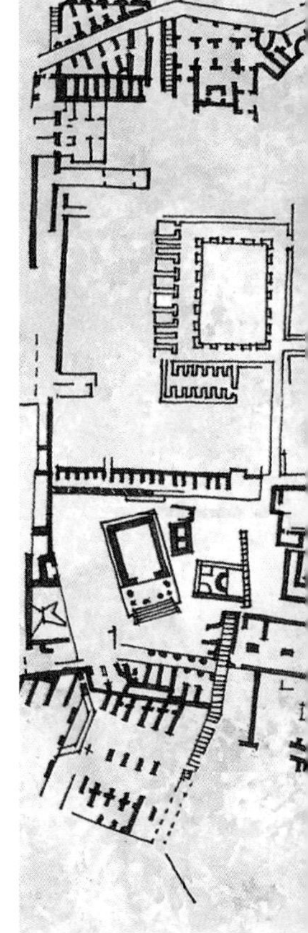

**A LABYRINTH OF BUILDINGS**
Reconstructed plan of the imperial *Palatium*. At the center is the peristyle with a fountain, and to the right the stadium of Domitian, both illustrated below.

## Domus Flavia *and* Domus Augustana

The decisive moment for the development of the *Palatium* was the Flavian period. In fact, part of the grand complex, the portion that people have attempted to identify (without complete certainty, however) with the "public" area set aside for the ruler's

**PERISTYLE WITH FOUNTAIN**
View of the large rectangular peristyle of the *Domus Flavia* with the "labyrinthine" fountain.

**THE HIPPODROME**
The hippodrome, which enclosed the east side of Domitian's palace, is 160 meters long and 80 meters wide.

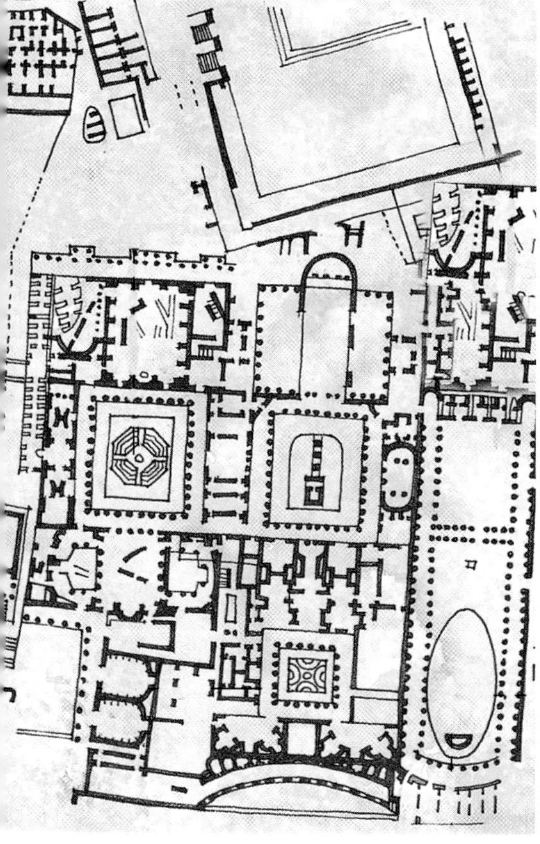

**Imperial Amusements**
Another view of Domitian's stadium, which probably was designed for strolling and for the emperors' sporting activities, particularly of an equestrian nature.

**Private Rooms**
The apartment of Livia, the wife of Augustus, was decorated with elegant paintings.

official activities, is called the *Domus Flavia*. To the side, another intricate complex was erected, the *Domus Augustana*, considered (again without proof) the "private" zone, reserved for imperial family life. Inside the residence were rooms of every type, peristyles, exedrae, gardens, temples, baths, even a stadium (hippodrome) reserved for the sovereign's recreational activities: an incredible, fascinating interweaving of spaces and functions, probably built in large part during the time of Domitian and then infinitely modified. We know the name of the architect for the initial project, a certain Rabirius, about whom we would like to know more, for he was able to conceive an impressive and innovative building, destined to become the model for all later palaces.

## ENTRANCE TO THE PALACE

The principal entrance had a monumental façade of which some pillars remain. According to a hypothetical reconstruction, three portals preceded by steps accentuated the verticality of the building. A row of windows brought light to the interior. The entire complex may have been surmounted by a colonnade in the form of a temple.

**A Continuous Evolution**
Another group of spaces that Domitian had built. After him, new grandiose projects were executed by Septimius Severus.

**The Room of the Masks**
Detail of paintings in the Room of the Masks in the interior of the *Domus Augustana*.

# The Forum, Heart of the City

Every Roman city had its forum, an open space at the center of the inhabited area, used as a location for the principal city temples, for the market, and for political demonstrations. But none could equal the Roman forum, the pulsating heart of the empire.

The Roman forum occupied a quadrangular area, once swampy, bound by the Palatine, Caelian, and Capitoline hills. Originally, it was the seat of numerous activities of a commercial, political, and ritual nature. With the passage of time and the increase in the city's prestige, however, mercantile exchanges, athletic competitions, and similar events moved to specialized markets, theaters, circuses, and amphitheaters. This left the forum a venue for political and major religious activities.

Until the fall of the empire, the forum functioned as the undisputed center of political, social, and religious life for the entire Roman world. Here stood temples dedicated to the major gods and also the most important basilicas. There were countless symbols of the empire, from the milestone, which served as a point of reference for all distances measured along the consular roads, to the house of the Pontifex Maximus and the vestals, to the Curia,

**Pagan Temple and Christian Church**
One of the most characteristic monuments in the Roman forum is the temple of Antoninus and Faustina *(right)*, erected in A.D. 141 by the emperor Antoninus Pius, who dedicated it to his wife Faustina. Today the building is incorporated into a church built in 1602.

**The Temple of Saturn**
*Below right*, view of the Roman forum with the ruins of the temple dedicated to Saturn in the foreground. Inside was a statue of the divinity, which was carried in a procession during triumphal ceremonies.

**Temple of Venus Genetrix**
Caesar, who maintained that he was a direct descendent of Aeneas, in turn the son of Venus, wanted a temple dedicated to Venus Genetrix in the forum. Three Corinthian columns remain *(left)* from the exterior colonnade.

where the Senate met. If there was one place in Rome sacred to the city's memory, it was the forum.

## *Caesar's Creation*

About 54 B.C., Caesar decided to build a new forum, the *Forum Iulium*, next to the Roman forum, to perpetuate the name of his family. The idea was practical (the forum at that point threatened to "explode" under the weight of all the functions it had to support, and an expansion was undoubtedly desirable), but unprecedented. Until then, victorious generals had built their own celebratory monuments in peripheral locations without daring to intrude on the city center. This step required a person of Caesar's immense ambition. The project was inaugurated, still unfinished, in 46 B.C., two years before Caesar was killed, and it was brought to completion by his successor, Octavian Augustus, and then was completely rebuilt during the reign of Trajan. Its regular form, dominated by the temple of Venus Genetrix, and even more its celebratory function, came to serve as a model. Indeed, the forum of Caesar was the first of a series of similar but larger creations connected to subsequent emperors, known collectively as the "imperial forums," which expanded the forum area as far as the Quirinal hill.

**The Charm of the Ruins** The ruins of the Roman forum in an engraving from the first half of the nineteenth century.

## *The Imperial Forums*

After the forum of Caesar, which acted as a bridge between the old Roman forum and the new creations, a series of forums were established by Augustus, Vespasian, Nerva, and Trajan. They were all based on the concept of a large, open, porticoed square around a temple or a public building of great importance. The forums fulfilled two important functions. On the one hand, they were colossal monuments that celebrated the ruler; on the other hand, they expanded and articulated the vital nerve center of the Urbs, the true center of Roman life and society. At its height, this apparently infinite expanse of columns, statues, temples, libraries, basilicas, and public buildings must have been impressive and contributed in no small degree to the fame and prestige of the imperial capital.

**Reconstruction of the Square of Trajan's Forum** The principal sources for the reconstruction of Trajan's forum are the fragments of the *Forma Urbis*, views of buildings depicted on coins of the time, brief descriptions by ancient authors, and architectural details still in situ.

# Hadrian's Villa, Anthology of Imperial Memories

A "city in the form of a villa" in an excellent state of preservation: Hadrian's Villa is one of the most fascinating monuments left to us by antiquity.

Hadrian was the promoter of an intense surge of building activity in Rome and throughout the empire. The results are seen most impressively in the villa he built near Tivoli, the Pantheon, and the mausoleum he erected along the banks of the Tiber. The villa, built in an area already occupied by a villa from the second century B.C., is a microcosmic complex. It is a small city devoted to imperial leisure, with large peristyles, porticoes and hidden porticoes, nymphaea, artificial lakes, temples, bath complexes, and recreation pavilions interspersed with open spaces and gardens.

The emperor wanted to reproduce in a free interpretation the famous places of antiquity that he had visited: the Lyceum, the Academy, the Canopus, the Poikilé, and the Prytaneum in Athens.

The Small Temple of Venus
*Right*, a reconstruction of the famous small circular temple of Knidos, the site of the statue of Aphrodite of Knidos by Praxiteles, a copy of which was found amid the ruins.

## WORKS OF ART

According to written accounts, Hadrian gathered a vast collection of artworks in his villa. These included Greek originals and Roman copies of paintings and sculpture, as well as masterpieces of the minor arts. Only a very small portion of these has been recovered, but they are sufficient to imagine the original magnificence of the imperial residence. Particularly noteworthy are two splendid centaurs in gray marble (now in the Capitoline Museum), masterpieces signed by two sculptors, Aristeas and Papias, and originally from the celebrated School of Aphrodisia in Asia Minor. The series of copies of Greek originals from Canopus are also memorable. The emperor's cultural passions are illustrated by the rich collection of copies of portraits of Greek philosophers. The splendid mosaic floors, particularly those in *opus sectile*, polychrome marble inlay, merit a separate discussion. This technique became extremely popular in this period and would find ample expression in late antiquity.

## *Strongly Innovative Architecture*

In the design of the villa (which, as far as we can tell from traces still visible in the structures, underwent numerous modifications and various adaptations over the years), Hadrian and his architects created a strongly original architecture. The choice of construction techniques (the revival of *opus reticulatum*, which had long fallen into disuse) and, above all, the planimetric and structural methods were significant. There was an extensive use of mixtilinear plans, of complex composite vaults and domes, and of visual perspectives that skillfully establish a network of relationships among the various parts.

HADRIAN'S VERSAILLES
*Above*, one of the reliefs discovered at Hadrian's Villa. Because of the dramatic aspect of its buildings and the wealth of artworks preserved there, the residence of the emperor Hadrian has been compared to the palace of Versailles.

## *A Synthesis of the Classical Cultural Legacy*

Unfinished upon the emperor's death and neglected by his successors, Hadrian's Villa is a true architectural legacy in which the cultural complexity of its creator can be glimpsed. The building program attempted through certain symbols to summarize the entire heritage of classical civilization. Through it, we can detect the cultural anxiety and chronic restlessness of the emperor, one of the most cultivated and problematic figures in Roman history.

THE GREAT BATHS
*Below*, the remains of the Great Baths, part of an imposing group of buildings situated in the central portion of Hadrian's Villa, which also included the Small Baths and the Vestibule.

THE MARITIME THEATER
*Left*, view of the Maritime Theater, perhaps the most unusual structure at Hadrian's Villa. It consisted of a circular court with a pool at the center of which was a sort of miniature villa with a small peristyle, triclinium, and a bath complex.

# Trajan's Column, Monument to Victory

Ideal center of the imposing *Forum Ulpium*, the largest and most complex of the imperial forums, the great column that celebrates the exploits of the emperor Marcus Ulpius Traianus has fascinated artists, literary figures, and pontiffs for centuries.

In A.D. 107, following his great victory against the Dacians, the emperor Trajan conceived a plan for a large forum in celebration of his feat. The project, entrusted to the architect Apollodorus of Damascus, was inaugurated in 112. The level area below the Capitoline was already completely occupied by the Roman forum and then by the forums of Caesar, Augustus, and Nerva, so a space connecting the Capitoline and the Quirinal was cleared and a gigantic complex erected. This included a large colonnaded square, an immense basilica (the largest covered space in Rome), a small square flanked by two libraries (one Latin, the other Greek), and a temple dedicated to the emperor. To the side was a gigantic exedra, designed to contain the new city markets. At the center of the entire complex was a fascinating monument, a celebratory column, as high as the hill that had been demolished to make room for the new forum. For centuries this column would stand as one of the symbols of Roman civilization.

**At the Top of the Column**
The statue of Trajan that crowned the column was lost during the sack of Rome by the barbarians. In the late sixteenth century, a statue depicting St. Peter was installed in its place.

## *A Filmstrip of Conquest*

Built from blocks of Carrara marble, the column is approximately 40 meters tall in all. The shaft alone is 100 Roman feet high (*columna centenaria*), corresponding to 29.78 meters. At the summit, which can be reached by an interior staircase, was a gilded statue of the emperor, now replaced

**War Chronicle**
The reliefs of Trajan's Column *(left and detail above)* merge elements from the Hellenistic tradition with typically Roman content involving the narration of historical events.

**Propitiatory Gesture**
Trajan, at the center, sacrifices a bull to Neptune before embarking on his campaign against the Dacians. The emperor appears some sixty times in the story sculpted into the stone of Trajan's Column.

## MONUMENT AND MAUSOLEUM

Trajan's Column is not only a monument that exalts the exploits of the emperor; for centuries it was also his tomb. The altar-shaped base, decorated with reliefs depicting weapons wrested from enemies, once contained golden urns that held the ashes of Trajan and his wife Plotina. This is the ultimate meaning of the column: a celebratory monument created during the emperor's lifetime, which, at his behest, became his memorial in eternal triumph.

## THE COLUMN'S FATE

Trajan's Column had the good fortune to be consecrated to the Christian religion and thus protected by the popes. Its unusual appearance and exceptional cycle of reliefs served as a model that was repeated in infinite variations. In the Renaissance artists had themselves lowered in baskets from the summit to copy the reliefs along the shaft and draw inspiration for their own work. The idea of a column decorated with spiral reliefs was taken up many times in antiquity (the Antonine Column in Rome and those of Theodosius and Arcadius in Constantinople) as well as in the modern era (as in Paris in the Place Vendôme and in London in Trafalgar Square).

by one of St. Peter. It is the first known example of a *columna cochlis*, a column with an interior staircase and exterior sculpture in a spiral format. It is also the first such monument to be completely decorated according to a scheme that later would be applied in other monuments: the sculpted band with projecting and irregular edges resembles a gigantic scroll of writing (*volumen*), such as those preserved in the two libraries that flanked the monument. It is an approximately 200-meter-long strip, entirely covered with reliefs that tell the story of the campaign against the Dacians. One might say it is a veritable "filmstrip" of Trajan's great undertaking. The emperor appears some sixty times, in military actions, addressing his troops, at sacrifices, and receiving homage from defeated enemies. Despite this evident glorification, his stance is always that of a man conscious of his role as commander, never that of an emperor endowed with divine power and attributes (as the sovereign would become in later Roman iconography).

**Polychrome Column**
This reconstruction of the north-south elevation of Trajan's Forum also includes the column. It was originally painted and embellished with metal friezes.

# The Aurelian Walls, the City's Defense

In A.D. 271 the proud city of Rome, which for centuries had not faced enemies on the Italian peninsula, had to confront the problem of creating a new masonry enclosing wall.

For centuries the Urbs had not needed to protect its agglomeration of built-up areas. Ruler of the world, it was totally open, undefended. Its only walls were those attributed to King Servius Tullius, which in reality had been built in the fourth century B.C. Long stretches of these survived; but, even in the time of Augustus, their value was totally symbolic, and they were preserved and repeatedly restored because they had sacred or legal rather than defensive value. Moreover, the city had long overflowed the walls to occupy an extensive swathe of surrounding territory. In the eighth decade of the third century A.D., however, the situation changed profoundly. In fact, in 270, an invasion of the Alemanni arrived as far as Pavia before being repelled with difficulty by the emperor Aurelian.

Porta Maggiore
Built by the emperor Claudius, at the intersection of the Via Prenestina and the Via Labicana, this later was enclosed within the Aurelian Walls.

For decades the Italian borders had been under constant threat, and the capital itself could no longer consider itself safe from enemy incursions. Its tranquility vanished forever.

## *Military Architects, Civilian Labor*

The plan for the walls was studied by military architects, probably under the supervision of the emperor himself. However, it was not the army, which was engaged at the borders, that provided the labor. Instead, civilians were called upon to participate in the undertaking. Members of all the urban associations in Rome became involved; in compensation for their labor, they received the title *aureliani*. Construction was carried out in brick, the material most easily available and usable. Kilns on the outskirts of the city produced the bricks, and numerous existing buildings were incorporated into the design and

Porta San Pancrazio
*Above*, the gateway erected in 1644 at the high point of the Janiculum corresponds to the ancient Porta Aurelia of the Aurelian enclosure, where the Aurelian consular road began.

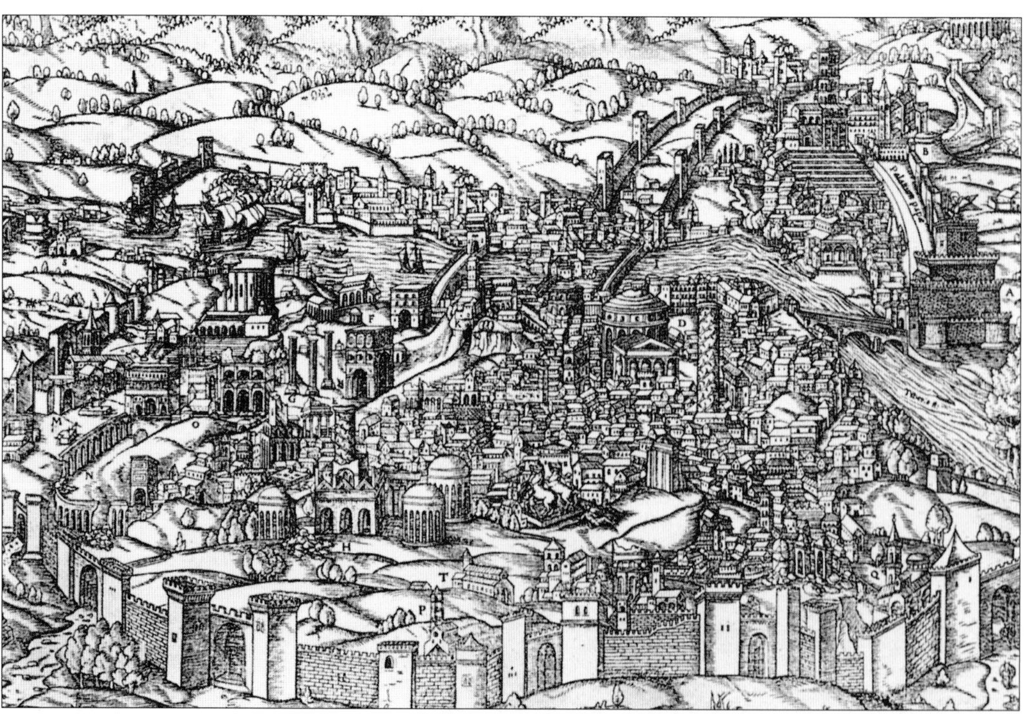

Rome in the Renaissance
In this engraving, which depicts the city of Rome in 1549, the masonry enclosure that the emperor Aurelian had built is easily visible.

**The Largest Gate in Rome**
Porta San Sebastiano, built to replace the ancient Porta Capena when Aurelian expanded the city walls, was the starting point for the Via Appia.

### PORTA SAN SEBASTIANO

The seventeen gates to Rome are some of the city's most fundamental architectural elements. One of the most significant is the Porta Appia, now known as the Porta San Sebastiano. Its structure dates from the time of Honorius (early fifth century A.D.), and it originally had two arches. One was later closed and incorporated into a new gate enclosed by semicircular towers. An internal court also was created with an interior door. San Sebastiano now contains the Museum of the Walls and is the starting point for a walk along the ancient ramparts, still in a good state of preservation.

equipped as strongholds for the new structure. Not only were the *Castra Praetoria* subjected to this fate but also the Amphitheater Castrense, the retaining walls for various private properties, and even tombs such as the pyramid of Gaius Cestius. The surface of the city thus defined remained unchanged for centuries, in practice until the unification of Italy.

## *The Structure*

Built in a maximum time span of eight years, the walls represent a colossal project. Originally about six meters high and three meters wide, they were fortified with square towers every thirty meters. They were reinforced and made higher under Maxentius and above all during the era of Honorius (395–423) so that they could accommodate platforms for maneuvering war machinery. Work resumed again after the siege of Alaric (410) and the attack of Totila (547), and the walls were restored numerous times during the Middle Ages and reinforced with new bastions in the Renaissance. They were and continue to be a fundamental point of reference for Rome's urban landscape.

**Porta San Giovanni**
This imposing and massive gate was created in 1574 by Jacopo Del Duca by order of Pope Gregory XIII.

# Villa del Casale, A Peaceful Sanctuary

One of the most opulent mosaic cycles we know of from late antiquity was discovered in a Roman villa outside Piazza Armerina in the Sicilian interior.

Sicily, the first Roman province, was for many centuries a depressed land, prey to periodic and devastating slave revolts and utilized by Rome as a large granary for the Urbs. Beginning in the late third century A.D., however, the senatorial aristocracy became increasingly interested in the island. Among the grand and luxurious villas that rose at the center of large landholdings was the Villa del Casale near Piazza Armerina. Known in ancient times by the name *Philosophiana*, it was built between A.D. 320 and 330 and abandoned definitively only in the twelfth century at the height of the Norman era. Within its walls, the villa contains the most complete and elaborate mosaic cycle from late antiquity that has come to light.

**Exterior View of the Villa**
Built on sloping terraces, the Villa del Casale covered an incredible expanse. Excavations thus far have revealed an area of approximately 4,000 square meters, of which 3,500 are covered with mosaics.

**Sound the Trumpets**
This musician belongs to the mosaics that decorate the gymnasium.

## *An Aristocrat Grandee*

The profuse mosaic decoration can be linked to African workshops, but the themes differ from those preferred by the artists connected with such work. In all likelihood, the figurative program was inspired directly by the owner of the villa, who wanted to surround himself with his own favorite subjects. We do not know the identity of this owner; the possibility of an emperor has been ruled out, but he must have been an important person. The numerous images of soldiers and military insignia imply that he may have held military offices, just as the numerous depictions of circus scenes may refer to the good works of the high magistrates who provided the populace with *panem et circenses*. The mosaics also contain many references

**Draft Animals**
Judging from the visual evidence, mosaics, such as this one of animals pulling a cart, must have been produced by artists from North Africa.

to literature, theater, and music. These characteristics taken as a whole have led archeologists to put forward the name Gaius Ceionius Rufus Volusianus, a senator of African origin who held important military posts under Maxentius and Constantine, and his son, Ceionius Rufus Albinus, a magistrate, literary figure, and intellectual who wrote on logic, geometry, history, and music (a *philosophus*, as such men were called at the time). The splendid villa would have offered him relief from the exile to which he was condemned for a certain period. Whoever the owner was, he left a legacy of the most moving and engaging evidence of late ancient Roman culture.

A TRITON
*Left*, in a detail from one of the villa's many aquatic-themed mosaics, a mythical sea creature called a Triton is surrounded by marine life.

THE CORRIDOR OF THE GREAT HUNT
*Below*, a ship traveling between Rome and Alexandria, part of the decoration of the Corridor of the Great Hunt, a space almost 66 meters long with an apse at each end.

# Clothing and Coiffure

Men attributed great symbolic value to clothing, which indicated the rank, age, and status of the wearer. Women, limited by law to their choice of garments, compensated with elaborate coiffures.

**Refined Elegance**
In Pompeian paintings, one can appreciate the elegance of Roman matrons belonging to the more affluent classes. The woman portrayed here wears earrings and rings, a gold hairnet, and a garment of precious fabric. Younger women preferred to wear white and pastel hues, while older women favored purple and neutral tints.

The traditional garment for the Roman man was the toga, a semicircle of wool or linen, scrupulously white, which could reach five meters in diameter and was draped around the body. This was a rather symbolic garment, attuned to the *gravitas* to which Romans set such store, but there is ample evidence as to its lack of comfort. In fact, Roman citizens freed themselves of it as soon as possible in favor of the much more practical tunic, which hung down to the knees and was cinched at the waist. If the climate so required, this garment was topped by a mantle, fastened at the shoulder. The toga was reserved for official occasions, where it was obligatory in part because requisite decorations (a wide red strip for senators, a narrower strip for knights) and the drapery indicated the rank and social status of the wearer. The passage from adolescence to adulthood also was emphasized by a change of garment. Adolescents wore the *toga praetexta*, edged in purple like the senatorial garment, whereas men had the right to wear the totally white *toga virilis*.

**Draped Toga**
*Above*, this statue clearly shows the drapery of the ample semicircular toga worn by Roman citizens.

**A Fabric Store**
The use of precious fabrics, particularly in imperial times, favored the spread of clothing-related professions, such as *lintari*, who made linen garments, and *setarii*, who worked with silk.

## *Women's Clothing*

The female equivalent of the toga was the stola, a floor-length, sleeveless garment, worn over a tunic. If a woman needed further protection from the elements, the stola was covered by a large mantle (*palla*), which could also go over the head. The severity of these garments was relieved by the use of colored fabrics, as well as by the infinite complexity of female coiffures.

### FABRICS

Wool, known and worn from the earliest times, was the most widely used fabric. Linen, produced and woven for the most part in Egypt, was considered particularly precious and therefore was reserved for the upper classes, as were the extremely fine and transparent veils that came from various Greek islands. Silk began to appear in Rome in the late republican era; the lengthy voyage from China and India to the Mediterranean made it extremely costly, accessible only to the wealthiest and to members of the imperial family. The Romans did not know how it was made; silkworms were not imported to Constantinople until about the sixth century A.D.

## *The Art of Coiffure*

According to Latin writers, the beauty of a woman depended above all on the care given to her face and hairstyle. There were infinite varieties of hairstyles, which were chosen to suit the shape of the face, the social class, the age, the mood, and the occasion. Traditional styles were relatively simple, with the hair drawn back and gathered into a bun or divided into strips at both sides of the face. But in the imperial era in particular, very complex hairstyles became fashionable, with braids of various types, curls, chignons, and the extensive use of jewels (diadems, gold chains, pins, and so forth).

The use of hair coloring was common, the most popular shades being blond (considered daring because it was the color typically used by prostitutes, who often were pointed out as women *flava coma*, with blond hair), black, and red. Wigs were also popular.

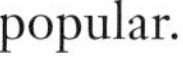

**Julia's Curls**
*Left*, in this portrait, Julia, the daughter of the emperor Titus and the wife of Domitian, wears a complicated coiffure of curls.

**Octavia's Style**
The most popular hairstyle in the early imperial era was the so-called Octavia style *(below)*, named for the sister of Augustus. This was characterized by a series of braids that spread out from a central point above the forehead and then were joined together in a chignon at the nape of the neck.

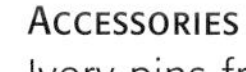

**Accessories**
Ivory pins from Roman tombs (first to second century A.D.). When needed, these items could be turned into tools of defense.

# The Art of Seduction

Women of all classes desired to be seductive. It mattered little that poets, moralists, philosophers, and sometimes even legislators and emperors sought to repress this feminine vanity.

The poet Ovid, the uncontested master of the sweet art of seduction, exhorted women to take care of their persons and present the best possible image. Following his teachings with enthusiasm, Roman women gave great importance to personal hygiene. With the growing popularity of baths, complete ablution became a daily routine, and—if the cleansers utilized (bicarbonate of soda and lye, accompanied by the continual rubbing of a pumice stone) were often abrasive—oils, unguents, and massages renewed the skin's elasticity and softness. Women doused themselves with perfume, often, willingly, and over their entire bodies: hair, feet, clothing, breath, even the nostrils. Pomades were produced by leaving flower petals to steep in animal fat; unguents were made by soaking aromatic substances in hot oil, which then was filtered. Essential oils were obtained by squeezing substances through a lathe, and perfumes were made by pulverizing plant substances. Beauty masques were

**Indispensable Accessory**
A silver mirror with motifs in relief and a cast handle, discovered at Pompeii (first century A.D.).

**At the Mirror**
In this second-century-A.D. mosaic, a Roman adorns herself with jewels.

**Bejeweled Woman**
The portraits of women discovered in Fayum, Egypt *(below),* provide thorough documentation of the jewels worn by Roman women during the imperial era.

particularly fashionable. Pliny relates that for her baths, the empress Poppea used the milk of five hundred asses, which she always brought with her. Those who lacked an empress's means could resort to lentils to eradicate blotches on the skin, narcissus bulbs for emollients and for whitening the skin, bicarbonate as a bleaching and healing agent, butter for acne, and cow placenta for wrinkles and ulcerations of the face, not to mention other less orthodox but equally popular remedies.

**Necklace with Medallion**
A necklace in gold and gems with a medallion on which the emperor Caracalla is depicted.

## *Accessories for the Toilette*

Objects for the toilette were kept under lock and key, beginning with the most important, the mirror. Square, round, or oblong, first made from polished metal, then with the addition of glass, it was every matron's faithful companion. Kept with it were containers for creams, perfumes, makeup, spatulas, tweezers, pestles, and combs: an arsenal equal to that of any present-day woman. A good makeup session began with an adequate preparation of the skin onto which was spread a layer of white lead, or ceruse, mixed with honey and an oily substance. If luminous skin was desired one could sprinkle the face with a gray blue veil of hematite powder. The eyebrow line was improved with a touch of pulverized antimony, as were the eyelashes. The eyelids were shaded and colored to emphasize the facial features. The cheeks could be brightened with red earth or another similar coloring, antecedent of today's cosmetics. Nor was it unknown for women to apply false beauty spots to their cheeks, something we think of as a typically eighteenth-century custom.

## *Jewels*

The Romans, both men and women, loved jewels of all types, with which they expressed their personalities. Unfortunately, much has been lost because precious gold was often melted down for reuse, depriving us of complete knowledge of one of the major productions in the ancient world. What remains, however, suffices to give an idea of artisanship of the highest quality; hairnets, hairpins, buckles, earrings, necklaces, bracelets, rings, and chains adorned the wrists, ankles, ears, arms, even the entire body. In fact, a Roman woman typically wore necklaces up to two and one-half meters long, wrapped around the neck, then crossed below the breast and attached at the back: a mischievous arrangement that invited the lover to undo the bejeweled defenses.

**Perfume Flask in the Shape of a Dove**
During banquets, it was customary for slaves to pour perfumes on the feet of the guests, on the walls, and sometimes even on the wings of doves, which then were set free.

### THE POET'S RECIPE

*Here is Ovid's recipe for making the skin "smoother than a mirror":*

- 2 librae (pounds; 654.9 g) African barley
- 2 librae (pounds; 654.9 g) bitter vetch (a legume similar to lentil)
- 10 eggs
- 1 sextans (54.575 g) deer horn
- 12 narcissus bulbs
- 1 sextans (54.575 g) mixture of resin and grain from Etruria (spelt)
- 9 sextantes (491.175 g) Italian honey

The barley was mixed with the bitter vetch, which had been macerated with the whole eggs. The mixture, once it had dried, had to be ground, added to the deer horn, minced, and passed through a sifter. Then the narcissus bulbs were peeled and mashed in a mortar, then added to the first mixture, along with the resin, the spelt, and the honey. The mixture, well blended, was now ready for application. With best of luck.

# Sickness and Health

Illness was a habitual companion to Romans of all classes, and remedies often were more illusory than effective. This is demonstrated by a startling fact: the average life span was around thirty years.

In his *Natural History*, Pliny the Elder states that the Romans had classified over three hundred illnesses with certainty, and new ones were being discovered nearly every day. These illnesses were of all types: diseases of the respiratory system (including a tubercular variety), gastrointestinal disturbances (dysentery, salmonella, typhoid fever), and rheumatic, ophthalmologic, and dermatological illnesses. From the time of Marcus Aurelius, plagues were frequent and particularly devastating. On the other hand, living conditions favored a rise in diseases. Diets were not particularly rich or varied and fell below subsistence levels in cases of famine. Residences were unhealthy, poorly lit, ill-ventilated, without lavatories, and often with polluted water. Hygienic precautions were scarce.

## *Cures*

In ancient times, cures were rather empirical and carried out in a family setting. Therapies, entrusted to the *paterfamilias*, called for a balanced use of curative herbs and magic formulas. Contact with Greece and its medical schools, however, also encouraged the birth of a professional body of physicians in Rome. For a long time, these were predominantly Greek and arrived in the Urbs as prisoners of war or

**The Study of Anatomy**
At the medical school in Hellenistic Alexandria, anatomy, with the dissection of human bodies, was the subject of systematic study for the first time. In Roman times, the work of Galen of Pergamum (A.D. 129–200) had enormous importance, and Galen's anatomical theories were refuted only after a millennium. *Above*, a silver cup (first century B.C. to first century A.D.) with a depiction of skeletons.

**A Visit to the Doctor**
The subject of this relief, dating from the second century A.D., is a patient visiting a doctor.

**A Visit to the Oculist**
Diseases of the eye were widespread, at least judging from the great number of physicians who practiced the profession of oculist. *Below*, a relief depicting a visit to the oculist (second century A.D.).

## THE DOCTOR'S RESPONSIBILITY

According to legal tradition in Rome, as in Greece, a doctor was not punishable for injuries caused to patients through therapies later discovered to be mistaken, at least if it was not demonstrated that he had acted with premeditation and malice. In the event that a doctor was accused of causing the death of a slave, however, he had to respond before a court to charges of damage to property, not to a person, and he risked only a monetary fine.

A SET OF INSTRUMENTS
Medical instruments generally were made of bronze. Iron was used for the manufacture of blades, and thanks to a specific treatment, it acquired the qualities of steel.

A VISIT TO THE DENTIST
This forceps (first century A.D.) may have been used for pulling out the roots of teeth or to extract splinters and extraneous objects from wounds.

to seek their fortune. Later, there were Roman professionals, as well. In the early decades after the birth of Christ, there was what could be described as a flowering of Roman medicine, although it was based on knowledge from the Greek world.

### *Illnesses and Social Classes*

Illnesses were not equal for all. The wealthy often had problems tied to dietary excesses; the urban plebs, who lived crowded into unhealthy, multistory housing blocks and ate little and poorly, were subject to respiratory diseases, malnutrition, dermatitis, and rheumatism. Farmers, who often came into contact with swampy environments, were subject to malaria. Moreover, like sailors, soldiers, and slaves, they suffered from arthritis, rheumatic illnesses, and hernias, due to strained positions, intense and prolonged exertions, and exposure to dampness. Toothache was a widespread and painful malady. Then there were some illnesses that are unusual today, such as lead poisoning, caused by the use of lead pipes to bring water into houses (an illness that often also caused sterility, to such a degree that it may have had an impact on the birth rate).

## THE WATER CURE

The Romans were convinced of the therapeutic value of cold-water baths. The principal champion of this cure was Antonius Musa, Augustus's personal physician. Using cold baths, he succeeded in healing the emperor, thereby gaining great fame both for himself and for his therapeutic methods. Cold hydrotherapy was considered curative for disturbances of the liver and the stomach, as well as for headache. This led Celsus to write, in the first century A.D., "nothing is better than cold water."

# Romans at Table

Gastronomy is one of the fields in which one most senses the distance between the tastes of antiquity and those of today. Lovers of strong and distinctive flavors, Romans used condiments and combinations that are unusual for us.

The Romans, like today's Italians, were great consumers of legumes and greens with which they also prepared tasty soups. Lentils, peas, chickpeas, and squashes were much appreciated, but cabbage was the king of the kitchen. It was eaten raw, dipped in vinegar, or boiled and dressed with cumin, salt, and oil. Onions and garlic were the "bread" of the poor, who put them to ample use. Olives, naturally, were never missing from the table and were the raw

**Fish Products**
This third-century-A.D. mosaic from Tunisia depicts fish and mollusks in a basket.

**In the Triclinium (Dining Room)**
A relief depicting a female servant who brings a plate laden with food to a woman and her child who are stretched out on a triclinium couch. The Romans used the expression *Ab ovo usque ad mala* ("From eggs to apples") to describe a complete three-course meal.

material for the typical Roman condiment, oil. Thus far, ancient tastes were rather similar to our own; but this is not true for meat (beef, pork, and both farmyard and wild fowl), which were seasoned with strong, highly spiced sauces that sometimes might set our teeth on edge. For example, *porcellum hortolanum* was typical. Despite its name, it was reserved for wealthy gourmands and was obtained by deboning pork and stuffing it with little meatballs of chicken, thrush, dates, smoked feather hyacinth, snails, beets, leeks, celery, boiled brussels sprouts, coriander, pepper, and pine nuts. If this dish was too "light," some fifteen or so eggs and a spicy *liquamen* could be added. The latter—also called *garum*—was a typical Roman preparation: a sauce made from the salting and steeping of fish entrails, which, despite its particularly acrid taste and odor, was much coveted. Fish and seafood were omnipresent on the Roman table: boiled eel accompanied by aromatic sauces, oysters from Lake Lucrinus (a small coastal basin in the Gulf of Pozzuoli), crawfish and shrimp, and boiled and roasted octopus. Our ancestors never did without these delicacies, even though, unlike us, they smothered meats in complicated sauces that prevented them from appreciating the natural taste of the food. Yet the products most favored in Latin gastronomy were also the simplest: bread, honey, and fruit. There were many different types of bread, ranging from white bread made from common wheat (*triticum siligeo*), to bran (*panis autopyres*), to "whole wheat" or black bread (*panis secundarius*), made from less refined flour. Honey was the sweetener par excellence in a society that did not know about sugar. As for fruit, choices expanded along with the empire's borders. Apples, grapes, and figs, typical of the Italian peninsula, were joined by specialties imported from the east: peaches, apricots, and cherries.

**Table Wine**
Bas-relief of a cellar with amphorae of wine. The Roman wine par excellence was Falerno, produced in Campania.

## *Wine, Gift of the Gods*

Like the Greeks, the Romans did not drink pure wine but mixed it in varying proportions with water, and they sometimes flavored it with honey or with resins. It was a beverage very different from today's wine, considerably more cloudy and rich in sediment. Yet it was highly valued not only for its taste but also for its intoxicating effects. It also was a principal item of trade in the Mediterranean, one of the Roman products known even beyond the borders of the empire. The barbarians began drinking wine instead of beer and hydromel (the Romans considered beer a beverage for children; hydromel was a fermentation made from honey). The wines produced on the slopes of Vesuvius were particularly renowned; the fertile volcanic soil there was cultivated almost up to the edges of the crater until the eruption of 79 A.D.

### RECIPE FOR *GARUM*

This was how *liquamen*, or *garum*, a typical sauce in Roman cuisine, was made:

"Throw fish entrails into a vessel along with some small fish, especially atherine, mullet, anchovies, and blotched picarel, taking care that they are all equally small in size, and salt them in the sun, stirring frequently. When the sun has ripened the brine, gather up the entire mixture and place it in a large, tightly woven basket, and the *garum* will run out from the basket. The solid part remaining will be the *allec*." The *allec* was the sauce that was used with oysters, seafood, and above all with mullet.

**Fruit on the Table**
Still life with fruit and glass vessels, from the House of the Stags in Herculaneum.

# Games and Sports

There was athletic activity, which the Romans considered essential for the harmonious development of the person, and there was *munus publicum gladiatorium*, the bloody circus spectacle that is so far removed from our own tastes. This complex and structured environment permeated many aspects of life in ancient Rome.

Physical activity occupied a very important place in the Roman world. In ancient times, the youth of the city met in the Campus Martius (at that time an expansive green plain between the forum and the bend in the Tiber) to run, swim, and ride. Swimming was almost universally practiced and was virtually obligatory for every young man. Along with athletics, it was considered an essential activity for preparation for wartime. In order to prove their strength, resistance, and skill, Romans enthusiastically adopted the Greek concept of athletic competition (*graecum certamen*), vying in races, wrestling, and boxing, and in *pancratium* (a combination of wrestling and boxing). Scrupulously regulated and followed with great passion, certainly more bloody than their modern equivalents (maiming and even death were frequent), these competitions were reserved for professionals, who participated with full awareness of the risks. But the basic rudiments were imparted to the majority of young men.

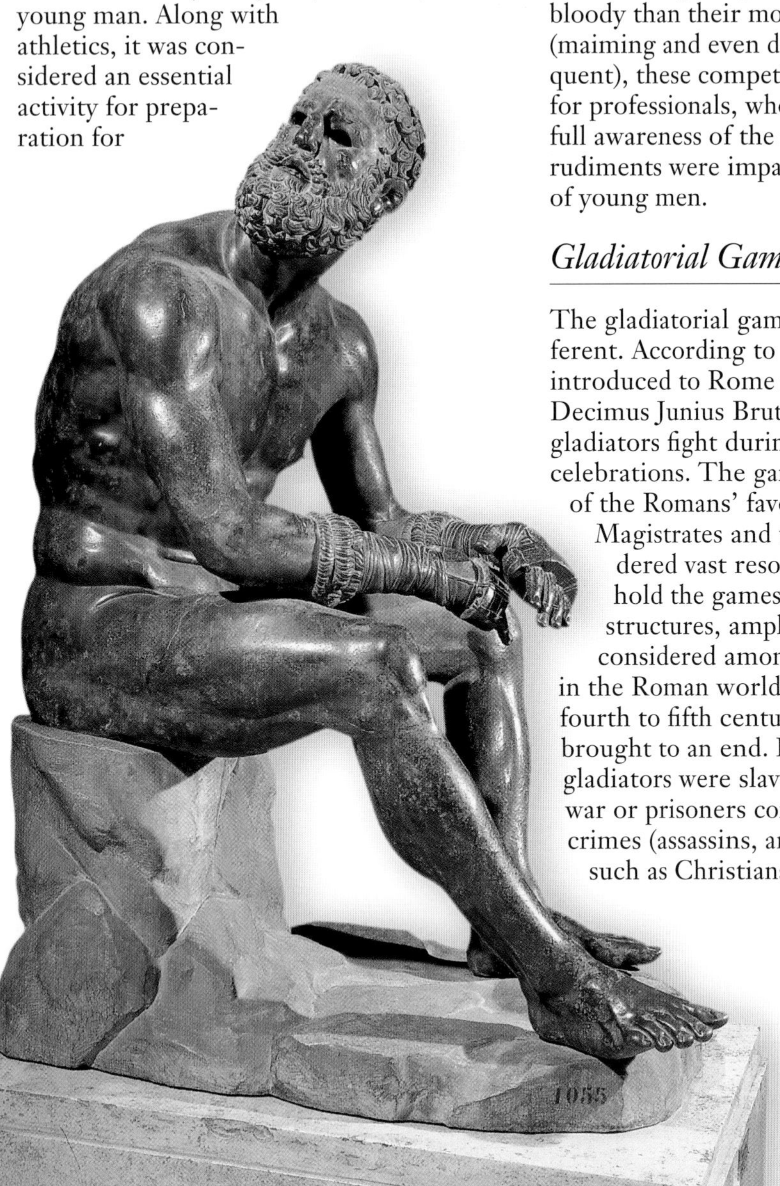

A Boxer's Weapons
*Left*, bronze statue of a boxer (first century B.C.). The athlete wears boxing gloves (*caesti*, hand bindings) studded with large nails and covering the wrists and forearms.

## *Gladiatorial Games*

The gladiatorial games were entirely different. According to tradition, they were introduced to Rome in 264 B.C., when Decimus Junius Brutus had three pairs of gladiators fight during his father's funeral celebrations. The games soon became one of the Romans' favorite pastimes. Magistrates and then emperors squandered vast resources to organize and hold the games. They created special structures, amphitheaters, which are considered among the major buildings in the Roman world. It was not until the fourth to fifth century A.D. that they were brought to an end. For the most part, gladiators were slaves and prisoners of war or prisoners condemned for serious crimes (assassins, arsonists, and heretics such as Christians). Sooner or later, the fate of death awaited them. However, there were also young men reduced to poverty or scions of families in disgrace who voluntarily chose the life of the arena in the hope of gaining fame, money, social prestige, and success with women. If they succeeded in surviving a certain number of combats, these gladiators had the possibility of "retiring" from the profession. In the imperial era, *venationes*, combats against wild animals, became popular, along with

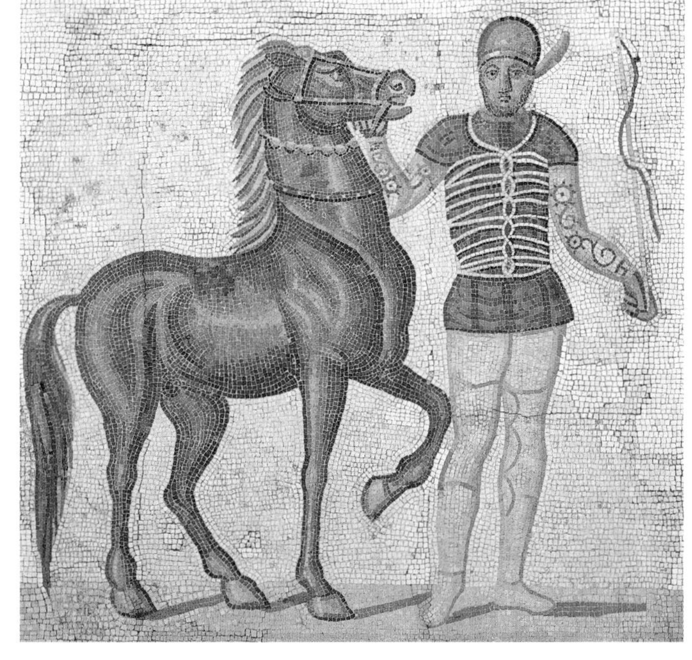

**Equestrian Sports**
Detail from a mosaic with a charioteer and a horse (fourth century A.D.).

## THE MORALISM OF TACITUS

The practice of athletic sports, instead of healthy gymnastic exercise and good training in arms, aroused indignation in Roman traditionalists, who used the historian Tacitus as their spokesperson. "Unfortunately the ancient customs, gradually suppressed, were subverted due to dissolute practices that arrived from other countries, so that one could see in Rome all those things that elsewhere had the possibility of corrupting and being corrupted. Under the influence of foreign customs, the young people degenerated. They began spending time at gymnasiums, became accustomed to idleness and amorous obscenities, encouraged in all this by the emperor [Nero] and by the Senate. . . . What was left but to go about naked and, grasping boxing gloves, to train for those gymnastic battles, instead of being a soldier or using weapons?"

**To the Death**
Duels between gladiators sometimes ended with the death of one of the two competitors, as this fourth-century-A.D. mosaic shows with dramatic realism.

sentences *ad bestias*, that is, to be torn apart by wild beasts without the possibility of self-defense. Gladiatorial games increasingly were transformed into orgies of blood, in which ferocious beasts, people condemned to death, and entire squads of gladiators were thrown into the arena. It was a violent and nauseating spectacle, yet one greatly loved by the public, which was obsessed with such events and debated them much as we today do with football or Formula 1 racing.

**Statue of Wrestlers**
Wrestling as a sport in the modern sense was first codified in Greece and, beginning in 708 B.C., became one of the Olympic games. In Roman times, it was quite popular and usually practiced by professionals in gymnasiums.

# Care of the Body

*Cura corporis*, "care of the body," is how the Romans referred to personal hygiene, a daily activity to which the ancient Quirites devoted much time and attention.

From the earliest times, a healthy daily bath was a nearly universal custom among Roman citizens of every social level. It eliminated odors caused by the use of heavy fabrics, which did not allow proper perspiration, it stimulated circulation, and it stretched the muscles, which were considerably more strained than those of today's citizens. Initially, people bathed in the cold waters of the Tiber, but there soon appeared, both in the private dwellings of the wealthy and at public facilities, places where people could wash with hot and cold water and avoid the muddy current of the river. As Seneca describes with regard to Scipio's bath, there were "small dark rooms" where people washed with unfiltered water, which, had there been a storm, might also be muddy, and where one was limited to washing work-soiled arms and legs, while the rest of the body was washed every *nundina*, that is, on market days, every nine days. By the late republican era, however, people could avail themselves of clean water, hot baths, which could be offered to mealtime guests, and daily ablutions followed by the skillful application of oils, unguents, and perfumes.

**Container for Unguents**
An agate cup probably used as a container for unguents and creams (first century A.D.).

**The Origins of Perfume**
The goddess Pietas often was depicted in the act of burning odorous substances on an altar. This action was described as *pro fumo tribuere*, "to offer by means of smoke," which led to the word "perfume." Thus, perfume originally had sacred significance. *Above*, detail of a fresco with a woman pouring perfume from a flask.

**Pair of Strigils**
Among the many items used for personal hygiene, strigils were considered indispensable. These were instruments used to scrape the skin clean after having rubbed it vigorously with oil, ashes, and pumice.

## STRAIGHT FROM THE POET'S MOUTH

In his treatise on the art of love, the poet Ovid dedicates some chapters to personal hygiene, considered indispensable for conquering the yearned-for "quarry." "The tongue should not be bitter, and the teeth cleaned of any russet color, the feet should not move about in shoes that are too large . . . the nails should not project too far out and should be free of filth, there should be no hair in the nostril cavities, nor should wretched breath emanate from a malodorous mouth." He also had advice for women: "She who has very fat fingers should accompany her conversation with very rare gestures, while she who suffers from bad breath should never speak before meals and should keep a certain distance from the face of her beloved."

## *Unguents, Perfumes, and Toothpastes*

After the bath, the use of unguents, perfumed oils, and perfume was common for both men and women. This was accompanied by the use of other cosmetics, such as toothpastes, for which a paste made from a base of sodium bicarbonate was used, as well as—to what advantage for the health of the gums we do not know—urine, which was thought to strengthen tooth enamel. To clean the mouth from residues of food, wood, bone, or metal toothpicks were widely used.

**Running Water**
In ancient cities an abundance of running water was a sign of prosperity not only for individual citizens but also for the entire community. *Above*, a fountain along a main street in Herculaneum.

## *Hygienic Services*

Hygienic services available to Romans were perhaps rudimentary compared to those of today, but surely they were far and away the most advanced in the ancient world. Group latrines outfitted with stone seats and small pipes with running water for washing away the excrement were often found in bath complexes and near the forums and the most frequented streets. They made up for the lack of running water in private dwellings, where people had to take care of their bodily needs with chamber pots (the contents of which were regularly emptied into the streets, a practice that continued in Europe until the eighteenth century). Rags, or often sponges soaked with water, were used for toilet paper. Rome boasted an efficient sewer system in which rainwater washed away the filth scattered in the streets. The various conduits flowed into a large collector, the Cloaca Maxima, which carried all the waste into the Tiber. Sewage from public buildings and from the latrines of patrician houses, which had similar plumbing systems, also flowed here. In short, there were rudimentary solutions alongside others that were highly refined, the likes of which Europe would not see until modern times.

**Public Services**
Excavations in Sabratah, Libya, have brought to light latrines, which were made from a stone or marble foundation on which seats were rested, all arranged in a row in close proximity to one another.

# The Baths and Social Life

In the imperial era, the bath facilities were an everyday meeting place for citizens of all ages and classes. Frequented by men and women, they were beneficial to both body and spirit.

The text of an ancient funerary inscription reads, "The baths, wine, and love corrupt our body but make life pleasurable." Faithful to this motto, during the first century A.D. wealthy Quirites were already taking great care with their private baths. As this taste spread to the common people, it tempted and often forced emperors and city magistrates to build grand public bathing facilities, which found their maximum expression in the gigantic baths of Caracalla and those of Diocletian, the most impressive ever to be created. Thus visiting these baths became a mass phenomenon; thousands of people flocked there every day not only to bathe but also to stroll, play, eat and drink, admire works of art, and attend public lectures and performances. Or they went simply to see and be seen, to gossip with friends about the day's events, and to eye and court pretty young women and attractive men. Usually the baths opened their doors around the fifth hour (11 in the morning), but it was not considered "in" to bathe before the seventh hour. Entry cost very little or even nothing, thanks to the patronage of many magistrates who shouldered the small entrance fee so that all could frequent the facilities, which thus took on the role of a first-rate social club.

## *Habitual Visitors*

There were many visitor "profiles," as we might say today. There was the health enthusiast, the libertine, the wealthy fop, the social climber, the scrounger, and so on. Each in his own way took advantage of the different services the baths had to offer.

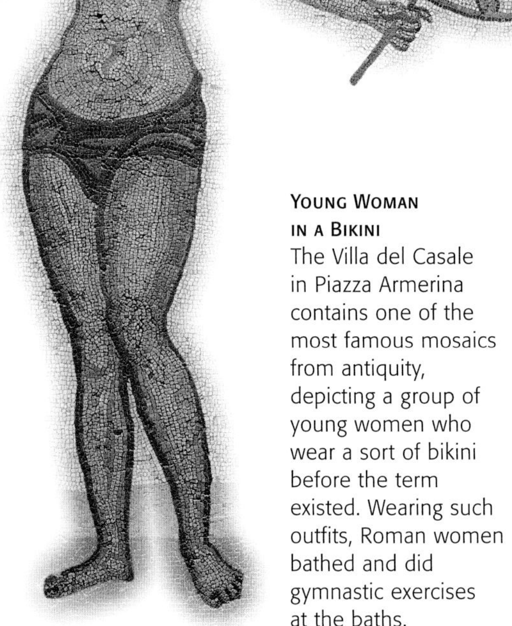

**Young Woman in a Bikini**
The Villa del Casale in Piazza Armerina contains one of the most famous mosaics from antiquity, depicting a group of young women who wear a sort of bikini before the term existed. Wearing such outfits, Roman women bathed and did gymnastic exercises at the baths.

**Constant Temperature**
*Below*, the calidarium of the baths of the forum of Pompey. The bath spaces were originally heated by large bronze braziers. Later, heating equipment was installed with the circulation of hot air beneath the floor and inside the walls.

### *MUSAEA ET AUDITORIA*

People went to the baths not only to restore the body but also to nurture the spirit. In many facilities, there were lecture halls and spaces set aside for conferences and musical performances. In others, as for example in the baths of Diocletian, clients even could avail themselves of a well-stocked library: clear proof that the baths fulfilled a cultural as well as a social function.

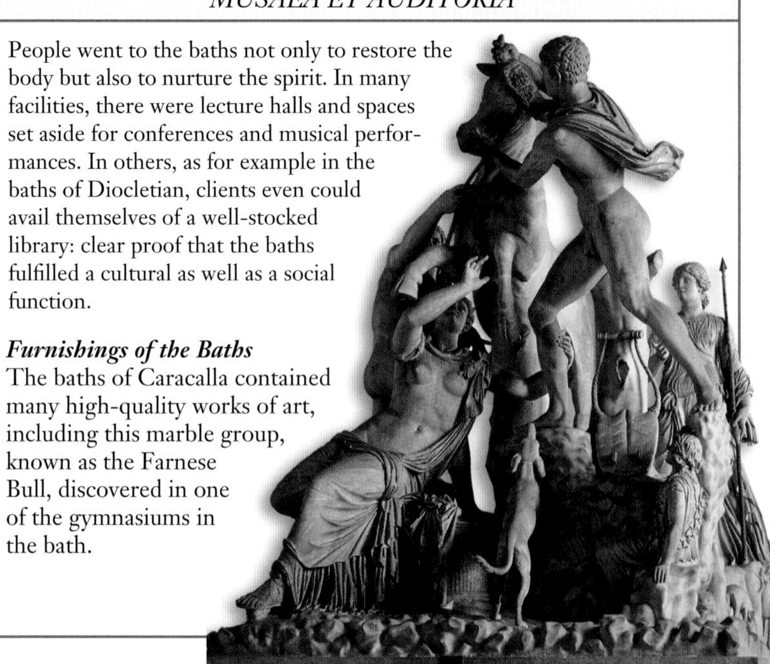

***Furnishings of the Baths***
The baths of Caracalla contained many high-quality works of art, including this marble group, known as the Farnese Bull, discovered in one of the gymnasiums in the bath.

**Baths in the Provinces**
*Left,* the Roman baths of Cyrene in present-day Libya. The city, annexed to Rome in 96 B.C., was a flourishing commercial center along the Mediterranean sea routes.

The health enthusiast was punctiliously methodical in approaching the four stages of the bath (preparatory gymnastics, slow and sumptuous immersion in the hot water of the *caldarium*, a pause in the *tepidarium*, and a resolute plunge into the cold water of the *frigidarium*, followed by a stimulating massage with perfumed oil). The libertine disdained bathing but sharpened his sights on his "prey." The brash social climber sought a dinner invitation from a likely source. The great number and diversity of people, all intent on their own affairs, made the bath environment a veritable beehive of activity, full of noise and confusion but also stimulating.

## *An Oasis for the Ladies*

The baths were also open to women but for a long time separate spaces or even separate facilities were set aside for them so that the two sexes would not mix. With the passage of time, however, customs changed; and women came in increasing numbers to the baths, along with men, leaving behind in the dressing rooms their sense of modesty along with their clothing. Scandalous situations became so frequent that the emperor Hadrian was obliged to impose once again a separation of the sexes, but he met with little success. Thus the baths remained places of promiscuity, where men and women met freely, although in the most traditional families women who frequented these establishments were considered, at the very least, to be lacking in virtue. Then, with the rise of Christianity and the decline of Roman society, both the baths and their habitués passed out of fashion.

**Extra Services**
Entrance to the baths cost little or nothing, but people certainly paid for extra services. They paid to have their clothing watched, for towels (if they had not brought them from home), for a massage, to have hair removed, to be shaved, for oil to apply to their skin, for soap for washing, not to mention for food consumed at places of refreshment. *Right,* detail of a nineteenth-century painting that depicts the women's *tepidarium* at the baths in Pompeii.

# Childhood and School

From birth onward, Roman life was difficult. In fact, to enter the family and society, newborns had to be recognized and accepted by the father. And it was from the father that children received the first rudiments of instruction.

When a son was born, the *paterfamilias* ritually expressed his acceptance by raising the infant up from the ground where the midwife had placed him. With this act, the newborn entered the family circle and acquired the rights belonging to a member of the human community. Babies that were rejected, because they were deformed, illegitimate, or suspected of being so, were exposed outside the door of the house or thrown out with the garbage. This was a legal practice, accepted by all social classes, based on the firm conviction that the right to life depended on recognition, not on birth. It was only toward the end of the second century A.D., with the rise of Christian morals, that this practice began to meet with disapproval, eventually becoming illegal.

**Nero's Childhood**
*Right,* a portrait of Nero as a young boy. His ambitious mother, Agrippina, entrusted his education to the best possible teacher, Seneca; but the young emperor greatly preferred poetry, music, and painting to rhetoric and philosophy.

## *Education*

Once accepted, sons were loved and protected. A son born to a wealthy family progressed from wet-nurse to tutor until, at the age of seven, he began his private education or school, under his father's supervision. Basic instruction, for males and very often also for females, lasted to the age of twelve, after which only males from

**Terracotta Toy**
The Romans considered play a right of children and also a formative activity until the age of seven, when school began. *Below,* a terracotta lamb.

**Mother and Son**
Fresco from Pompeii *(left),* depicting a heroine of Greek mythology, Danae, with her son, Perseus.

affluent families continued their studies. Daughters, at that age, were considered ready for marriage, and by fourteen they were often already married. Not many subjects were taught: the Latin and Greek classics and rhetoric, as well, of course, as sports. All the rest, it was presumed, offspring would learn from their fathers and from experience, life's irreplaceable teacher.

## *Subjects and Teachers*

Over time and above all in the imperial era, schooling became more complex and refined. The first stage was *ludus letterarius*, from the ages of seven to thirteen. Lessons, often imparted through rigidly mnemonic and fact-based criteria, taught students to read, write, and do arithmetic. Those who continued on studied with a *grammaticus*, who taught the art of rhetoric, essential for a political career but also for making a good appearance in society, because a cultivated Roman had to know how to express himself in correct Greek as well as in Latin. More or less in-depth studies of history, geography, and natural science were also given. All this generally was accomplished through the reading of selected passages by poets, philosophers, essayists, and historians. The last stage of instruction was the school of *rethor*, what we would call university, which taught the art of eloquence, the logic of debating, and how to extricate oneself from political and legal situations. All in all, this was training for political activity—the only occupation worthy of an upper-class Roman.

### THE BILINGUALISM OF THE ROMANS

In aristocratic families, it was normal practice to speak Greek. The language of Homer was widely known in the Roman world because it was spoken throughout the eastern portion of the empire, because it was considered indispensable for the highest manifestations of culture, and, finally, because of the growing presence of Greek slaves, tutors, teachers, doctors, and rhetoricians in every upper-class Roman home. Women also spoke Greek correctly, and it seems that among lovers it was considered very chic to exchange endearments in this language.

**Public Scholar**
As early as the time of Plautus, the people understood the Greek words that were used in abundance in the texts of comedies. *Left*, detail of a mosaic depicting a theater mask.

**Lesson in the Schoolroom**
During the *ludus letterarius*, the schoolmaster taught his students how to write. *Below*, bas-relief from Trier with a school scene.

# The Role of Women

They were married off while still children, often to much older men; they became mothers, ran the risks of childbirth, and were under the protection of their fathers or husbands. Yet women in ancient Rome were very important, indeed extremely so.

The *paterfamilias* expressed his acceptance of a newborn girl by ordering that she be nursed. If not accepted, the baby was left outdoors to die. This was only the first of many risks encountered by a Roman female. To begin with, her childhood was very short: at the age of twelve or fourteen she was considered ready for marriage, and even before reaching the age of matrimony she often was sent to the house of her future husband (chosen, naturally, by her father) in order to become accustomed to her new family. A bride was expected to be absolutely faithful, reserved in behavior, and utterly subordinate to her husband. She went from living under the *patria potestas*, power of her father (who, however, remained partially in her life, for example, with the right to remove a daughter from an unworthy husband), to that of her spouse. Even her property, if she had any, was managed by her husband, although with time, custom if not law recognized the right of women to manage their own assets or to leave them to an heir. A wife who had proven fertile could be temporarily "ceded" to a friend or a political ally who needed a child.

**Roman Matron**
Statue of a Roman matron from Colonia Cirta in present-day Algeria.

## *Motherhood*

A woman's entire world revolved around motherhood. In a society in which infant mortality was very high, up to twenty percent, "producing" many children was an imperative (although the upper classes sought to have no more than one male heir to avoid dividing up inherited property and even gave up "excess" male babies for adoption into sterile families). The law prescribed that free women should generate at least three children if they wanted to enjoy a range of benefits connected to their legal status. But pregnancy was very risky.

**Ubi Tu Gaius ego Gaia**
With these words ("Where you are Gaius, I am Gaia [feminine version of husband's name]") the Roman bride committed to take the name of her husband, to follow him wherever he might go—to be completely his. As soon as she pronounced this phrase, the woman was lifted and carried into her husband's house, while careful not to touch the threshold (a custom, reserved for a first marriage, connected to the virginity of the bride). *Left*, relief depicting a marriage, from a sarcophagus.

About ten percent of women died during childbirth or from related complications (hemorrhages, puerperal fever). The extremely young age established by law for the marriage of girls exposed their not yet mature bodies to further risks. Indeed, this led families to celebrate a marriage with a commitment not to consummate the relationship for a certain period. The result was that Roman women, who at twenty or twenty-five years of age had already given birth to the three children imposed by law, often took refuge in sexual abstinence to avoid risk of further pregnancies.

**Too Good to Be True**
Curiously, the Romans regarded with suspicion a legitimate couple who had generated the three children required by law but lived in mutual fidelity. A husband too tied to his wife lay himself open to the criticism of being considered *uxorius*, submissive to his spouse *(uxor)*, in other words, lacking in virility. *Above*, detail, a husband and wife, from a third-century sarcophagus.

**Numerous Offspring**
The law called for a series of benefits for free women who gave birth to at least three children.

**Small Talk Among Friends**
Detail of a fresco from the House of the Hunt in Pompeii, depicting three women talking.

## *Law and Custom*

As often happens, laws and customs did not always coincide. Weak and precarious in legal terms, the condition of the Roman woman was often on much more solid ground in reality. For example, Cornelia, the mother of the Gracchi, raised her two "jewels" with a firm hand (they were the only survivors of twelve children born to her), and cases like hers were not infrequent. The need to rule houses and often extensive properties while their husbands were far away, sometimes for years, gave wives an opportunity to assert their personalities. Furthermore, in the imperial era, the role of the *paterfamilias* gradually diminished, making way for a more equal relationship. In any case, never, not even during the time of the Republic, was a Roman woman subjected to the conditions of her Greek counterpart, who was closed off in her own house and "erased" from social life. In Rome women circulated. And they mattered.

# Love in Rome

At first it was rather stormy, with the rape of the Sabines. Later, Roman customs related to love entered a realm of "respectability," but once again became exuberant toward the end of the Republic and during the imperial era.

A collective abduction—the rape of the Sabine women, lured to the city under pretext—lay at the origins of Roman love life, at least according to legend. After this dramatic beginning, amatory relationships entered a period of calm: rigorously proper families, austere female figures dedicated to raising sons devoted to their country, fine examples of conjugal virtue. Customs did not evolve until the late republican era, when Roman conquests in the East brought home perfumes, luxury goods, and cosmetics, which introduced Roman women to the game of seduction.

## *Licentiousness in the Empire*

In the late republican era and during the time of the empire, sentimental relationships became audacious and numerous. In the scandalous shadows of the porticoes and above all in theaters (according to Ovid, the designated venue for amorous intrigue), romances were carried out with increasing frequency, apparently between partners married to others. Again according to Ovid, "property belonging to others is more alluring than one's own." Caesar was a well-known conqueror of female hearts, even though he divorced his wife because she "could not have even the appearance of suspicion." Many empresses

**Queen of Hearts**
Among the many lovers of Julius Caesar, the most famous was undoubtedly the Egyptian queen Cleopatra, depicted here in a relief. She also turned Marc Antony's head.

**Legendary Lovers**
A Pompeian fresco *(right)* depicting Venus and Mars, together with Cupid, who is to the right of the two other divinities.

**Spicy Scenes**
Detail of a painting *(left)* from the Villa of the Mysteries in Pompeii. A large fresco with scenes of initiation into the Dionysian mysteries, famous for explicit subjects of an erotic nature, was discovered in this building.

were queens of the dolce vita; the name of one, Messalina, went down in history.

## *The Problem of Prostitution*

In any case, relationships between the sexes remained extremely unbalanced. Roman noblewomen might be able to be unfaithful to their husbands, but men were actually encouraged, pushed, almost forced by social custom to "keep busy." It was considered normal to keep a concubine or to hire a courtesan for any period of time (the subject of *Asinaria*, a famous comedy by Plautus). Prostitution was widespread and flagrant. It moved through the channels of slavery with little girls as the principal victims, then thrived in veritable "sex quarters," where everything could be found, and reached sophisticated levels with highly placed "professionals," installed in luxurious dwellings on the Aventine. Prostitution was considered "healthy," because it provided an outlet for male instincts, "preserving the chastity of married women," as Cato said. Even severe censors such as Saint Augustine considered it necessary: "Banish prostitutes from society and you will reduce society to chaos," wrote the famous author of the *Confessions*. But no one really thought about banishing them.

**Professional in Love**
The official term that Romans used for a prostitute was *meretrix*, "she who earns." In a society that banned women from paid jobs, the prostitute was basically the only female "professional." *Right*, mosaic from the third century A.D., depicting two prostitutes.

**Unexpected Accomplice**
In a letter described by Suetonius, Marc Antony made fun of Augustus for his passion for young women. The emperor's wife, Livia, depicted here in a marble sculpture, allegedly knew of and tolerated his behavior. Indeed, according to gossip, she sometimes even procured young virgins for her husband.

### DIVORCE "ROMAN STYLE"

While they did not allow a marriage to be terminated by mere whim of the spouses, Romans broke and renewed conjugal relationships with notable ease. Divorce, especially for men, was not difficult. One had only to find an excuse that was valid and acceptable to the family (obviously the form of excuse varied with the passing of the centuries and with changing customs) and then bring together a *consilium amicorum* (council of family friends), who had the task of taking note that the divorce had occurred. For women, naturally, things were a bit more complicated. A request for divorce was justified by mistreatment so serious and unmotivated that it required immediate intervention by the head of the family that the wife originally belonged to. He was the only one who could make a petition to the council of friends for the ratification of the dissolution of the marriage bond.

# Furnishings

Ancient Romans lavished attention on the home, which had to mirror the rank and office of the owner, and they furnished their dwellings in much more elaborate fashion than one might think.

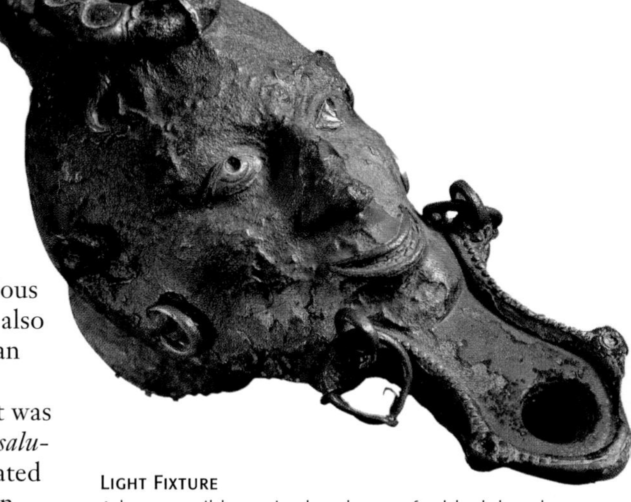

**Light Fixture**
A bronze oil lamp in the shape of a black head with silver incrustations, from Ampurias in Spain.

Our knowledge of the interior design of Roman houses is limited. Much of what we know is derived from the luxurious homes at fashionable Herculaneum and Pompeii that were buried by the eruption of Vesuvius. The essayist Marcus Vitruvius Pollio gives us a more detailed description of these residences, one that has been confirmed in archeological excavations: "Tall, regal vestibules, spacious atriums and peristyles, extensive gardens and luxurious and imposing porticoes." This scheme also was linked to the demands of the Roman patron-and-client system, whereby the house of a wealthy man or an aristocrat was thronged with *clientes* for the morning *salutatio*. As a result, these clients consolidated relationships with their protector and in turn made themselves available to him for the day. Stone benches were arranged outside the house, where clients could await the opening of the doors and the appearance of the *patronus*. Beyond the entrance door (*fauces*), lay the core of the *domus*, the atrium. It was characterized by an *impluvium* (central basin) where rainwater collected, a *lararium* (altar to the household gods, or *lares*), a *cartibulum*, a marble or bronze banquet table with zoomorphic supports, which was one of the prized pieces in the house, and *arcae*, studded wood or bronze strong-boxes that held the family jewels. Behind the atrium, opposite the entrance, were the public spaces of the house. These were the *tablinum*, the owner's study, and the *triclinium*, or dining room. The former space was dominated by a large, tall chair, a veritable throne with back and armrests. This was reserved for the *dominus*, or head of the household; seated here he received clients and visitors. The triclinium contained couches, usually three, arranged in a **U** shape around a central table. These refined pieces of furniture made from wood with bronze incrustations, were generally created by skillful workers who came from Greece or southern Italy.

**Sumptuous Interior**
In this detail from a nineteenth-century painting entitled *The Gladiators at the Triclinium*, one can appreciate the precise reconstruction of the interior of a Roman *domus*.

**The Furnishing of the Triclinium**
This relief shows a group of banqueters, stretched out on triclinium couches arranged in a U around a circular table.

## *Reclining to Eat*

The presence of triclinium couches, adapted to the Roman habit of eating in a reclining position, is perhaps the feature of Roman interiors most different from houses of today. Originally, only the *paterfamilias* ate in a reclining position, while his wife sat at the foot of the couch, his children on chairs and stools. Then it became customary for male table companions to dine on triclinium couches, while women sat opposite. It was not until much later that women were also permitted to eat while reclining. Toward the end of the third century A.D., the triclinium couch was replaced by the *sigma*, a single semicircular sofa.

**The Ficoroni Cist**
A cist was a cylindrical container with feet and a lid, lined in leather on the inside, where women's clothing was stored. The one illustrated here is distinguished by fine workmanship and also bears the names of both the craftsman who created it in Rome in the fourth century B.C. and the woman who gave it to her daughter.

**Statuette with Bells**
Houses had to have amulets against the evil eye. It was thought that bells, particularly anthropomorphic ones *(right)*, had this power.

## *Cubicula*

Furnishings for bedrooms (*cubicula*) were much more modest than those for the public spaces of a house. The beds were simple pieces of wood furniture with a webbing of leather strips as a support for the mattress. In the late imperial era, it became customary for beds to have a headboard, or head and sideboards surrounding three sides, making them comparable to sofas. Armoires were also very simple with panel doors framed by wood cornices. All this mattered little to the Romans, who led their lives for the most part outdoors.

### VISITING A ROMAN HOUSE

If we could enter a complete and functional *domus* from the imperial era, perhaps we would be most struck by the lack of illumination, which came from interior courtyards and from oil lamps or candelabra. The next thing we might notice would be the contrast between the superabundant decoration of floors and walls and the scarcity of furniture. Finally, if we were to turn our attention to the furniture details and design, we would notice a series of solutions that, all things considered, seem familiar (supports shaped like animal paws, sphinxes, beds and sofas with curved backs). All these elements were revived during the neoclassical era on a wave of enthusiasm for the discovery of Herculaneum and Pompeii.

**Cat's Paws**
A round table in bronze with three legs that end in cat's paws.

**Immersion in Nature**
Frescoes were a fundamental decorative element in Roman houses. Often porticoes that faced onto the garden featured paintings with landscape themes, such as the one illustrated below. In this way, someone strolling through had the real garden on one side and painted vegetation on the other.

# The Traffic Problem

In imperial times, like today, Rome was paralyzed by traffic. The first attempt to regulate the flow of traffic dates back to 45 B.C., but it was futile.

Throughout most of its history, Rome was a many-tentacled city with narrow streets wedged between tall and looming buildings and an urban layout in an inextricable tangle. There were very few wide streets, and for the most part there were unpaved alleys, steep flights of steps that climbed up the hills, and passageways no more that three meters wide, made even more suffocating by balconies that projected out from facades. Moving about in this perennially obstructed maze was exasperating. In 45 B.C. Julius Caesar faced the situation head-on. His *lex Iulia municipalis* prohibited, among other things, any movement of animal-drawn vehicles in the city streets between dawn and dusk, restricting them to nighttime hours. In order to "drain off" traffic, he also created special parking areas (*areae carruces*) near the entrance gates to the city. This was not sufficient, but it did accomplish something.

## *Everyone Out in the Street*

The problem was not just vehicles. All Rome lived outdoors, where unspeakable levels of noise and confusion were reached. The stands of vendors and merchants of every type occupied much of the street level, so that pedestrians, litters, and sedan chairs were forced to jostle each other and collide in the remaining space. During the night, there was a deafening and uninterrupted clatter from carts, porters employed to load and unload merchandise, draft animals, and animals headed for slaughter. On the other hand, the problems of supply were enormous. Every day, food, wood, and raw materials had to be brought into the city for over a million inhabitants who were crammed into a territory that was hilly in some areas and swampy in others—a veritable nightmare.

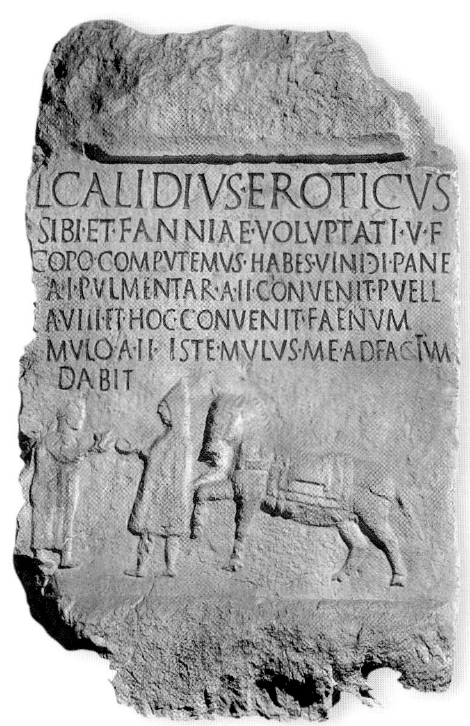


**The Bill**
This stele depicts an innkeeper preparing the bill for a customer who is about to depart with his mule.

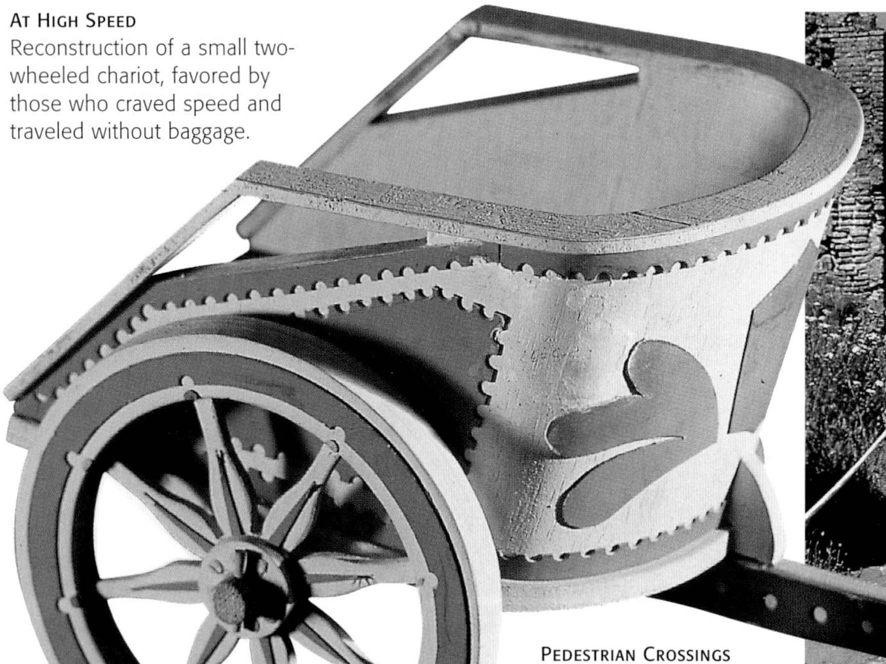

**At High Speed**
Reconstruction of a small two-wheeled chariot, favored by those who craved speed and traveled without baggage.

**Pedestrian Crossings**
*Right*, view of the Via Augustali, Pompeii, with boulders to mark off a pedestrian crossing.

**To Faraway Places**
Reconstruction of a four-wheeled covered cart for long voyages.

**A Ban on Traffic**
*Left*, a farmer going to market with his cow. The few exceptions to the ban on daytime traffic in the city included vehicles used to transport garbage and building materials.

## URBAN POLICE AND NIGHTTIME GUARDS

Augustus entrusted the control of public order in Rome to two different security corps: urban and evening guards. The former acted as urban police during the day and were posted in various parts of the city. The commander, a *praefectus urbi*, was a very high dignitary who reported directly to the emperor and had broad judicial powers. In fact, he could pass judgment summarily not only in cases of disturbing the peace but also for questions regarding relationships between slaves and owners, public morals, unlawful appropriations of legacies, and criminal associations. The role of nighttime security, however, was turned over to special police who patrolled the city streets, seeking to thwart the numerous episodes of violence, with little result, if we are to believe contemporary accounts.

## *Means of Transport*

The wealthy moved about the city in a *lectiga* carried by six or eight slaves. They traveled stretched out below a sort of canopy, generally closed off by curtains. Two or four slaves sufficed for a *sella gestatoria* in which the occupant traveled seated. Due to restrictions on daytime traffic, funerary transport was also by hand-carried litter, replaced, when the deceased was poor, by a simple stretcher. Outside the city, however, carts and two- or four-wheeled gigs were used. For quick drives or trips, a two-wheeled *essedum* with a coachman was used. The *cisium*, *covinnus*, and *birotus* were extremely light, rapid coaches favored by young speed demons. For slower journeys and those that involved baggage, the *carruca*, a four-wheeled vehicle drawn by four mules or horses was suitable. For long voyages, there also were *carrucae dormitoriae*, the antecedents of sleeping cars, where those who could tolerate the jerking of the vehicle might sleep. Finally, goods, agricultural foodstuffs, and building materials were shipped by *plaustrum* or *sarracum*, archaic but sturdy vehicles with two solid, iron-bound wheels (*tympana*), drawn by oxen, mules, or donkeys.

**Making a Stop**
*Below*, relief with a scene of the arrival at a *mansio*, a post house. Generally *mansiones* were equipped with hotels, warehouses, and stables.

# Music and Dance

In Rome, at least initially, music did not enjoy the same consideration and popularity as in Greece, but over time it became a significant component in the city's social life.

In the Roman world, the art of song accompanied by music and dance was at first limited to public and solemn demonstrations: religious ceremonies, funerals, triumphs. Beginning in the second century B.C., with the conquest of Greece, Greek actors and musicians arrived in Rome. In addition to performing personally, they taught their art to young Romans. The moralists did not approve of this innovation, but it took root nonetheless, and became an integral part of the education of younger generations. Even severe matrons devoted themselves to the art of dance, albeit discretely and "without aiming for artistic perfection." In the late republican era and then in the imperial period, the practice of hiring musicians who could play various instruments became widespread among the wealthy. Performances by professional musicians and dancers were then in high demand, and they often commanded astronomical fees. Even one emperor, Nero, did not shirk from presenting himself as a musician who took pleasure in his art.

## *Stars and Acrobats*

Along with famous stars such as the well-known flautist Tigellius, favored by Caesar and Cleopatra, or the court citharist Terpnos, a favorite of Nero, a vast array of strolling acrobats and musicians also prospered in Roman society. Earning their living in the streets, they were called *circulatores* because the public they encountered by chance would form a circle around them and throw some coins at the end of the performance. Music became so important that it earned a famous invective from the historian Ammianus Marcellinus

**Performance by *Circulatores***
A group of strolling musicians (*circulatores*) in a mosaic from Pompeii.

**Stringed Instrument**
*Above*, a relief with two musicians playing a stringed instrument. The strings, made from gut or hemp, were plucked with a plectrum.

**Divine Music**
*Below*, a Pan's syrinx, or flute, in wood; the reeds are hollowed out from a single plank, the surface of which has geometrical inlays.

**Musical Performance**
Marble relief with a scene of music and dance in honor of Isis.

(fourth century A.D.): "Houses that in the past were illustrious for devotion to studies now resound with songs and with the tinkling of cithara. Instead of a philosopher, today one becomes a singer, instead of an orator, a master of stage arts; the libraries are like tombs, closed forever, while they are building hydraulic organs and enormous lyres."

## *Musical Instruments*

The use of wind instruments was prevalent in the Roman world: the bronze *cornu*, used as a military instrument and in religious ceremonies; the *lituus* of Etruscan origin; the *bucina* made from a cow horn; the *tuba*, which accompanied the maneuvers of the infantry; the *syrinx*, beloved by Pan; and various types of flutes. Among the stringed instruments, the *lyra* and the *cytara* were very popular. Both were made up of a sound box from which projected two wood struts, joined at the top by a horizontal traverse: an invention said to date back to the god Hermes.

**The Tuba**
One of the most popular musical instruments was the tuba, or pipe, also used in the army.

**Concert for Cymbals**
Detail of a fresco depicting a Silenus figure, a mythical inhabitant of the woods, who plays the cymbals. This instrument *(below)* was made from two concave pieces of metal that, banged against each other, emitted a very high-pitched sound.

### THE INVENTION OF THE HYDRAULIC ORGAN

Sources attribute the invention of the hydraulic organ to Ctesibius of Alexandria, who lived about the mid-third century B.C. In the first century, it already was being used in Rome with great frequency at circus games and in theatrical performances. Archeological finds, along with descriptions by Hero of Alexandria and Vitruvius, have allowed us to understand how the instrument functioned. Water pressure was used to bring air into the body that contained the mechanism for opening and closing the valves applied to the connection of each pipe. In the early period of the empire, the bellows organ was popular; bellows were attached to the main body and pushed compressed air directly inside.

# The Calendar and the Measurement of Time

From the first Roman calendar, attributed to Romulus, to the one ordered by Julius Caesar and destined to last until the Renaissance, Rome always had a complicated relationship with the measurement of time.

The historian Varro attributes to Romulus the creation of the first Roman calendar. This was based on the phases of the moon and was made up of 304 days, divided into ten months, of which six had 30 days and four (March, May, July, and October) had 31. The year began in March and ended in December. According to tradition, Romulus's successor, Numa Pompilius, added the months of January and February to the primitive Romulan calendar, creating a 355-day year divided into twelve months (four of 31 days, seven of 29, and one of 28). To reconcile the lunar-based system with the solar path defined by the succession of the seasons, an additional inserted month of 22 or 23 days was added periodically to February, which put the two systems in balance.

## *The Julian Reform*

The insertion of the additional month, which allowed the term of magistrates in office to be prolonged, was entrusted to the Pontifex Maximus, who was anything but immune to political passions. Thus it was crucial that there be some verification of a series of abuses that, in the mid-first century B.C., had created a three-month displacement between the calendar and the cycle of the seasons. And so in 46 B.C., Julius Caesar, upon consultation with the astronomer and mathematician Sosigenes of Alexandria, instituted a radical reform. The solar year was regulated on the Egyptian system with a duration of 365 days and the insertion every four years of a supplementary day, called *bis sexto Kalendas Martias*, the origin of leap year.

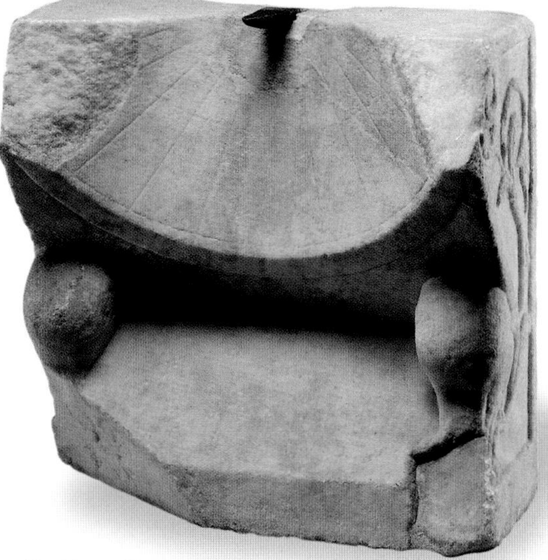

**The Solar Hour**
A marble sundial with a bronze gnomon (first century A.D.). The base terminates in two lion's paws, and the sides are decorated with plant motifs in relief.

**Market Scene**
Every seven working days, the Roman calendar called for one day dedicated to market.

## *The Calculation of Days*

The months were divided into intervals of *nundinae*, that is, market intervals of eight days each: seven for working and one for market and city activities. The days of the week were given the names of planets: *Lunae dies*, *Martis dies*, *Mercuri dies*, and so on, up to *dies Saturni* and *dies Solis* (these then would become *Sabbatum* and *Dominica*, the day of the Lord). The calculation of days was not done in progressive fashion as we do now but rather by counting backward, to see how many days were left before the three precise moments of the month: the *calends* (the first of the month), the *nones*, the fifth or seventh), the *ides* (the 13th or 15th). It was a complicated system, archaic in origin, and still based on the phases of the moon to which there was added a distinction between days that were favorable to activity, those that were unfavorable for religious reasons or because of custom, and those that were set aside for meetings, when it was legitimate to carry out political activities and convene the popular assemblies. One also had to take into consideration days considered unfavorable in the early hours but favorable by midday.

**The Tower of the Winds**
This building from the first century B.C. still stands in the Roman agora in Athens. Now called the Tower of the Winds, it originally contained a water clock.

### THERE ARE HOURS AND THEN THERE ARE HOURS

Unlike our own clock, whereby we measure the hours of the day beginning from midnight and dividing the day into equal intervals, the ancient Romans calculated time by dividing the period between sunrise and sunset into twelve intervals. Thus noon corresponded to the sixth hour, and sunset to the twelfth. Accordingly, of course, the hours varied in length every day, and summertime hours ended up being almost twice as long as winter hours. This made the functioning of tools for measuring time rather aleatory. In fact, in addition to the sundial (which, however, only worked in the absence of clouds), the ancients were familiar with the hourglass and also ingenious water clocks; how the latter were calibrated is still not clear. However, the Romans did not give time—or, to be more precise, the measurement of time—the absolute and authoritative value that we grant it today.

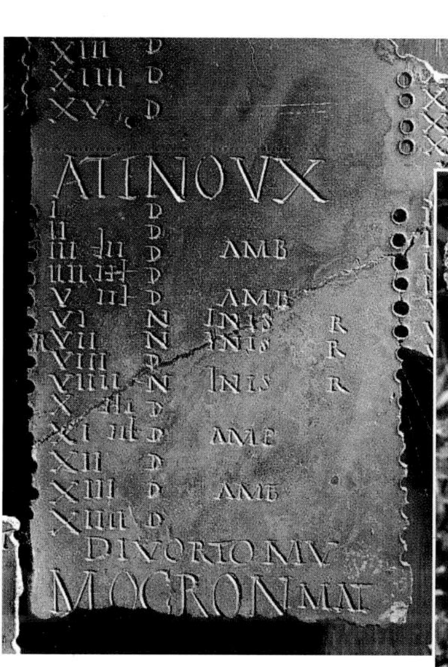


**The Phases of the Moon**
*Above*, a Gallic lunar calendar from the first to second century A.D. The days of the month were calculated based on the phases of the moon.

**Public Clock**
*Below*, a solar quadrant with the face of a divinity, discovered in Timgad, Algeria.

**Bronze Calendar**
A Celtic calendar on bronze sheets, dating from the first century B.C. The Julian reform, which increased the days of the year from 355 to 365, is from this era.

# Glossary

*This brief glossary, which has no pretensions to being complete, serves the purpose of clarifying the meaning of some of the more specialized or unusual terms that appear in this book or those with meanings profoundly different from analogous terms used today. This is meant to provide the reader with a tool to understand the text with greater ease.*

## A

***Ab urbe condita***
A term that means "since the founding of Rome," an event traditionally agreed upon as April 21, 753 B.C., the date from which Romans counted the years.

**Acheron**
Name of a river in Epirus, which probably entered the cosmogony as the infernal river because its course lay underground. For Romans it represented the entry to the afterlife.

**Acropolis**
The high, fortified portion of ancient cities. Along with military installations, it also contained the temples of major divinities and other public buildings.

**Acroterium**
An architectural term for the ornaments placed above the pediment, at the corners, or along the apex of temple structures.

***Aes***
A term the Romans used to signify both bronze and copper, the materials used to mint the most ancient coins. This is the derivation of *aerarium*, the Latin word for public treasury.

***Ager publicus***
Lands taken over by the state following wars or specific punishments inflicted on rebel cities. In the last days of the Republic, this was the subject of fierce social clashes.

**Agger**
A Roman field fortification built to protect encampments. It consisted of a wall erected with planks and tree trunks, thickened and protected with earth and stones.

***Annona***
A term originally used to designate the wheat crop for a year (*annus*), then, gradually, for any other foodstuffs produced by a territory in a year.

**Antefix**
A terracotta ornament, generally semicircular or pedimental, attached to the edges of the roofs of temples or other ancient buildings.

**Aphrodite**
Greek goddess of beauty and love, identified with the Phoenician goddess Ishtar, who later entered the Roman pantheon by the name Venus.

**Aquila**
The eagle, symbol of Rome's power. Gaius Marius made it the principal emblem of the legions, imbuing it with almost sacred value.

**Ara**
For Romans, the altar used in public sacrifices, usually made from stone and quadrangular in form.

**Architectural order**
A concept typical of classical architecture, indicating a standardized formal and proportional association among the various elements of the column and trabeation; used in Greece as a structural, weight-bearing system, in Rome it became a typically decorative motif.

***As***
The most ancient Roman coin, which originally had a weight equal to one pound (approximately 327 g.).

**Asclepius (Latin: Aesculapius)**
Greek god of medicine, son of Apollo and the nymph Coronis. He was worshiped in Rome by the name Aesculapius.

***Astati***
Soldiers in the front line of the Roman legions, chosen from among the youngest and most robust.

**Atellana**
A type of vulgar farce, greatly in vogue among the plebeian classes. According to tradition, it originated in the Oscan city of *Atella* (Acerra).

**Augurs**
Priests in ancient Rome, whose task was to interpret the will of the gods through the observation of the flight or song of birds or other signs.

**Auxiliaries**
Soldiers who served in separate units, made up of allied forces, originally Italic, then later from the provinces. Used for the most part in actions alongside the legions.

## B

**Bagaudae**
Farmers from Gaul who, organized into bands, fought against wealthy landowners and Roman rule between the third and fourth centuries A.D.

**Bellona**
Roman deity of war (from the Latin *bellum*, "war"), also called *Duellona*. She was worshiped in a sacred wood on the Capitoline hill and in a temple outside Rome.

**Bona Dea**
Roman divinity venerated on the first of May and on an unspecified day in December.

**Bulla**
A sort of bipartite capsule in which an amulet was kept, worn as an ornament around the neck by young Etruscans and Romans.

## C

***Calends***
The initial day of the month for Romans.

***Caldarium***
The area in Roman baths reserved for hot baths.

***Calumnia***
A false accusation. A citizen who was accused (*querelato* in Italian, from the Latin *querela*, "complaint") and then absolved could institute proceedings against his accuser for *calumnia*.

***Cardo***
A Latin term that indicates the north-south axis road of Roman cities and territories.

***Causidici***
A pejorative term for third-rate lawyers, similar to "shyster" or "pettifogger" in English. They had a tremendous gift of gab but very few scruples and lured easy marks in the forum, convincing them, with visions of large profits, to sue their neighbors, relatives, and acquaintances, to the great advantage of the lawyers and with disastrous consequences for the naïve victims.

**Cenotaph**
An empty sepulchral monument, usually erected in honor of those worthy of remembrance, whose remains were not recovered or were buried elsewhere.

***Censeo* (census-taking)**
Recognition of the income (*census*) and rights of every citizen, which was calculated every five years. This was essential for the functioning of military conscription and for the enjoyment of political rights, which depended on a Roman citizen's status.

**Censor**
The name of the Roman magistrates who carried out census-taking duties. Another task of the censors was to control public morals, with the authority officially to disapprove of citizens' behavior through a *nota censoria*.

**Centuriation**
System of regular measurement and division of territory into square lots, called centuries, which constituted the land-surveying basis for the assignation of Roman state lands.

**Centurion**
In ancient Rome, an officer of a lower rank, the commander of a "century" in a legion.

**Ceres**
Roman goddess connected to the growth of edible plants and grains (from which the word *cereal* is derived).

**Charon**
In ancient Greek religion, the deity of the underworld. He ferried the deceased across the Acheron, and they had to pay him an offering. For this reason, coins were placed on the eyes or in the mouths of corpses, to pay for their passage to the next world.

***Circulatores***
The name given to strolling acrobats and musicians, whose street performance would attract passersby to gather around them in a circle, and afterwards perhaps leave money in appreciation.

**Citizenship**
A right acquired by birth, adoption, or concession by the people to individuals. Only those who held Roman citizenship could enjoy political rights.

***Civitas***
The totality of citizens in a place and, at the same time, the legal status that made all citizens subject to laws and duties.

***Cliens* / Client**
For the Romans, this term designated an individual who had recognized obligations of loyalty, aid, and obedience to an important citizen (*patronus*). The meaning of client was by no means negative. For example, the clients of important men of politics such as Marius, Caesar, Crassus, and Pompey included bankers, senators, generals, and even sovereigns.

***Cognomen***
Family name—for example, Caesar or Scipio—which was added to the name (*nomen*) of the *gens* and the nickname, such as Africanus or Caecus ("blind"), which a person was given because of some great exploit or a physical characteristic.

**Cohort**
A tactical unit of the Roman army, made up of 600 men and subdivided into 6 centuries.

***Collegium***
A state-regulated association that grouped together those who carried out a specific occupation or profession.

***Columna cochlis***
A typical Roman celebratory column with an interior spiral staircase and an exterior frieze that followed in the same direction.

**Corona**
The most important of the Roman military decorations. Of the various types—*muralis, obsidionalis, vallaria*—the most coveted was the *graminea*, made of woven grass, which was awarded to a general who, by his actions, had saved an entire army.

***Cubiculum***
Literally signifies a "lying-down position." This was the name given to the bedrooms in a Roman dwelling.

**Curial offices**
The most significant administrative offices in ancient Rome (consul, praetor), which gave access to the Senate (Curia).

***Cursus honorum***
The political "career" in ancient Rome, made up of a totality of posts of increasing importance to be held according to an obligatory sequence.

## D

***Decumanus***
A Latin term that indicates the east-west street axis of Roman cities and territories.

***Deductio***
In ancient Rome, this term meant literally the "leading away" of a colony: its foundation, carried out by moving settlers there from the mother country.

**Diadem**
A circular gold band that fitted around the head as a symbol of great civil or religious authority.

**Diana**
Latin goddess of the hunt, corresponding to the Greek goddess Artemis. Her most famous sanctuary, in the extremely distant past, stood at the foot of Mount Albano (present-day Monte Cavo).

**Dilectur**
Regular conscription, to which all Roman citizens were subject upon reaching the age of eighteen.

**Dioscuri**
In Greek mythology, the name for the twin deities Castor and Pollux.

**Dis**
Roman divinity soon assimilated into the Greek god Pluto, both as god of the underworld and as distributor of riches.

***Domus***
The typical Roman single-family house, laid out around a central atrium.

**Dròmos**
In archeology, an access corridor to underground tombs (for example, in Etruscan necropolises) or rocky tombs (as in the Mycenean *tholos* tombs or in Hellenistic necropoleis).

## E

**Eponym**
In the classical world, someone who gave his name to something; it could be a god, the founder of a city, or the founder of a clan or family.

**Equestrian order**
This was made up of knights, citizens wealthy enough to serve in the cavalry divisions.

## F

***Familia***
In Latin this term had a much broader meaning than our own, and it indicated not only the various generations of a family line living together under the authority of the oldest male (the *paterfamilias*) but also the servants and slaves.

***Familia rustica***
The totality of slaves used to cultivate the fields under the supervision of a steward (*vilicus*).

***Familia urbana***
The slaves who worked in personal service to the owner and his family (doorkeeper, barber, scullery worker but also tutor, secretary, or administrator).

***Favissa***
In Italic-Roman sanctuaries, an underground and separate space where obsolete or extra votive objects were stored.

**Fescennine songs**
Songs of rustic origin, both obscene and playful, where there were opposing verses that the farmers exchanged on the occasion of country festivals or nuptials. The name comes from the Etruscan city of Fescennia.

**Frigidarium**
The area in Roman baths set aside for cold baths.

## G

***Garum***
A sauce (*liquamen*) made from macerated fish entrails, not to the liking of today's palate but a favorite in ancient Rome.

**Genius**
In the Roman religion, this was a person's guardian from birth. The Genius of the Roman people and, in the imperial era, that of the emperors, was the object of public worship.

***Gens***
The family line, dating back to a common ancestor, whose name the entire line adopted, and through which a Roman family group was recognized: *gens Iulia, gens Cornelia, gens Fabia*.

***Gentilis***
Related to a family line; in Latin onomastics the name of the family (*gens*).

***Gladius***
Typical hand-held weapon of the Roman infantry, with a rather short blade, sharpened point, and double edge.

**Gnomon**
Vertical staff whose shadow, projected by the sun, marks the local hour on a graduated scale appropriately laid out on the ground.

**Gravitas**
Literally, "seriousness"; a term used to indicate not only an attitude but a model of serious and dignified behavior, which constituted an integral part of the essence of a Roman citizen.

**Groma**
In ancient Rome, the most widely used tool for measuring land, dividing up lands, or laying out encampments, streets, or city facilities.

## H

**Haruspication**
The art of divination, Etruscan in origin, involving the examination of the entrails of sacrificial victims and the interpretation of lightning and of various other phenomena.

**Hercules**
Latin name for the Greek god Herakles, son of Alcmena and Zeus, who was known for his exceptional strength.

***Heredium***
A small farm, two jugers in area, the origins of which are attributed to Romulus himself. For a long time, this constituted the working unit for Italic farmland.

***Homo novus***
"New man": the designation for a citizen who was the first in his family to achieve curial office (praetor, consul, censor), thereby joining the ranks of the nobility. Well-known *homines novi* included Marius and Cicero.

**Hoplite**
A Greek soldier in the heavy infantry. A hoplite was armed with a lance and a sword, carried a large shield, and wore armor made up of a helmet, breastplate, and leggings.

**Hortus**
A sort of courtyard arranged at the back of the *domus*, used as a garden more than as a vegetable garden in the modern sense of the term. Sometimes it was expanded to take on the form of a colonnaded courtyard, or peristyle.

**Hypocaust**
A Greek term indicating the layout of centralized heating for bath facilities and for wealthy Roman houses. It consisted of an underground stove the smoke of which was sent through pipes running beneath the floors, thereby heating the spaces above.

# I

***Ides***
In the Roman calendar, the 13th day of the months of January, February, April, June, August, September, November, and December, and the 15th day of March, May, July, and October.

**Imperator**
Holder of an *imperium*. The term soon came to indicate the bearer of a particular military command, granted to soldiers after an exceptional victory.

***Imperium***
Generically a military command but also the government of a city, province, or state, In particular, the *imperium proconsulare* was the command of military forces.

***Ingenuus***
An individual born free, either because he was the son of a duly married free father or because he was the son of a free mother, even if born outside marriage. Roman law placed such people in an advantageous position compared to a freedman.

**Insignia**
A staff surmounted by a cloth or by another object that served as a guide or identifying symbol of a military division.

***Insula***
Literally "island" or "block," this was the name given to the multistory residential buildings typical of Roman cities, as opposed to the single-family *domus*.

**Intercalary month**
A month of 22 or 23 days that periodically had to be inserted between the end of February and the beginning of March to synchronize the ancient Roman calendar, which was lunar based, with the rhythm of the solar seasons.

***Ius imaginum***
This was the coveted "right to images," which allowed a nobleman who had attained a curial post to exhibit publicly his portrait and those of his ancestors who also had attained this rank.

# J

**Janus**
Roman god of beginnings and passages to new conditions, who gave his name to the first month of the year (*Ianuarius*, "January").

**Juno**
Latin goddess in whom the human female condition was ideally projected, particularly with regard to women who achieved the rank of wives.

# L

***Laqueum***
A noose that many aristocrats always carried so that they could resort to the extreme act of strangling themselves, were they to fall into disgrace with their princeps. Suicide avoided the family's becoming involved in such disgrace.

**Legate**
In the Roman army, an officer authorized as commander in chief or governor of a province with duties comparable to those of today's Chief of General Staff.

**Legion**
The principal tactical unit of the Roman army. Originally, it was made up of 3,000 foot soldiers and 300 knights, but over the course of the centuries the number of regulars varied considerably.

**Liber**
Ancient Roman god identified with the Greek god Dionysus, sometimes paired with the goddess Libera (in turn identified with the Greek goddess Persephone), both depicted as children of the goddess Ceres.

**Libera**
Ancient Roman goddess of fertility.

**Libertus**
An individual freed from the state of slavery. Freedmen remained in an inferior position compared to citizens who were born in freedom. It was not until the imperial era that they were granted similar status.

***Limes***
The boundary line—or, more precisely, the defended area—that separated the lands of the Roman empire from barbarian territories.

**Lupa**
Literally, "she-wolf." In ancient Rome this term often was used to indicate a prostitute. This was the derivation of the word *lupanar*, "brothel."

**Lustrum**
A religious festival that marked the end of the census-taking operations, which took place every five years; its meaning evolved to signify a five-year period.

# M

***Maenianus***
The sections, descending in height, into which circuses and amphitheaters were divided.

***Meretrix***
Literally, "she who earns," who merits payment. This is what prostitutes were called in Rome, for they were the only women who "earned" a living in a society that prohibited women from practicing any paid profession.

**Metope**
A rectangular strip of stone, marble, or terracotta, smooth, painted or decorated in relief, inserted between the triglyphs in the frieze of a Doric Greek temple.

**Mithras**
An Indo-Iranian sun god, whose cult spread throughout the Roman empire, finding followers especially among soldiers, which perhaps is a testament to the god's original warrior function.

***Mos maiorum***
This was the "way of life of the ancients": the totality of pre-existing traditions and behavioral models connected with the Roman way of life and political customs, to which every citizen was expected to conform.

***Municipium***
A term originally used for those who immigrated to Rome and who enjoyed only civil rights. Later, it also was used to designate a community of Roman citizens with full rights, with administrative jurisdiction over a broad territory.

**Mystery**
Originally, the name of an initiatory cult practiced in ancient Greece at the sanctuary of Eleusis and elsewhere. Secrecy (from *myo*, which means "I am closed") was its most characteristic feature.

# N

**Nenfro**
A volcanic tufa stone similar to peperino, gray or reddish in color, used as a building material.

**Neptune**
Roman god of the seas and water in general.

**Nomen**
The name derived from that of the *gens* to which an individual belonged—for example, Julius—and which constituted a person's principal name (the only name for women of that family).

**Nomenclator**
In ancient Rome, the slave who acted as his owner's "rubric," reminding him of the name, profession, and details about people he met and should know.

***Nones***
The 5th or 7th day of the month.

# O

**Odèion**
A building reserved for musical performances and public readings, similar to a theater, from which it was distinguished by its covered roof.

**Olpe**
A type of jug, a variation of *oinochóe* (an ancient Greek vase used for wine), much in use in proto-Corinthian and Corinthian ceramics in the seventh and eighth centuries B.C.

***Onerarium***
A boat used for mercantile transport, particularly amphorae of wine, oil, or grain.

**Onomastics**
The assignment and use of names. The Roman system was particularly complex. Males had at least two names: their own name (*praenomen*) and the name of the family or *gens* (*nomen*)—for example, Publius Cornelius. These often were accompanied by the name of the family branch within the *gens* (*cognomen*)—for example, Scipio. In certain cases these three appellatives were joined by an *ad personam* name, derived from an individual's exploits—for example, Africanus. The famous general who vanquished Hannibal thus came to be called Publius Cornelius Scipio Africanus. In formal circumstances, he was referred to by *praenomen* and *nomen*; in informal situations, by only the *praenomen* or the *cognomen*. Women went by a single name, that of the *gens*: Iulia, Claudia, Cornelia. To avoid confusion within the family, names of endearment were used: Iulilla, Lia, etc.

***Oppidum***
The Roman name for fortified villages, first on the Italic peninsula, then in Gaul, Spain, and the barbarian territories. Over time, many *oppida* became *municipia*.

***Opus***
A word, followed by an adjective (*incertum*, *reticulatum*, *sectile*, *latericium*), used in the Roman world to indicate the manner in which a masonry surface was created (with irregular stones, square stones, slabs of marble, or bricks).

***Opus caementicium***
A mixture of stone aggregate (*caementa*) bound by a resistant mortar made of quicklime and sand.

***Opus incertum***
A masonry technique that involved facing the inner core of a wall with irregular and irregularly arranged stones.

***Opus signinum***
Compact mixture obtained from combining minute shards of amphorae, tiles, etc. with lime; this was used by the Romans to face floors, walls, and terraces.

***Opus tessellatum***
This was the name Romans gave to classical mosaic made from colored tesserae, which, beginning in the third century B.C., replaced the older pebble mosaics.

**Ovation**
A sort of lesser triumph, during which the victorious general sacrificed a sheep on the Campidoglio.

# P

**Pales**
Name of an ancient roman divinity connected to the sanctity of the Palatine hill and titular deity of the festival known as *parilia*, when the birth of Rome was celebrated (April 21st).

**Palliata**
This was the word for Greek comedy, from the name of the typical mantle—the *palliolum*—worn by the protagonists.

***Palla***
An outer garment made from a large fabric rectangle or square, which Romans wore over a tunic; it was attached beneath the chin or on one shoulder with a buckle.

**Panoply**
A complete set of armor, particularly the armor of the hoplites in ancient Greece.

***Paterfamilias***
Generally, the man belonging to the eldest generation of a family line, who exercised more or less absolute authority over the members of the family (see *familia*).

***Patres conscripti***
A traditional formula whereby senators were selected. Some occupied seats by virtue of lineage (*patres*), while others had won seats by being elected to one of the curial posts (*conscripti*).

***Patronus***
"He who holds the position of father": this was the term for an important citizen in relationship to his clients—that is, to those citizens who acknowledged obligations of loyalty and subordination to him.

**Peristyle**
A courtyard surrounded by columns placed at the back of the largest and most luxurious *domus*.

**Phalera**
A decoration of valor, consisting of a metal badge hung from ties or ribbons on the armor of a legionnaire.

**Plebiscite**
Voting by the plebs that, with certain limitations, had the power of law. Certain innovative men of politics, such as the Gracchi, resorted to the plebiscite in order to overturn a veto by the Senate.

**Pomoerium**
The sacred boundary of the city of Rome, which consisted of an uninterrupted strip of land that surrounded the city.

***Pompa triumphalis***
A solemn procession that accompanied a victorious general to the Capitolium.

***Pontifex maximus***
The highest member of the pontifical college, who had the task of interpreting and handing down legal-religious traditions and supervising demonstrations of worship.

**Portorium**
An indirect tax, comparable to our customs, which was applied with variable rates on goods entering or leaving the city.

***Potestas tribunicia***
The power conferred upon tribunes of the plebs (originally 2 or 4, later increased to 10).

**Pozzolana**
Sand from Pozzuoli, favored by the Romans for making *opus caementicium*, because they considered it to have exceptional static qualities.

***Praefectus praetorio***
Until the time of Constantine, the head of the troops chosen to protect the person and general surroundings of the emperor.

***Praefectus urbi***
Commander of the urban cohorts, employed directly by the emperor and granted broad judicial powers.

***Praenomen***
The "personal" singular name of an individual, which distinguished him within a *gens*—for example, Gaius or Publius. A person's complete name was given by the sequence *praenomen-nomen-cognomen*: for example, Gaius Julius Caesar.

**Praetorians**
The select corps of soldiers who acted as the emperor's personal guard. Created by Augustus, it was dissolved by Constantine.

***Praetorium***
Part of the Roman military encampment where the tent of the commander, also called the *praetorium*, was located, along with those of the principal officers.

***Princeps***
In the republican era, the eldest patrician senator, a former censor. From the time of Augustus on, this was the highest position in Rome.

***Principia***
The second line of legionnaires, entrusted with the principal stress of battle, after the *astati* had absorbed the first blows.

**Proconsul**
A consul whose powers were extended beyond the one-year term. In the final years of the Republic, provincial governors were proconsuls or propraetors. In the imperial era, governors of senatorial provinces were proconsuls.

**Protome**
A decorative element of architectural structures or of objects of various types (vases, jewelry, weapons, etc.), made up of the head and sometimes part of the chest of an animal or, in rare cases, a human figure.

# Q

**Quaestor**
In ancient Rome, perhaps also under the monarchy, this was a magistrate of a lower order who had jurisdiction over criminal matters. With Sulla the quaestor gained entry to the Senate.

**Quirinus**
One of the oldest and most important Roman gods. With Jupiter and Mars he formed an archaic triad that can be considered the divine representation of the Roman state.

# R

**Rostrum**
A metal or wood beam with a metal point, used on Etruscan and Roman ships to strike, damage, and drag enemy ships; the speaker's platform they adorn.

# S

***Sacellum***
In ancient Rome, a small enclosed area or small building with a sacred altar to a divinity, most often of a private nature.

***Saepta***
The enclosures within which the Roman people voted.

***Salii***
A priestly association in ancient Rome, whose service was connected to the cult of the god Mars.

***Salutatio***
A typical Roman custom according to which the clients of a powerful man (*patronus*) went in the early morning to his house to offer him their services and to receive his gifts (*sportula*).

**Senatorial order**
The order grouping senators and their family members. They entered this order by birthright or by election to the highest curial positions. To maintain membership in this order, however, they had to possess considerable wealth.

**Serapis**
An Egyptian god in Ptolomeic times. In keeping with traditional Egyptian methodology, this god is a fusion of Osiris and Apis. Like Osiris, he has a relationship with Isis and with the world of the dead.

***Servile supplicium***
The "punishment for slaves," or death on a cross, considered particularly defamatory and reserved for slaves.

**Sesterce**
The most typical Roman coin, having the value of two and one-half asses.

***Socius et amicus populi romani***
"Ally and friend of the Roman people," a traditional phrase used to indicate kings or peoples who were tied to Rome by a client-patron bond, recognizing Rome's supremacy in exchange for aid and protection.

**Solidus**
A gold coin issued by the emperor Constantine.

**Soranus of Ephesus**
Greek physician (c. 90–c. 150). Follower of the school of Asclepius, he made major contributions to the field of pediatrics and especially obstetrics and gynecology.

**Stilicon, Flavius**
Roman general of Vandal origin (365–408). *Magister militum* (394) of Theodosius and tutor (395) of his sons Arcadius and Honorius. Stilicon fought for the territorial integrity of the empire, which had been divided into West and East. He perished during a military rebellion that broke out in Ravenna.

**Stipis**
According to archeologists, offerings of various types dedicated to a divinity.

**Strabo**
Greek historian and geographer (Amasia, Pontus, 64 B.C.–c. A.D. 20). He wrote the 17-volume *Geographia*, which is of considerable importance because of the quantity of information it contains, going beyond pure geographical science.

**Suetonius, Gaius Tranquillus**
Latin historian (first to second century A.D.). His most famous work, *De vita Caesarum*, is an 8-volume biography of the first 12 emperors.

**Sylvanus**
An ancient Italic god, very similar to Faunus but protector only of the woods. Pine and cypress were his sacred essences.

# T

**Tacitus, Publius Cornelius**
Latin historian (c. 55–120), remembered for the *De origine et situ Germanorum*, about the life and customs of the Germans, and for his 12-volume *Historiae*, of which only 4 remain intact, which recount the history of Rome from 69 to 97.

**Tertullianus, Quintus Septimius Florens**
Christian apologist (Carthage c. 155–c. 222). His masterpiece is the *Apologeticus*, perhaps the very first text in Christian Latin literature.

**Theodoric**
King of the Ostrogoths (454–526). An Arian by religion, he ruled over Italy, establishing the capital in Ravenna. He adopted a policy of rapprochement between the Ostrogoths and the Romans, but suspecting agreements between the senatorial aristocracy and Byzantium, he sentenced the most distinguished members, including Boethius, to death.

**Theseus**
The principal hero in Athenian mythology, famous for having killed the Minotaur in Crete.

**Thetis**
A sea creature in Greek mythology who married a mortal, Peleus, and gave birth to Achilles.

**Tholos**
A round structure with a conical roof, used for funerary or civic purposes.

**Troy**
Ancient city in Asia Minor, founded as Ilium, according to legend. It was supposedly besieged for approximately nine years by a Greek army to avenge the abduction of Helen (who was betrothed to the king of Sparta) by Paris, son of the king of Troy.

**Ulpianus, Domitius**
Roman jurist (Tyre, third century A.D.). A great legal scholar, he wrote numerous books that later would constitute the principal source for the compilation of Justinian's Digest.

# V

**Velleius Paterculus, Gaius**
Latin historian (c. 19 B.C.–after A.D. 31). He wrote a concise general history in two volumes that covers the period between the Trojan War and A.D. 30.

**Verro, Gaius**
Roman man of politics (c. 119–43 B.C.). Having amassed immoderate wealth, he was accused of corruption and condemned. He went into exile voluntarily before being banished by Antony.

**Vesta**
One of the most important goddesses in the public religion of ancient Rome, she had a circular temple in the forum where an eternal flame was kept burning. Her cult was overseen by six Vestal Virgins.

**Victory**
Roman goddess venerated as the giver of victories in war. Her most ancient temple stood on the Palatine.

**Vitruvius, Pollio**
Roman architect and essayist (first century B.C.), he is known above all as the author of *De architectura*, the only ancient architectural treatise to have survived to the present day.

**Vulcan**
Roman god of fire and craftsmanship; identified with the Greek god Hephaestus.

**Zealots**
Followers of a Jewish political-religious movement in the first century A.D.

**Zosimus**
Byzantine historian (fifth century A.D.). He wrote, in a tone free from preconceptions, a six-volume *Historia nova* that covers the period from the age of Augustus until A.D. 410.

# Index